MY SECOND-FAVORITE COUNTRY

D1602539

My Second-Favorite Country

How American Jewish Children Think About Israel

Sivan Zakai

NEW YORK UNIVERSITY PRESS

New York

NEW YORK UNIVERSITY PRESS
New York
www.nyupress.org

References to Internet websites (URLs) were accurate at the time of writing. Neither the author nor New York University Press is responsible for URLs that may have expired or changed since the manuscript was prepared.

Library of Congress Cataloging-in-Publication Data
Names: Zakai, Sivan, author.
Title: My second-favorite country : how American Jewish children think about Israel / Sivan Zakai.
Description: New York : New York University Press, [2022] | Includes bibliographical references and index.
Identifiers: LCCN 2021039790 | ISBN 9781479808953 (hardback) | ISBN 9781479808984 (paperback) | ISBN 9781479809073 (ebook) | ISBN 9781479808991 (ebook other)
Subjects: LCSH: Jewish children—United States—Attitudes toward Israel. | Israel—Study and teaching.
Classification: LCC DS132 .Z35 2022 | DDC 956.94—dc23
LC record available at https://lccn.loc.gov/2021039790

New York University Press books are printed on acid-free paper, and their binding materials are chosen for strength and durability. We strive to use environmentally responsible suppliers and materials to the greatest extent possible in publishing our books.

Manufactured in the United States of America

10 9 8 7 6 5 4 3 2 1

Also available as an ebook

For my children
Eytan, Ilan, and Liam

And for all the children
who contributed to this book

CONTENTS

LIST OF ILLUSTRATIONS

Introduction

"What Kids Say Is Important": Israel and the Education of American Jewish Children

Five-year-old Maya Glaser knows what she likes: shiny rocks, mint chocolate cupcakes, and going to visit her grandparents. By the time Maya is eight years old, her list of preferences has evolved into favorites and second favorites. In terms of colors, blue is her clear top choice, but she also likes red, and friendship bracelets in both colors adorn her arms. Her favorite food is pizza, but pasta takes a close second. And when she thinks about countries, the ranking is also clear: The United States of America is her favorite country and Israel is her second favorite.

Eight-year-old Maya is tall for her age, and she speaks with confidence. "This place, America," she explains, "is my home, and I'm happy that I live in America. America feels like it's a place for everybody. You can believe whatever you want to." She smooths out her clothes while she talks, adding, "Although I am happy that I am in America and that it's my home, I also love Israel. It's a really special place, and I feel happy that Israel even exists. Outside, in the real world, it takes a long time to get there. But inside me, I feel like it's really close." She taps her heart and continues, "Like it's right here."

As a Jewish child living in the United States, Maya understands that the state of Israel is geographically remote, but it nonetheless touches her own life. She knows this at age 5, when she can first describe the symbols of the Israeli flag, and at age 8 when she begins watching newsclips about Israel, and at age 11 when she starts to download Israeli pop music. As Maya grows, her conceptions of Israel change, but one thing remains constant: She views Israel as both distant from and part of her own experiences.

I first met Maya in September 2012, when she was heading off to kindergarten. That month, speaking at the Democratic National Convention in Charlotte, President Barack Obama accepted the Democratic Party's nomination to run again for the highest office in the nation. In Silicon Valley, Apple unveiled the new iPhone 5, and in Chicago, 26,000 public school teachers went on strike. But in Los Angeles, Maya packed her new backpack and headed off to begin elementary school, thinking not of the national context or historical moment in which she was operating, but only of whether she would like her teachers and make new friends. The weather was unseasonably warm, even for Southern California, and as the sun beat down on her classroom, the smell of fresh paint and sharpened pencils wafted through the air.

Maya is part of a group of 35 children who, as kindergarteners, first agreed to participate in a longitudinal study of American Jewish children.[1] Even in kindergarten the children were an eclectic bunch, with varying interests and different behaviors in their new schools. Some, like Maya, tumbled into the halls with an eagerness to begin learning. Others were more reticent, cautiously exploring their classrooms. Some instantly gravitated to one corner of the room, finding the painting supplies or the books or the Legos, while others stood at the edge and examined their surroundings.

When the children look back at themselves years later, as they are finishing elementary school, they will barely recognize these young 5- and 6-year-old selves. They will have learned to speak with confidence, even the shiest among them throwing back their shoulders and projecting their voices. They will all know how to read and write in English and, to some degree, also in Hebrew. Many of them will have developed specific talents and interests as artists, athletes, musicians, or coders.

In these intervening years, the children won't only have learned more about themselves and about their schools, but also about the larger world they inhabit. They will all consider themselves patriotic American citizens and proud Jews. Most of the children will have begun to voice political beliefs, and all will be aware of the hotly contested political climate of Trump's America. They'll talk about matters of general interest to today's youth—Internet safety and global warming—but also about issues specific to the Jewish community—antisemitism and the Jewish character of the state of Israel.

Children in the United States are coming of age at a time of digital connectivity, in a nation of hyphenated identities, and in an era of increasing political polarization. Growing up in this context requires children to make sense of a deluge of information, much of it conflicting, about what it means to be a good citizen, a responsible community member, and a grounded individual. How do children navigate this complicated reality? How do they think about the collective and the personal? How do children interpret history and current events? And how ought they be educated in order to help them better understand and cope with the world in which they live?

This book presents Jewish children's learning about Israel in the United States as a rich case for understanding both the complexity of children's thinking and the forcefulness of children's desires to be included in conversations about important civic and political matters. While the empirical study on which this book is based spotlights a particular group of children in a specific religio-cultural context, it illuminates a broader relationship between children, who often want to be taken seriously as deep thinkers, and educational systems that rarely treat them that way.

In tracing the thoughts and feelings of a group of American Jewish children over the course of elementary school, I argue that children invest a great deal of intellectual and emotional effort in making sense of how countries and societies do and ought to function. Yet even as Jewish children build foundational conceptions of civics, history, and politics in both the United States and Israel, they also express deep frustration because they feel ill-equipped to make sense of contested issues in contemporary Jewish and Israeli life. Taking children's ideas seriously requires a shift in educational practices in order to help children better navigate a world in which people disagree.

The claim that children think in deep and complicated ways may, at first, appear counterintuitive. Even though children have complex spiritual (Coles, 1990; Heller, 1988), moral (Coles, 1986a; Damon, 1988; Paley, 1992), emotional (Bosacki, 2008; Doherty, 2008), and political lives (Coles, 1986b; S. W. Moore et al., 1985), "elementary" is often equated with simplistic or uncomplicated. Yet, as this book shows, elementary school students spend considerable effort contemplating the very concepts that adults often assume they are not developmentally ready to discuss: the intricacies of identity and belonging, conflicting ways of framing the past, the intractability of geopolitical conflict, and the demands of civic responsibility.

While schools and other educational institutions have long been places that children inhabit, they have not always been places that honor children's ideas and ways of meaning-making (Paley, 2004). This is in part because, as scholar of elementary mathematics education Deborah Ball explains, "making sense of children's ideas is not so easy. Children use their own words and their own frames of reference in many ways that are not necessarily congruent with [adults'] ways of thinking" (1993, p. 385). Yet it also reflects a larger trend in education that pushes schools to teach children what adults think that children ought to know about the world (e.g., Hirsch, 2016, 2020) rather than structuring learning around the questions that children are curious about or the ideas that children find both intriguing and confusing. To argue that educational institutions ought to take children's ideas seriously reflects both a commitment to better understanding children's thinking and an educational philosophy that schools ought to be places not only made up *of* children but also made *for* children.

To make this argument, I draw upon the experiences, thoughts, and feelings of a group of American Jewish children as they developed over childhood. From the age of 5, these children offered thoughtful reflections about themselves, their communities, and the larger world in which they lived. As they matured, the children built increasingly complex theories and developed a growing range of emotions and viewpoints. Like other longitudinal studies that highlight how children form ideas (e.g., S. W. Moore et al., 1985) and make sense of their own lives and communities (e.g., Morrow & Crivello, 2015), this research offers one illustrative case for understanding how children develop ideas and beliefs about self, community, nation, and world.

The Context

This book traces the thoughts and feelings of a group of Jewish children in the United States as they developed ideas, beliefs, and questions about

Israel over the course of elementary school. American Jewish children's learning about Israel offers a particularly variegated case for understanding both the complexity of children's thought and the profound questions that children's experiences raise about educational practices precisely because Israel plays a role in American Jewish life that is, at once, central and contested.

Israel functions as the "symbolic homeland" of the American Jewish community (Kelner, 2010), occupying a place in American Jewish life that is both integral and often ambiguous (L. Grant, 2018). As such, Israel sits at the intersection of the real and the symbolic, the personal and the collective, the past and the present.

For children who receive a Jewish education in the United States, learning about Israel has become part of what historian Ivan Marcus (1996) calls "rituals of childhood," the ways that children are acculturated into shared communal norms and values. Thus, American Jewish children's conceptions of Israel function as a prism for understanding how the youngest members of a community come to develop ideas and beliefs about core issues of the human experience: communal affiliation, national identity, contemporary geopolitical events, and collective heritage.

Israel has not always played such a prominent role in the experiences of American Jewish childhood. While learning about Israel has been part of Jewish education in the United States since before the foundation of the modern state (Krasner, 2003), only over time has it moved from the periphery to being a central component of the education of young American Jews (Krasner, 2005b, 2006). A series of changes—some in the American Jewish community and the structure of Jewish education in the United States, and some in the evolving nature of childhood itself—have resituated Israel as a core aspect of American Judaism and experiences of American Jewish childhood.

Israel's Shifting Role in the American Jewish Community

The American Jewish community's relationship to Israel has waxed and waned over time, at moments functioning as a major preoccupation of American Jews, and at other times simmering in the background of attempts to cultivate Jewish life in the American context. At each juncture, American Jews have had to redefine how Israel should function in their own lives and communities.

As the ideas of political Zionism began to gain traction in Europe in the late 19th century, American Jewish leaders were splintered in their beliefs about the merits of a future Jewish state. Some American Jews were explicitly anti-Zionist, privileging Jewish religious expression over Jewish nationalism (Kolsky, 2010; Raider et al., 1997). Other Jews in the United States embraced a distinctly American form of Zionism, proclaiming their Zionist commitments to be the Jewish version of American liberal ideals (Urofsky, 2020/1975). Others still set forth a vision of Zionism that rejected Jewish statehood even as it reaffirmed the national cohesion of the Jewish people (Pianko, 2010). As vociferous debates about Zionism played out on the public stage, American Jews reaffirmed—albeit in different ways—their allegiance to cultivating Jewish life in the United States.

Yet in the wake of the destruction of Europe's Jewish community in the Holocaust, American Jews began to band together to throw their political and financial support behind the Yishuv, the prestate Jewish community in British Mandate Palestine. American Jews played a central role in providing the Yishuv money and arms, persuading the Truman administration to support the United Nations' plan to partition Palestine into a Jewish and an Arab state, and resettling Jewish refugees to the newly established state of Israel (Rosenthal, 2001). Responding to the needs of the fledgling Jewish state, as historian Arthur Goren explains, American Jews displayed "a unity of purpose on a scale unprecedented in the modern history of the Jews" (1999, p. 188).

Soon after the new state had formed, however, American Jewish relationships to Israel became simultaneously more pervasive and more insecure. On the one hand, Israel began to permeate the homes, cultural institutions, and fundraising efforts of American Jews (E. A. Katz, 2015; D. D. Moore, 1996). On the other hand, many American Jewish leaders became increasingly "uneasy" about what the new state would portend for their own American Jewish community (Ganin, 2005). Concerned about accusations of dual loyalty from their fellow Americans, they vocally and vociferously proclaimed their allegiance to the United States (Ganin, 2005) and reiterated their commitment to developing a robust Jewish community on American soil (Barnett, 2016). At the same time, as the new Israeli government assumed sovereignty, the leaders of American Zionism expressed concerns that they had been sidelined in conversations about the policies of the new Jewish state (A. E. Katz, 2015). Thus, cautiously and hesitantly, American Jews attempted to situate their relationships to Israel as part of a larger expression of American patriotism and a belief that Israel could be an important friend and ally of the United States.

Caution turned to unabashed support by the conclusion of the 1967 Six-Day War, as any remaining ambivalence American Jews may have expressed about Israel had all but vanished. Voicing pride in the military victories of the Jewish state, American Jews poured financial and political resources into supporting Israel and its government. The decade between 1967 and 1977 marked a "golden era" in which American Jews were passionate devotees of the Jewish state (Sasson, 2014). Israel had become "the new civil religion of American Jews," uniting Jews of different denominations and political persuasions (Woocher, 1986). Any objections that did arise—most notably from members of Breirah, a Jewish organization that called for the establishment of a Palestinian state in the aftermath of the 1973 war—were tamped down by American Jewish leaders and institutions as part of a crackdown "aimed at silencing public Jewish dissent before it could spread" (D. Waxman, 2016, p. 77).

Over time, American Jews continued to mobilize financial and diplomatic support for Israel, yet consensus began to give way to dissent over Israeli government policies. As American and Israeli Jews developed distinct cultural practices (D. D. Moore & Troen, 2001), differing approaches to religious observances (Rebhun & Levy, 2006), and divergent beliefs about democratic societies (Gordis, 2019), American Jews began to voice skepticism about the choices of the Israeli electorate. At first, this dissent was merely a trickle as some liberal Jews pushed back against the growing power of the Orthodox Israeli rabbinate and expressed concern about Israel's fraught relationship with Palestinians in the wake of the 1982 Lebanon War and the First Palestinian Intifada of 1987–1991 (Sasson, 2014).

The more that American Jews had access to Israel—through travel, media, Jewish education, and the rise of Israel Studies programs on university campuses—the more they began to explicitly critique aspects of

Israeli society and politics that conflicted with their own values and beliefs (D. Waxman, 2016). Throughout the 1980s and 1990s, as the pendulum of Israeli politics shifted, so too did the American Jewish response; American Jews on the right pushed back during left-leaning Israeli governments, and American Jews on the left did so when the Israeli government leaned right (Sasson, 2014).

In the early 21st century, on the heels of the Second Palestinian Intifada, a new reality emerged: Substantive public disputes *between* American Jews and Israelis were joined by growing divides *within* an American Jewish community increasingly fractured in their beliefs about what Israel ought to be (D. Waxman, 2016). Thus contemporary American Jewish relationships with Israel can best be understood as the confluence of two factors: the prominence of Israel as a symbolic presence in the American Jewish community, and the increasing polarization of American Jewish attitudes toward Israel.

Israel functions as a "preeminent symbol" for American Jews (Sasson, 2009, p. 26), a place simultaneously emblematic of contemporary Judaism and distant—both geographically and metaphysically—from their own American Jewish lives. On the one hand, Israel is an ethnic Jewish state, offering rights and protections not only to its citizens but also to Jews around the world (Smooha, 2002). Israeli governments, past and present, do not function solely as the mouthpiece of their citizens; they also speak on behalf of the global Jewish people. On the other hand, most American Jews do not speak the language of Israel, neither literally nor metaphorically; they are not conversant in Hebrew, nor are they comfortable with the ways that Judaism functions in the Jewish state (Gordis, 2019). While the United States has a sizable Israeli expatriate community (Rebhun & Ari, 2010), most American Jews are not Israeli— nor do they want to be. Israel is, at once, a part of and apart from American Jewish life.

While Israel has long served as a symbolic touchstone in American Jewish discourse, it has expanded its reach in the digital era as the Internet has become a tool for creating and sustaining homeland-diaspora relations (Brinkerhoff, 2009). Not only have new technologies made it easier to physically travel across the globe, but they have also made it possible to be simultaneously physically removed from and emotionally present in a faraway place (Fortunati et al., 2013). Thus contemporary American Jews are not only visiting Israel more frequently,[2] but they are also able to connect from afar. As they do so, they are more likely than ever to consume Israeli news and entertainment and to invest time and money in influencing Israeli policies (Sasson, 2014).

Yet at the same time that American Jews are more invested in experiencing and influencing what happens in Israel (Sasson, 2014), they are also increasingly polarized about what that influence ought to yield. Most contemporary American Jews do not believe that support for Israel necessitates automatic support for the Israeli *government*; instead, they express support by advocating for a particular vision of what Israel could be, and by offering political and financial backing for the subset of Israelis who are working to enact that vision (Barnett, 2018; D. Waxman, 2016). While many American Jews are politically liberal (Newport, 2019), others—especially among a growing American Charedi (Ultra-Orthodox) population (Trencher, 2020)—are conservative on both U.S. and Israeli political issues. Because American Jewish political ideology is not monolithic (Weisberg, 2019), American Jews on the political left work toward a vision of Israel that is more in line with their own values of liberal democracy and pluralism, and American Jews on the political right advocate for an Israel that is a safe and secure center of Jewish life. Both seek to influence Israeli policies, and as political scientist Dov Waxman explains, the result has been "a rancorous and divisive debate pitting left against right, critics against defenders of Israeli government policies, Jews against Jews" (2016, p. 10).

This growing polarization of American Jews reflects trends in both the U.S. and Israeli political contexts. In the United States, increased partisan rancor has resituated Israel as a major source of political strife. Israel—once viewed by Democratic and Republican administrations alike as the primary U.S. ally in the Middle East (Ross, 2015)—has become a wedge issue between Republicans and Democrats, and within the Democratic Party itself as its centrist and progressive flanks offer differing visions of the U.S. role in the Middle East. In a way unimaginable a generation ago, today American public figures are engaged in highly contentious debates about whether an alliance with Israel constitutes a strategic asset (Foxman, 2007) or a liability for the United

States (Cordesman, 2010). Scholars have long argued that American Jews' conceptions of Israel have been shaped by the values that Jews have embraced in the American context as much as by Israel itself (e.g., Goren, 1996; Sarna, 1994, 1996). As Israel has become a wedge issue in the American political system, American Jews' conceptions of Israel have reflected those divisions, reframing Israel as a politically contentious issue.

The growing polarization of the American Jewish community also reflects a response to political trends within Israel itself. As American Jews have increasing access to, and interest in, the internal political discourse of Israelis, they have, in the words of sociologist Theodore Sasson, "gone from passive fans sitting in the bleachers to active players on the field of contentious Israeli politics" (2014, p. 163). Despite their physical distance and lack of voting rights, American Jews—like Israelis themselves—have made acrimonious debates about key issues in Israeli policy a central part of their own practice.

In fact, discussions of Israel-related politics have become so contentious that Israel now sits as *the* primary source of intracommunal strife within the American Jewish community. Today Israel is "so deeply ideologically rooted and so divisive" (Gordis, 2019, p. 18) that it has become "one of the most contested issues" confronting American Jewish institutions (Wertheimer, 2018, p. 195) and the one "most likely to destabilize" those institutions and their leaders (Kurtzer et al., 2019). As Waxman explains, "Israel used to bring American Jews together. Now it is driving them apart" (2016, p. 3). As American Jews are increasingly divided in their approaches to Israeli politics, they have built and sustained a growing number of niche Jewish organizations, each with its own political bent (Sasson, 2014), a trend that simultaneously reflects and reinforces the political divides within the American Jewish community.

The result of this polarizing climate is twofold: Any *individual* American Jew can now make choices about how to spend their time and money in ways that more closely reflect their own personal values and views about Israel. Yet as a *collective*, the American Jewish community has lost political capital. Intentionally or not, American Jews are now working at cross-purposes with one another as the causes and organizations that they support vie for radically different visions of Israel and American Jewish relationships to it.

Young Jews have become the symbolic exemplars of the American Jewish community's anxiety about this loss of collective capital. The pages of the American Jewish press and a growing body of Jewish Studies scholarship are brimming with arguments and laments about the uncertain future of the American Jewish relationship to the Jewish state. In this context, today's young Jews are seen as harbingers of what is to come. Some worry that rising intermarriage rates and a collective drop in Jewish tribalism among young Jews portend a future in which American Jews will no longer feel attached to Israel (e.g., S. M. Cohen & Kelman, 2007, 2010).[3] Some bemoan that right-leaning Israeli governmental policies consistently alienate young, overwhelmingly liberal Jews (e.g., Beinart, 2012). Others insist that young American Jews are, in fact, "still connected" to Israel (Sasson et al., 2010), but their growing concern for Palestinians (D. Waxman, 2017) and their willingness to take a stance on internal Israeli policy issues (Sasson, 2014) set them apart from their parents' and grandparents' generations.

Uniting these very different assessments are two commonalities: a belief that young Jews hold the key to the future of the American Jewish relationship to Israel, and a tendency to define "young Jews" as those between the ages of 18 and 35. Yet American Jews in their teens, 20s, and 30s are not the only young Jews assessing their relationships with Israel; American Jewish children do so as well, and their voices have been conspicuously absent from Jewish communal discourse.

It is in childhood—not in young adulthood—that American Jews are first inducted into communal conversations about Israel. It is as children that they begin to make sense of the complex and increasingly contentious intra-Jewish politics vis-à-vis Israel. In synagogues and community centers, schools and camps, at home and online, Jewish children are learning about Israel and forming their own thoughts, beliefs, and feelings about it. They do so in large part through a system of American Jewish education that has moved Israel—slowly over time—from an ancillary role to a core aspect of the socialization of American Jewish youth.

Israel's Changing Role in American Jewish Education

Teaching American Jews about Israel and Zionism has long been a part of Jewish education in the United States. Even before the founding of the modern Israeli state, Jewish educational leaders engaged in public debates about whether Jewish educational institutions ought to focus on creating vibrant Jewish culture embedded in the pluralism of the United States, contributing to Jewish nationalism in Palestine, or both (Krasner, 2005a). Once a new Jewish state was a reality, American Jewish educators turned their arguments to what it meant to enact—and to teach—Zionism in the Diaspora in light of that state (Krasner, 2005b).

Despite the musings of Jewish educational thought leaders, Jewish institutions were slow to adopt Israel as a formal part of Jewish schooling in the United States. A full decade after the 1948 establishment of the state, few Jewish educational institutions had integrated Israel into their curricula (Krasner, 2005b), and a decade after that, the majority of Jewish schools still had no explicit policy regarding the study of Israel (Schiff, 1968). It took three decades after the founding of the state for Israel to take its place as a part of the curriculum of most Jewish educational institutions, and even then, Jewish educational thought leaders lamented that pedagogy generally "reflect[ed] no ideological principles, beyond the assumption that Israel is important" (Chazan, 1979, p. 10). There Israel remained, solidly ensconced in American Jewish education yet undertheorized and uneven in practice, until the turn of the new millennium.

Two shifts in the early 21st century have resituated Israel from the periphery to its new place as a major force in the education of young American Jews. Both of these shifts—the rise of educational travel to Israel, and the emergence of a new class of "Israel educators" devoted to teaching about Israel from the United States—have fundamentally altered the Jewish educational landscape and positioned Israel as an integral part of American Jewish education. Responding to fears that "the socialization of young American Jews into a deep and meaningful connection with present-day Israel is not as self-evident or as natural as it was 40–60 years ago" (Horowitz, 2012, p. 2), the American Jewish community has poured substantive financial and institutional resources into teaching young American Jews about the Jewish state.

The first major shift has been the meteoric rise of Israel educational travel, which has brought hundreds of thousands of Jewish young adults to visit and learn in Israel (L. Saxe et al., 2013). While small-scale educational travel experiences to Israel have long been a part of endeavors to connect young American Jews to the Jewish state (Chazan, 2002), the establishment and proliferation of Taglit-Birthright, which has offered American Jewish young adults access to a philanthropically funded Israel trip, has left an indelible imprint on Jewish education. It has done so by situating "homeland tourism" (Kelner, 2010) as a core and common experience of American Jewish young adults (L. Saxe & Chazan, 2008). In fact, although Taglit-Birthright is relatively new in the long history of American Jewish education, it has quickly established itself as a major institutional force; participants have come to see it as part of the American Jewish establishment, and those on the political left in particular have begun pushing for educational travel "alternatives" both within and outside of the parameters that Taglit-Birthright itself offers (Maltz, 2019; Pink, 2019).

The ascent of Taglit-Birthright has ushered in two concomitant shifts in Jewish education. First, it has heralded renewed focus on social scientific research as a tool for understanding American Jewish relationships to Israel and Jewish education. Taglit-Birthright has demonstrated a firm and lasting commitment to research and evaluation, documenting the short- and long-term impacts of educational travel and igniting a larger social scientific discourse (e.g., Sasson et al., 2014; L. Saxe et al., 2019, 2013). Second, even as Taglit-Birthright has offered unprecedented firsthand access to Israel for young adult American Jews, it has also pulled focus away from the educational experiences of Jewish teens (Bryfman & Cohen, 2015a, 2015b) and children (Zakai & Cohen, 2016). Philanthropy, Jewish educational resources, and Jewish Studies scholarship have all focused on young adults, often to the exclusion of even younger Jews.

Responding to the same concerns as Taglit-Birthright but taking a different tack, Jewish institutions in the United States have pushed for "a more deliberate, systematic approach" to the education of Jewish youth and to the professional preparation of their educators as part of an endeavor that has come to be called Israel education (Horowitz, 2012). The shift to Israel education—a departure from earlier Jewish educational approaches to "Zionist education" (e.g., Allen, 1995; Schenker, 1966; Schiff, 1994;) or "teaching about Israel" (Chazan, 2015)—is more than rhetorical; it connotes a commitment to situating Israel as its own sub-field of Jewish education, substantively different from teaching prayer, classical Jewish texts, or Jewish rituals and holidays, and also separate from the political enterprise of Israel advocacy (Attias, 2015; Horowitz, 2012). While many of the questions of contemporary Israel education have been part of the Jewish educational discourse over the course of many decades—including disagreements about the goals and purposes of teaching American Jews about Israel and conversations about the necessary professional qualifications for doing so—there are also important ways that the new Jewish educational landscape is a departure from prior generations (Zakai, 2014).

The most striking difference has been the development of a new cadre of "Israel educators," a term now used to connote an educator who has specific content and pedagogical content knowledge about Israel. Although one can be both an "Israel educator" and a "Jewish educator," Israel educators are not simply Jewish educators "who also happen to know about, or have visited Israel" (Sinclair et al., 2012, p. 2). Instead, they are expected to have a deep understanding of Israel *and* to engage seriously with the intellectual, social, emotional, and spiritual challenges of teaching Israel to their learners (Backenroth & Sinclair, 2014). These educators have developed in large part thanks to the efforts of a growing number of institutions committed to supporting and professionalizing the work of Israel education. The Chicago-based iCenter for Israel Education, the Atlanta-based Center for Israel Education, the Jewish Agency for Israel's Makom, and others have developed both curricular resources and professional learning experiences for inducting Israel educators and supporting their continued growth as Jewish professionals.

As a result, Israel education occurs in virtually every kind of Jewish educational institution that exists in the United States today: early childhood centers (Applebaum & Zakai, 2020), Jewish day and supplementary schools (L. Grant, 2007; Pomson et al., 2014), camps (Kopelowitz & Weiss, 2014), adult education programs (L. Grant, 2001), and central agencies (Gerber & Mazor, 2003). Although there is no consensus about either the goals of Israel education (L. Grant et al., 2012; Zakai, 2014) or the educational practices that best support its varied purposes (Isaacs, 2011), there is agreement that learning about Israel is "an essential part of Jewish education" (L. Grant & Kopelowitz, 2012, p. 167).

Thus, at the same time that Israel has become an increasingly partisan and polarized topic in the American Jewish community, it has also solidified its standing in American Jewish education. This confluence of factors has meant that Israel is, at once, unifying and divisive; it is increasingly a core aspect of the education of young Jews even as it highlights deep fissures in the American Jewish community.

One of those fissures exists in the ways that educators and educational institutions frame the purpose of their work. There exists no common answer or shared language to the fundamental question that lies at the heart of Israel education: Why should young Jews in the United States learn about Israel? To tie them to an ancestral homeland (Attias, 2015) and/or a normative vision of contemporary Jewish life (Alexander, 2015)? To cultivate in them a personal connection (Chazan, 2016) and/or a sense of collective responsibility (Sinclair, 2013; Winer, 2019)? To give them a deep understanding of the past (Stein, 2020) and/or a gateway to participating in the conversations of the present (Gringras, 2020)? To orient them toward patriotism and/or cosmopolitanism (Ariel, 2020)? To prepare them to defend Israel in the court of public opinion (Dershowitz, 2004) and/or to work toward a more just vision for Israeli society and Israeli–Palestinian relations (L. Zimmerman, 2016)? A lack of consensus around the goals of Israel education has meant that just as different segments of the American Jewish community are often working at cross-purposes when it comes to Israel advocacy and philanthropy, so too are educators and educational institutions when it comes to Israel education.

Further complicating this contested terrain is the fact that there is little empirical evidence to illuminate how Jewish children themselves think and feel about Israel, and thus little understanding of what types of learning experiences might be interesting, meaningful, and developmentally well suited to them. This lacuna has shaped the contours not only of academic scholarship but also of the practice of Israel education in homes, schools, synagogues, and camps, as conversations and curricula are often rooted in deep philosophical commitments and scant empirical understanding of how children learn.

Developments in American Jewish Childhood

One additional factor is essential for understanding the experiences of contemporary American Jewish children. For it is not only that Israel and its role in American Jewish life and Jewish education have shifted over time; so too has the very nature of Jewish childhood itself. Historians and sociologists have shown that childhood is culturally contingent; it is experienced and understood in different ways in different societies across time and space (Corsaro, 2017; Heywood, 2017; Stearns, 2016). Contemporary American Jewish children, growing up in digitally connected and demographically diverse communities, have childhoods that differ in significant ways from those of their parents and grandparents.

The primary difference lies in the access that today's children have to digital technology, which is so omnipresent in children's lives that it appears unremarkable to them (Plowman et al., 2010). Even before children are old enough to enter school, digital interaction is part of their daily lives (Zevenbergen, 2007; Zevenbergen & Logan, 2008). Around-the-clock connectivity has meant that children can lead parallel lives in real and virtual spaces (Craft, 2012), often using their digital presence in order to support or expand their offline interests (Chaudron, 2015).

One of the many capabilities that the digital world has made possible is to connect to remote places on the globe. Even very young children are able to use connective technologies to build ties to distant people and places (e.g., Kelly, 2015), and in a way unimaginable a generation ago, today's youth have opportunities for "connected presence" in places that are geographically distant from their own homes (Licoppe & Smoreda, 2005). Thus, in an era of global connectivity, Jewish children who do not live in Israel can—and do—experience the sights and sounds of life there through video-conference platforms, social media, livestreamed newscasts, and other forms of digital communication.

In the digital age, children are consumers, curators, and creators of online content. At their fingertips, they have access to information—and misinformation—unknown to children of prior generations. Yet children are more than passive recipients (Jenkins et al., 2009), often crafting online experiences for themselves and their peers. Children tend to view the Internet not only as a place to find information but also as a place to share their own ideas about the world (Friedrich et al., 2017), and they create digital content starting at a very young age (Lankshear & Knobel, 2003). For contemporary Jewish children, digital technologies offer not only ways of learning *about* Jewish life but also ways of *being* Jewish. Many of the children in this book viewed digital information as a primary source of their learning about and relating to Israel, at times supplementing or even supplanting their formal educational experiences.

Digital access is not the only aspect of Jewish life that distinguishes between contemporary American Jewish children and their progenitors; so do the changing demographics of American Jewish families. Jewish parents today are cisgender heterosexual and LGBTQ; endogamous, intermarried, and single; and from a wide array of ethnic and racial backgrounds (Eichler-Levine, 2018; Kim & Leavitt, 2016; Limonic, 2019; Pew Research Center, 2021; Pomson & Schnoor, 2018; Wertheimer, 2018). As children are growing up in this increasingly diverse American Jewish community, they view as normative the fact that Jews engage in a range of practices, beliefs, and customs. As they turn their gaze toward Israel, they do not expect to see a monolithic Jewish culture; they would never imagine such a thing might exist in the minds of others.

American Jewish Children and the State of Israel

Children pay careful attention to the conversations of adults. As both U.S. politics and Jewish communal discourse grow increasingly polarized, and as Israel plays a prominent role in both conversations, American Jewish children are—at the same time—encouraged to learn about Israel and often shut out of conversations that would allow them to do so.

In one direction, children are pushed to view Israel as central to Jewish expression and commitment. Jewish educators often frame Israel as integral to Jewish life and an essential part of the experience of being a Jew in the United States (L. Grant & Kopelowitz, 2012). Conversations about Israel are omnipresent in American Jewish communities. As political commentator Peter Beinart (2014) explains, "American Jews are inundated with commentary about Israel. They read about it in newspapers and websites. They hear about it on TV and radio. They attend lectures about it at their local universities and Jewish Community Centers." While children may not be the target audience of these conversations, they observe and listen as the adults in their communities situate Israel as a core aspect of the American Jewish experience.

In the other direction, children are pulled by the ambivalence of American Jewish leaders, who are often fearful to speak about contentious Israel-related issues, even in adult company. Rabbis in the United States frequently describe feeling "hesitant," "afraid," and "muzzled" to engage their congregations in deep and meaningful conversations about Israel, fearing political backlash from their own communities (Goodstein, 2014; Sirbu, 2013; Troy, 2011; Yoffie, 2014). Jewish educators worry—often with good cause—that speaking about Israel with their students will bring complaints from parents whose views on Israel differ from their own (Zakai, 2011, 2012). As historian Jack Wertheimer explains, "As a matter of public discussion [Israel] is handled in a gingerly fashion" in contemporary Jewish institutions (2018, p. 199). Thus Israel is, at once, pervasive and often glossed over in conversation, simultaneously ubiquitous and taboo. Young Jews often interpret this as a situation in which people in the Jewish community are always talking about Israel without ever *really* talking about Israel (Zakai, 2011).

Compounding this hesitance to talk about Israel is the fact that when Jewish communal leaders call for more meaningful conversations about Israel with Jewish youth, they rarely include Jewish children; instead, they focus exclusively on teenage and young adult Jews. Scholars and Jewish communal leaders who agree about little else when it comes to American Jewish relationships to Israel are virtually united in their belief that teenagers and college-age Jewish students ought to have access to educational programs that help them better learn about Israel (e.g., Bryfman & Cohen, 2015a, 2015b; Koren et al., 2015). As Rabbi Janet Liss explains, the central questions of American Jewish adults are, "How do we talk to our teenagers about Israel? How do we prepare our college-bound students and how do we support our college students as they confront the challenges of powerful oppositional voices on campus today?" (2017, p. xiii). Young children do not even factor into the list of most adults' concerns about Israel and Israel education even though childhood, not adolescence, is when people begin to take on the "stories, beliefs, and observances that symbolize belonging to [a] community" (Fowler, 1981, p. 149).

When Jewish communal leaders *do* consider the questions and needs of children, they are often at a loss about how to speak with children in developmentally appropriate ways about key issues in contemporary Jewish life. Some adults adopt a gut-level reaction about how Jewish children ought to be inducted into communal conversations. For example, Peter Beinart (2017) argues that children ought to learn "love first, truth later," a philosophy adopted by many Jewish educators and parents but one that lacks empirical understanding of children's ways of thinking about patriotism, nationalism, and community. Others still have no words at all for including children in important conversations about contemporary Jewish life. Novelist Dara Horn (2019), for instance, wrote after the deadly shooting at a synagogue in Poway, California, "I don't know what to tell my children." When communal leaders struggle to speak with their own children, how can they be expected to address the needs of other people's children?

Yet as adults hesitate to speak with children about important issues, children themselves are turning to other sources of information. Today's American Jewish children have unprecedented—and often unmediated—access to information from across the globe. Because they understand that Israel holds an important place in their own community, and because they view the adults in their lives as insufficiently prepared to speak with them about Israel, they often turn to online sources of information, most of which were never constructed to be sites for children's learning. At times, children are sophisticated information consumers, actively stitching together a patchwork understanding of Israel and its role in American and Jewish communities, past and present. At other times, they flail about in the absence of adult guides who could help them better understand the world.

The result is that children who receive a Jewish education in the United States have been socialized to view Israel as a central part of Judaism and take seriously the task of learning about it, yet at the same time they receive insufficient adult guidance to help them process and make sense of information about Israel. A Jewish community that has long been interested in the transmission of values, beliefs, and knowledge to its youth, and that has invested considerable resources in understanding and cultivating teens' and young adults' relationships to Israel, has also overlooked the experiences of Jewish children as they struggle to make sense of what has become a central part of the American Jewish experience.

Scholars of Jewish education have repeatedly voiced concerns that current approaches to educating Jewish children about Israel are inadequate. There is widespread consensus that Israel education must become "more developmentally attuned" (Horowitz, 2012, p. 12) because current practice often inadvertently "communicat[es] developmentally inappropriate messages" to young learners (Pomson et al., p. 48). As educational philosopher Alex Sinclair explains, one of the most important next steps for the field of Jewish education is to "develop language that helps us talk about and teach about the complexities of Israel with children, including young children, in developmentally-appropriate" ways (2014, para. 9).

Yet if adults are to better respond to the concerns, needs, and questions of children, they will require a deeper understanding of how children themselves think, feel, and develop over time. For any attempts to support children must be built upon a foundational understanding of children's learning and development.

Children's Learning and Development

At the heart of children's learning sits a paradox: Each individual child is unique and, also, children often develop along common trajectories. Children's cognitive, social, and physical development each follow "reasonably predictable patterns" (Wood, 2007, p. 12). At the same time, there is considerable individual and cultural variation among children (Bjorklund & Causey, 2018; Gutiérrez & Rogoff, 2003; Rogoff et al., 2017; Rogoff et al., 2015). To understand the interplay between children's commonalities and their idiosyncrasies, it is important to recognize both the locations and the ways in which children's learning occurs.

Children's learning occurs in a large and complex ecological system and cannot be isolated to a single source or educational experience (Bronfenbrenner, 1979; Kress & Elias, 2008). Children learn in so many places, of which formal schooling is only one (Waite, 2017). They stitch together ideas and build theories about the world as they travel from home to homeroom, from the playground to online. As Jewish children learn about Israel, many do so in part through Jewish institutions that are explicitly engaged in the work of Israel education—synagogues, day and supplementary schools, camps, and youth movements—and in conversations with family members (AJC Survey of American Jewish Opinion, 2021). Yet they also learn about Israel from a myriad of other sources: picture books, television, social media, Internet searches, peer-to-peer conversations, and more. Like detectives scouring their environments for clues about the world (Acer & Gözen, 2020; Ainslie, 2000), children actively construct new understanding by gathering information and making sense of what they encounter (e.g., Bruner, 1966; Narayan et al., 2013; Piaget, 1954).

As children learn from an array of sources and interactions, they acquire some skills that are subject-specific and some that are generalizable across contexts, which is often referred to as domain-specific and domain-general learning (Bjorklund & Causey, 2018; Rakison & Yermolayeva, 2011). Just as a child learning to play an instrument practices both transferable skills like focus and executive functioning along with specific skills such as rhythm and pitch, so too does a child learning about Israel gain knowledge and skills that are both specific to and transcend the particular subject matter. Because learning about Israel requires learning in multiple disciplines—including history, political science, literature, art, Hebrew language, and more—as Jewish children learn about Israel, they draw from and further develop a wide range of domain-specific and domain-general knowledge and skills.

Yet children's learning is never purely a cognitive endeavor. As children learn about countries, nations, and societies in particular, they develop *both* a deeper understanding of subjects like geography, politics, history and culture, *and* an emerging sense of national affiliation (Barrett, 2007). Even very young children are capable of developing both initial theories about how countries function (Applebaum et al., 2020) and emerging conceptions of collective belonging (Wastell & Degotardi, 2017). As they continue to learn over time, children simultaneously exhibit common patterns and considerable variation in their understanding and identification (Barrett, 2007). Thus children from different national contexts may develop common ideas and stereotypes about nations and the people who constitute them (Barrett, 2005) even as children whose families have similar cultural backgrounds may develop dissimilar beliefs about belonging and affinity (Pustulka et al., 2016). For Jewish children in the United States, making sense of Israel requires a complex and ongoing negotiation between place(s) and self, understanding and belonging. It requires them to consider and navigate a host of interconnected questions: *What is Israel? What is the United States? What is the Jewish people? Who am I?* As sociologist Shaul Kelner explains, this process entails "creating their understandings of themselves and of Israel in the meeting of the two" (2010, p. 198).

This book examines how one group of children in a particular religio-cultural minority community in the United States develop ideas, theories, and beliefs about a specific place, illuminating how they piece together learning over time. It tells a story about how children, as they grow, simultaneously affirm and question communal norms, developing their own sense of collective affiliation, obligation, and belonging. In doing so, it sheds light on contemporary childhood and the distinct ways that children of the digital age understand and interpret the world.

The Study

The 35 children whose stories and experiences sit at the heart of this book have made it possible to understand the unique ways that American Jewish children, geographically distant from yet remotely connected to Israel, understand and make sense of it. Throughout the course of their elementary school years, from their initial kindergarten experiences in the 2012–13 school year up through the culmination of fifth grade in the 2017–18 school year, my research team and I worked with the children in order to understand their thoughts and feelings about Israel.[4]

Much of the time, children's interactions with adults are prescriptive. Adults, usually operating from a place of love and good intentions, guide children's learning and behavior and carefully construct their physical and psychological environments. In this case, however, our work with the children was descriptive. We set out not to guide or shape, but to understand: What did the world look like through the children's eyes? As they thought about Israel, what did they understand about it and what did they believe it to be? As they reflected on their own lives, how did they position themselves vis-à-vis Israel? What questions, feelings, and concerns arose for the children as they considered what it meant to be a Jewish child living in the United States, looking at Israel from afar? And how did the children's answers to these questions shift as they grew older?

In order to understand the children's beliefs and experiences, we sought what scholars of education call "windows into children's thinking" (McGee, 1996; Wright et al., 2008): glimpses into the ways that the children themselves viewed Israel and its place in their own lives. We interviewed the children, asking them directly to explain their thoughts, beliefs, and feelings.[5] We showed the children images and played them sound clips of places and events in Israel, asking them to articulate what these prompts elicited for them.[6] We invited the children to tell us stories about Israel, past and present.[7] At times, we collected artwork or school projects that the children had produced, or asked the children to describe and explain what they had made.[8] As developmental psychiatrist Robert Coles explains, "The heart of [this] work is listening, years of it, and then describing what has been heard—selecting the most revealing excerpts, I hope, from the endless stories children have to tell" (1986b, p. 17).

At various points throughout the years, we checked in with the children's parents and teachers to give us a greater context for understanding the children's words.[9] At times, those adults confirmed and added texture to the children's perceptions. At other moments, however, adults' explanations directly clashed with the children's reports, and at those times our analysis has, without exception, favored the viewpoints of the children. Because the purpose of this research is to illuminate children's ways of experiencing the world, we sought to understand the children's perceptions even when they did not match those of the adults in their lives.

Partnering with children in the service of research relies on an ethical and methodological stance that respects children as people who are capable of offering worthwhile, believable accounts of their own lives and worldviews (Alderson & Morrow, 2011). Researchers, like myself, who hold this view aim to help children "give voice to their own interpretations and thoughts rather than relying solely on our adult interpretation of their lives" (Eder & Fingerson, 2001, p. 181). The goal is to conduct research *with* children rather than research *on* children, empowering children to offer their own explanations of the worlds around and inside of them (Christensen & James, 2017). In the words of one child in this study, Avigail (grade 5), "Any time that we have a conversation or an interview, it makes me feel more in touch with Israel and how kids' minds can share what they believe [about] Israel. It makes me think that kids' thoughts matter, and what kids say is important."

All of the children who lent their thoughts to this book did so over the course of multiple years. In the pages that follow, most children appear at six different grade levels, kindergarten through fifth grade. As is the case with Avigail (5) above, whenever a child is directly quoted, the grade level at which the child made those particular comments will be given in parentheses after their pseudonym. This convention is an attempt to balance two priorities: to allow the children, as much as possible, to speak in their own words, and to allow the reader to follow their development over time.

The Children and Their Stories

Who are these children, and why, in the words of Avigail, do their thoughts matter? To understand the particular children in this study, it is first important to realize that they are not a uniform group. While the children themselves are all U.S. citizens, collectively their parents hail from eight different countries, and their grandparents were born in twice as many places. Six distinct languages are spoken in their homes. The 17 girls and 18 boys include oldest, youngest, middle, and only children. Some are loquacious extroverts, while others are more private and reserved. Table 1.1 provides basic demographic information about these children.

TABLE I.1. Participant Demographic Information

	Participant	Gender	Denominational Affiliation	Parents' Birthplace(s)	Primary Language(s) Spoken in the Home
1	**Ari**	M	Reform	United States, Israel	English, Hebrew
2	**Avigail**	F	Modern Orthodox	Israel	Hebrew, English
3	**Bella**	F	Reform	Iran	English, Farsi
4	**Brent**	M	Traditional	United States, Iran	English, Farsi
5	**Caleb**	M	Traditional	United States, Iran	English, Farsi
6	**Carly**	F	Reform/Conservative	United States, Iran	English
7	**David**	M	Reform	United States	English
8	**Dina**	F	Orthodox	South Africa, Israel	English, Hebrew
9	**Elliott**	M	Traditional	Iran	English, Farsi
10	**Esther**	F	Conservative	Iran	English, Farsi
11	**Gabe**	M	Reform	United States, Iran	Farsi, Hebrew, English
12	**Gia**	F	Reform/Conservative	United States	English, Farsi
13	**Hannah**	F	Just Jewish	United States	English
14	**Hayim**	M	Traditional	Iran	English, Hebrew, Farsi
15	**Isaac**	M	Traditional	Iran	English, Farsi
16	**Isabelle**	F	Unaffiliated	United States, Israel	English, Hebrew
17	**Jacob**	M	Orthodox	Israel	English, Hebrew, French
18	**Julia**	F	Conservative	United States	English
19	**Keren**	F	Conservative	Canada, Israel	English, Hebrew
20	**Kevin**	M	Conservative	United States	English
21	**Lailah**	F	Unaffiliated	Israel	Hebrew, English
22	**Lior**	M	Just Jewish	Israel	English, Hebrew, French
23	**Maya**	F	Unaffiliated	Israel, Czech Republic	English, Hebrew, Czech
24	**Micah**	M	Conservative	United States, Israel	English, Hebrew
25	**Naomi**	F	Reform	Unites States	English, Spanish
26	**Noah**	M	Unaffiliated	United States	English
27	**Olivia**	F	Conservative	Israel, Peru	English, Hebrew
28	**Owen**	M	Unaffiliated	United States	English
29	**Pearl**	F	Chabad	United States, Israel	English, Hebrew
30	**Peter**	M	Just Jewish	United States, Israel	English, Hebrew
31	**Rina**	F	Reform/Conservative	United States	English
32	**Ryan**	M	Reform/Conservative	United States	English
33	**Samantha**	F	Reform	United States	English
34	**Seth**	M	Reform	Argentina, Israel	Spanish, Hebrew, English
35	**Tzvi**	M	Conservative	United States, Israel	English, Hebrew

The children have had varying exposure to and experiences with Israel. Some of them have never been to Israel, while others have visited for extended periods. Some have relatives living in Israel, others do not. The children's families sit at various points on the political spectrum, and their parents have differing ways of situating Israel in their own lives, ranging from "Zionist, no equivocation" to "mostly ambivalent."

As a collective, the children have only four things in common: they all identify as Jewish, they are part of a subpopulation of American Jewish children who actively participate in Jewish learning, they all grew up in the Los Angeles metropolitan area, and they are all part of the same grade cohort. Each of these commonalities, as well as the shades of difference among the children, are important for understanding who the children are and how they have developed over time.

1. Jewish Children

All of the children in this study identify as Jewish, though not all of their parents do. From the earliest days of kindergarten and through early adolescence and beyond, these children have situated themselves as members of the Jewish community and express pride in their affiliation as Jews. As Maya (2) explained, "We are Jewish, and we like being Jewish."

Even so, the children's ideas and beliefs about Judaism differ, with some children viewing being Jewish as a central part of their lives and others considering it a more peripheral piece. Their families affiliate with Reform, Conservative, Modern Orthodox, and Chabad synagogues, and some have no synagogue affiliation at all. They celebrate Jewish holidays with Ashkenazi (Eastern European), Sephardi (Spanish), and Mizrachi (Middle Eastern) customs and foods, and a handful come from homes that blend Jewish ethnic traditions. Thus even their common Jewish heritage is not monolithic.

2. Jewishly Educated Jewish Children

In addition to self-identifying as Jewish, all of the children in this study are Jewishly educated Jewish children. While Jews are often considered to be a highly educated group as a whole (Hackett et al., 2016), not all

Jews are learned about Judaism itself. In fact, over half of children living in U.S. Jewish households receive no formal Jewish education at all.[10] The children in this study are all part of the subset of Jewish children who *are* engaged in learning about Judaism, though the institutional contexts in which they do so are not uniform.

In kindergarten, all of the children attended a private Jewish day school. It is in their kindergarten classes that I first encountered the children, having partnered with three Jewish day schools who agreed to give us access to the children and their parents.[11] The particular schools were invited because they cater to different segments of the Jewish community. The goal was to enlist a set of participants that varied in their Jewish practices and affiliations, as well as in their experiences and relationships to Israel. Thus, these schools have different denominational affiliations: one is Reform, one Conservative, and one a nondenominational community school.[12] The ethnic background of the school's typical families also varies; one has predominantly Ashkenazi children, one has a sizable Persian Jewish population, and one serves a large number of Israeli expatriate families. Children who attend Jewish day schools are often viewed as exemplary, rather than typical, Jewish learners because they receive consistent formal Jewish educational instruction over time. Yet while some of the children are now day school graduates, others have taken different paths.

In the years since kindergarten, the children have scattered well beyond their original schools.[13] As parents have made different choices for their children as they grow (Pomson & Schnoor, 2018), the children's own educational experiences have diverged. Several attend suburban public schools. One child is homeschooled. Another moved to Israel with her family before returning to the United States to attend public school. Many are still enrolled in full-time Jewish schools, but even those who aren't continue to be engaged in some form of Jewish learning: in synagogue-based supplementary schools, in Jewish camps, or with tutors at home.

3. Growing Up in Jewish Los Angeles

All of the children grew up primarily in the Los Angeles metropolitan area. Los Angeles is home to the fourth largest Jewish population of any city in the world, trailing only Tel Aviv, New York City, and Jerusalem (K. S. Wilson, 2013). To grow up as a Jewish child in Los Angeles means being part of a large and diverse Jewish population generally clustered in Jewishly dense neighborhoods (Phillips, 2007). As historian Karen Wilson explains, "Los Angeles has developed arguably the world's most varied Jewish population, with representatives from Israel and virtually every diasporic community asserting Jewish identities that range from religious to ethnic to political to social" (2013, p. 4). Los Angeles Jews—like the city's residents as a whole—are a multiethnic, multilingual group. The city is home to Jews who are recent immigrants and to those whose family trees have been rooted in the United States for multiple generations. Of particular note are the city's large Persian Jewish and Israeli expatriate communities (Gold, 2006; Herman, 1998).

For the young Angelenos in this study, the heterogeneity of their Jewish community is not mere happenstance; it is deeply ingrained in the way that they experience their surroundings. The Jewish institutions in their neighborhoods celebrate Nowruz (the Persian New Year) and Yom Ha'atzmaut (Israeli Independence Day) along with Rosh Hashanah (the Jewish New Year) and Shabbat (the Sabbath). The children all know Jews from ethnic and denominational backgrounds different from their own, and many of them speak freely about the foods and traditions of other Jewish communities. As one child, Gabe (4), explained, whenever a kid in his day school class has a birthday, all the children sing birthday songs—first in English, then in Hebrew and Farsi, and then, depending on the year and who is in the class, in Spanish or another language.

In addition to its cultural diversity, Jewish Los Angeles is known for innovative and creative expressions of Jewish religion and culture (Windmueller, 2017). The city is home to a wide variety of Jewish arts and cultural institutions, summer camps, mega-synagogues, independent spiritual communities, political advocacy institutions, and the West Coast hubs of both the Reform and Conservative movements. Private Jewish day schools play an outsized role in the city's Jewish institutional landscape. As historian of Jewish education Sara Smith explains, "The sheer scale of the day school system and the geographic area the schools serve is beyond that of any other city" (2017, p. 282). Los Angeles boasts more than two dozen Jewish day schools, and their presence is both prominent and unabashed. Yet the city's high levels of day school attendance may reflect parents' skepticism about the particulars of the LA public school system more than a deep commitment to Jewish learning (Smith, 2017). Thus in their approaches to Jewish education, LA families with children enrolled in day schools may be less exceptional and more similar to those whose children learn primarily in Jewish supplementary schools and camps than is the case in other cities.

4. Children with a Shared Grade Cohort

The final attribute that unites all of the children is that they are part of the same grade cohort, having started kindergarten in the 2012–13 school year. Cohort studies offer a rich way of understanding how people change over time (G. Payne, 2006) and have been used to explore various aspects of child development in different national and cultural contexts (Pirus et al., 2010). Yet while studies of Jewish populations have recognized the importance of longitudinal research for understanding how Jews develop conceptions and experiences of Jewish life over time (Pomson & Schnoor, 2018), existing longitudinal research about North American Jews has focused on teens and young adults (e.g., Keysar & Kosmin, 2004; Kosmin & Keysar, 2000; L. Saxe et al., 2009). The children in this study offer a rare glimpse into the ways that some of the youngest members of the Jewish community understand and make sense of their own Jewish lives.

Although cohort studies are well suited for understanding how a group of individuals changes over time, they are also generationally situated, accounting only for the experiences of those born at a particular time and place. Thus they must be understood contextually. As the children in this cohort study traversed elementary school, world events happened at the same moments in all of the children's schooling. The children were, for example, all rising second graders during the 2014 war between Israel and Gaza, and they were all in fourth grade during the 2016 Trump–Clinton presidential election. Their reflections on global events are rooted in particular moments in time and in particular phases in the children's own growth. The historical and the developmental are inexorably intertwined in their reflections, which illuminate how children's developmental capacities can interact with particular global events to shape children's perceptions of the world.

Learning from the Children

These children—from ethnically, denominationally, and politically diverse Jewish backgrounds, and united by grade cohort, geography, and the presence of Jewish education in their lives—have been reflective and articulate narrators of their own experiences. They have both beautiful idiosyncrasies and striking commonalities, and they have been in equal measures serious and playful about the years-long task of illuminating their own ideas and beliefs.

This book frames the children's reflections and development over time as a rich case that sheds light on key issues in contemporary education (Yin, 1994). I make no claims that these particular children's experiences are universal nor that they represent all children or even all Jewish children in the United States. Young people's development is deeply rooted in culture and context (Lave & Wenger, 1991; Nasir, 2012; G. Saxe, 1999) and reflects different lived experiences of the world (Wenger, 1998). Therefore, throughout the pages of this book I use the terms "the children" or "these children" to refer to the particular children in this study. When I use more generic phrases like "children's theories" or "children's thoughts and feelings," it refers to a larger body of knowledge that reflects the experiences of multiple groups of children in a variety of contexts. This convention is an attempt to recognize the commonalities in children's developmental trajectories without overstating the homogeneity of children's experiences (Alldred, 1998).

The children in this study thought deeply about how countries and societies do and ought to function, and over the course of elementary school they built increasingly sophisticated foundational conceptions of civics, history, and politics in both the United States and Israel. Yet the children also expressed anger and frustration about the limits of their own understanding about one question in particular: how to make sense of contested issues in contemporary Jewish and Israeli life. These two pillars—the depths of the children's thinking, and the profound intensity of their frustration—undergird the argument that if educational institutions are to take seriously children's thinking, they must shift in order to better help children navigate a world in which people disagree. This argument is simultaneously rooted in, and transcends, the experiences of the particular children in this study. The claims I make all arise from years of listening to the specific children who shared their thoughts and feelings with me. At the same time, they illuminate a much broader set of educational questions that emerge from children's attempts to understand a complex and increasingly politically polarized world.

Chapter 1 begins to illuminate the depth of children's thoughts about how societies function by exploring how children develop an understanding of, and beliefs about, countries and nations. Examining the children's developing ideas and beliefs about Israel and the United States, I argue that children invest considerable effort in mapping the conceptual boundaries of countries—what countries are, what values they represent, and who calls them home. I distinguish between children's cognitive ideas about countries—which follow a developmental pattern shared by different children in this study—and children's affective beliefs about belonging—about which the children were much more idiosyncratic. Both children's cognitive ideas and their affective beliefs demonstrate that children can, and do, reflect on complex questions about home and homeland.

Turning from children's understanding of the present to their thinking about the past, chapter 2 highlights how children tell origin stories, which function as another window into children's thinking about countries and societies. I demonstrate how the children in this study narrated the "same" story about the history of Israel in different ways at different ages, and I reveal how older children were able to deliberately craft distinct stories for different audiences. I argue that children begin to build foundational ideas about historical narrative and audience even when their stories about the past are not chronological or evidentiary.

Chapter 3 continues to illuminate the depths of children's thinking, yet it also begins to explore how and why educational practices need to pivot in order to better help children understand and participate in a world in which people disagree. It does so by focusing on children's understanding of geopolitical conflict, a topic that children think about from a surprisingly early age. By highlighting these children's ideas about Israel's relationship with Arabs, and especially Palestinians, I challenge the belief that geopolitical conflict is not an appropriate topic for children. I argue that children need and want more adult guidance as they navigate a world in which such conflict exists, and that providing such guidance requires a delicate balance between helping children better understand the world as it is and working to recreate the world as it ought to be.

Chapter 4 focuses on children's understanding of civic and political issues that extend beyond violent conflict, and it spotlights children's expressions of anger and frustration. Although children express civic awareness from a very early age, only in middle childhood do they begin to understand that political engagement is one key avenue for civic participation. Yet the children in this study remained unaware of Israeli civic and political issues long after they began to understand the politics of American life. The result was that, when children *did* encounter civic and political questions relating to Israel, they were caught off guard, unable to make sense of important and contested issues in contemporary Jewish and Israeli life. Recounting the children's feelings of profound anger when this occurred, this chapter situates the frustration of American Jewish youth not as a sign of disillusionment with Israeli policies but rather as a desperate plea for a new approach to education.

The book concludes by offering next steps for both elementary education writ large and Jewish education about Israel in particular. I argue that in order to be sensitive to the ideas, beliefs, and questions of children, educational practices will need to help children make sense of disagreements both within and between countries and communities. Doing so will require shifting from transmitting to children the knowledge that adults already have about the world, to helping children ask, investigate, and deliberate about important questions, including those for which the answers are still unknown or unsettled. In the particular context of Jewish education, this will require reorienting both the aims and the practices of Israel education, focusing less on helping young people forge a personal connection to Israel (Chazan, 2016; Horowitz, 2012) and more on helping them understand and participate in collective discourse and disagreement.

Each of these chapters differs in three important ways from existing scholarship about American Jews and Israel. First, this book gives voice to the American Jewish children who have been consistently absent from prior attempts to gauge American Jewish relationships to Israel. It does so not only because children are in the process of becoming future adults who will someday shape society, but also because children already are human beings in their own right (Uprichard, 2008). Children have beliefs, opinions, conceptions, and misconceptions, like all people, and these are worthy of inclusion in the broader discourse about American Judaism.

Second, the children themselves—not their families (cf. Pomson & Schnoor, 2018, 2008) or their educational institutions (cf. Aharon & Pomson, 2018; Pomson et al., 2014)—are the focus of analysis. While children are necessarily influenced by their environments, including both the formal and informal contexts in which they learn, this book does not attempt to untangle the myriad educational influences on a child's process of development—though it does raise questions about the ways that adults can shape opportunities for, and obstacles to, children's learning. Instead, this book endeavors to capture children's views of the world as they develop at specific historical moments and within a particular religio-cultural milieu. In so doing, it frames childhood not as the yield of educational tilling by families, schools, and communities but rather as a human experience of sense-making and meaning-making.

Third, this study pivots from the educational philosophy that undergirds much of the sociological literature on American Jewish youth. Many existing studies operate on a deficit approach grounded in a theory of cultural literacy. This approach, rooted in the tradition of education reformers like E. D. Hirsch (1988), assumes that there is a body of knowledge that literate Jews must know and a set of beliefs that Jews ought to hold about Israel (e.g., Troen & Fish, 2017). Measured against those standards, today's American Jewish youth manifest a severe "deficit" (Koren et al., 2015, p. 20).[14]

Whether or not they do so intentionally, scholars who focus on the deficits of American Jewish youth reflect both the philosophy and the metaphors of what educational philosopher Paulo Freire calls the banking model of education—an approach that views young people as receptacles into which knowledge may be deposited. In Freire's words, this approach "interpret[s] a certain historical moment of the [young] people's consciousness as evidence of their . . . deficiency" (2018/1968, p. 166). Yet children, no less than adults, work to actively construct their own understanding of the world; they are, as Freire explains, "critical co-investigators in dialogue" with adults (p. 81). Viewing them as such builds upon a long tradition in democratic education that recognizes young people as capable of understanding, and taking action to influence, their communities (e.g., Dewey, 1916; Rugg, 1921).

Departing from a banking approach, this book aims to uncover not what American Jewish children don't sufficiently know or feel about Israel but rather what they *do* think and feel, and how they articulate what Israel means in their own lives (Levisohn, 2016). It follows the work of sociopsychologist Bethamie Horowitz (2002), who argues that in order to better understand American Jews, scholarship ought to move from questions that assess "How Jewish are American Jews?" to those that uncover "How are American Jews Jewish?" This book attempts to make a similar shift in the study of American Jewish relationships to Israel, asking not "How knowledgeable about or connected to Israel are young American Jews?" but rather "How do young American Jews know and connect to Israel?" This approach conceives of knowledge and connection as fluid over time and as continually constructed by individuals and communities.

It also honors "children's ways of knowing" (Robertson & Gerber, 2001; H. Wilson, 1998), recognizing that even when children do not use the language or concepts that adults do, they nonetheless merit inclusion in the broader discussions of American and Jewish life. As renowned education reformer Deborah Meier explains, "We all have more in common with five-year-olds than we imagine; adults remain, in Piaget's terms, 'concrete thinkers,' and little kids, lo and behold, are capable of some very fancy abstractions" (2002/1995, p. 47). This book is an attempt to illuminate children's "fancy abstractions" and to trace how children's ideas and feelings change and develop over time. It is also a testament to what remains unchanged throughout childhood: the depth of children's emotions, and the seriousness of their thought.

1

"The Place Where I Belong"

Children's Conceptions of Home and Homeland

In Caleb's 6-year-old mind, there are three kinds of places in the world: the United States of America, other countries to which his family is connected, and everywhere else. He calls the United States "our world" because it is the only world he has ever known. He has never traveled outside of the United States nor has he ever lived anywhere but Los Angeles. The rest of the world is foreign. He understands that there are many countries, each with its own leaders, languages, and customs, but he doesn't think much about them.

It is the middle category—other countries to which his family is connected—that trips him up the most. As a Persian Jew and the first generation in his family born in the United States, Caleb understands that his family has ties to places outside of the U.S. When I ask him about Israel, he is excited to tell me his family's story.

"Do you know what? My dad used to be in Israel," he explains, "and there used to be a mean president, and my dad had to leave. He used to have trophies, but his [mom said he had to leave and pack a suitcase]. His clothes were in it, and he couldn't put his trophies in, so he just left— left his trophies there."

Caleb's story about his father's previous life "in Israel" is, in fact, a story about his father's departure from Iran, but there is little difference between the two in Caleb's mind. He is learning both Farsi and Hebrew, but he can't yet tell their alphabets apart even though he knows that neither is English. He understands that his family talks about both Israel and Iran, and he "likes" both these places, but he doesn't see them as distinct.

Five years later, as a fifth grader, Caleb tells the story of his family's journey to the U.S. quite differently. "Way, way, way back like 30, 40 years ago," he begins, my whole family lived in Iran, but then [there was] the king. He was a bad king, and so my dad and his family all tried to escape, and now they all live here. . . . My dad was about my age. My grandpa and grandma decided to send my dad and my [youngest] uncle to England to a boarding school to be safe, and they sent my oldest uncle to LA. After a couple of years, my grandpa and grandma picked [up] my dad and uncle from England and they all met up in LA and they spent the rest of their life here. And it was just a horrible case, because their whole life was in Iran. My dad loved Iran. All of his friends were there.

Caleb's reflections on Iran as an 11-year-old show the evolution of his thinking over time. It is not only that he can distinguish between the U.S., Iran, Israel, and other countries such as England, but that he frames these places very differently in relation to his own family story. He understands that his family is "Persian and so are Iranians in Iran," but he doesn't think of Iran as his home in any way. By contrast, he views both the United States and the state of Israel as "my country." He claims the U.S. as his own because "we are U.S. citizens and we live in the U.S." He views Israel as a "home for the Jewish people," and he explains, "I think [Israel's] my country because we are one and all the Jews are together."

For Caleb, as for all children, childhood is a time for sorting through what it means to be part of a world that is divided into distinct countries and communities. How, then, do children like Caleb think about what countries are? How do children conceive of their own national identities? To what and to whom do children view themselves as connected, and what do they believe constitutes belonging?

This chapter addresses these questions by examining how the children in this study have thought and felt about the United States, the state of Israel, and other countries to which their families have ties, tracking how the children's thoughts and feelings have developed over time. Scholars have long been interested in children's development of national and collective identity, understanding childhood as the time when both ideas about and affiliations toward nations and national groups emerge (Barrett, 2007). For the most part, studies of children have been cross-sectional rather than longitudinal.[1] Examining the thinking of large numbers of children at a particular moment in time makes it possible to understand children's developmental *stages*, pinpointing differences among children of different ages. Yet tracing children—even relatively small numbers of children—over time makes it possible to see children's developmental *pathways*: how development shifts over time in ways that are both common among children and particular to an individual child. It is those pathways—which at times converge and at times diverge—that form the basis of how children experience the world.

Tracing children's developmental pathways over time, I argue that children invest considerable effort in mapping the conceptual boundaries of countries—what countries are, what ideals and values they represent, and who calls them home. This process of conceptual mapping, which contains both cognitive and affective components, is one facet of children's complex thinking about how communities do and ought to function. The children in this study shared a set of cognitive developmental steps as they attempted to understand what it means to call a place a country and a homeland. Yet as the children worked to make sense of "the place where I belong" (Dina, 2), they situated themselves in many different ways. Their pathways, at times shared and at times idiosyncratic, illuminate the complexity of children's thoughts and relationships to country and nation, home and homeland.

The Favorite Countries of American Jewish Children

A child's primary job is to figure out the world and how it functions (Bruner, 1990). Children actively work to make sense of a wide range of ideas and concepts: family, the rules of the natural world, the routines of daily life, and more (Piaget, 2007/1928). Among the many complex ideas that children attempt to sort through is how countries and communities function (Piaget &Weil, 1951).

As children develop initial ideas and beliefs about countries, they often begin to express a clear favoritism toward their own home country. In early childhood, before the age of 7, children's beliefs about countries are relatively idiosyncratic. They may like a particular country because it sounds exotic (Jahoda, 1962) or because a relative has visited it (Piaget & Weil, 1951). Yet beginning at age 7, and continuing throughout childhood, children from a wide range of national and cultural contexts exhibit a clear preference for their own country over all other countries (e.g., Gimenez et al., 2003; Jaspers et al., 1972; Johnson et al., 1970.) Children prefer the countries in which they live precisely because they understand them to be "my own country" (Piaget & Weil, 1951, p. 566).

Thus it is not surprising that as the American Jewish children in this study reflected on the world, they expressed a clear preference for the United States beginning in first or second grade. As 7-year-olds, they began to explicitly state, "I love America" (Naomi, 1) and "I stand proud 'cause I'm in America" (Brent, 1). Like other American children (e.g., R. D. Hess & Torney, 1967), they spoke of being "proud of America" (Tzvi, 2), "proud to be American" (Olivia, 3), and "proud of my country" (Ryan, 4). Unprompted, the children would frequently make patriotic gestures such as reciting the pledge of allegiance (Esther, K) or singing patriotic songs like "You're a Grand Old Flag" (Lailah, K), "Yankee Doodle" (Esther, 2), and "America the Beautiful" (Samantha, 2). Expressions of pride continued throughout elementary school as children made comments like "I'm proud to be an American" (Samantha, 4), "My favorite colors are red, white, and blue" (Maya, 1), and "America rules!" (Seth, 4).

Yet the children also clearly exhibited a preference for Israel, viewing Israel as "better than" other countries (Maya, 3). Mirroring the language they used to describe their own home country, they spoke of being "proud of this really important place" (Gia, 2) and "proud of Israel" (Rina, 5). Ryan (4) explained that just looking at the Israeli flag "I have pride in me." In Olivia's words (5), "Israel makes me feel very proud."

Thus, at the same developmental stage in which children worldwide tend to exhibit a preference for their own country, these American Jewish children were expressing a two-tiered preference for *both* the United States *and* Israel, in that order. The children referred to the United States as "my first favorite place" (Maya, 3; Carly, 3) and Israel as a "second favorite place" (Ryan, 2; Lailah, 4). Regardless of whether they had ever visited Israel, and irrespective of whether they had any Israeli family members, the children viewed Israel as "another special place" (Seth, 2) or "also a very important place" (Ari, 2).

Even the children who could clearly identify their own family's journeys to the United States from places other than Israel expressed this two-tiered preference. Like Caleb in the opening anecdote of this chapter, these children understood that their families had ties to countries that were neither the United States nor Israel, yet they consistently ranked the United States and then Israel above the countries from which their families migrated. For example, Maya (4) explained that the United States is "my home, it's my first home. Israel's my second, and then third, Czech Republic." Similarly, Brent (5) described his three-tiered ranking as follows: "Iran is basically our other homeland, but just not as holy as Israel is.... Israel is a good place to be, and a holy place, and America is the best, really, really great." The children consistently classified their own homes in the U.S. above Israel, and Israel above other places in the world.

How, then, did the children think about these two "favorite" countries? How did they understand the United States and Israel, and what ideas and values did they believe these places represent? The children were united in their conceptions of their two favorite countries and remarkably consistent over time: They viewed the United States as a free country welcoming to all and Israel as a special Jewish place.

The United States: The Land of the Free and the Home of Everybody

Children are engaged in a continual process of national enculturation, a developmental process through which they are inducted into the heritage, values, customs, and practices of their national groups (Barrett, 2007). As children work to understand and to participate in their communities, they seek to make sense of the geography (Matthews, 1992), economy (Webley, 2005), political structure (Berti, 2005), and historical narratives (Barton, 2001a) of their national groups.

In order for children to develop a sense of national identity, they must first know of the existence of a national group and they must locate themselves as a member of that group (Barrett, 2007). As they thought about the United States, the children in this study did both from the earliest days of elementary school. They understood that "I live in America!" (Kevin, K) and that "America is my state!" (Micah, K). They viewed the United States as "my country where I live" (Rina, K) and identified themselves as "one of the American people" (Ryan, K).

Yet even at age 5 or 6, the children understood that the United States is more than a physical place; it also represents a set of ideals. As the children thought about the United States, and what distinguished "our country" (Samantha, K) from other places in the world, they consistently described the United States as a "free country" (Samantha, 3). In the first years of elementary school (K–1), the children used generic language to explain that "America is freedom" (Hayim, 1) and "America is free" (Keren, 1). Yet what did it mean, in the children's minds, to call the United States a "country that's free" (Carly, K)? In kindergarten and first grade, the children could not explain what makes the United States "free." Consider, for example, a conversation with kindergartener Hayim as he was looking at a photograph of an American flag.

> INTERVIEWER: What does it make you think about when you see this?
> HAYIM: America.
> INTERVIEWER: What about America?
> HAYIM: America's a free state.
> INTERVIEWER: What makes it a free state?
> HAYIM: Because . . . I can't [answer]. I don't know.

In these early years of elementary school, the children embraced the characterization of the United States as a place of "liberty" (Esther, K), but they had not yet developed a sense of what that concept might mean.

Beginning in second grade, however, the children began to develop initial theories about what makes the United States "a free place" (Maya, 2). Some children associated American freedom with the abolition of slavery. "I'm free and there's no more slavery," explained Gia (2), and Naomi (3) equated American freedom with the Passover story of liberation from slavery "when they [be]came free." Other children believed that the United States was free because "we are not ruled over" (Keren, 3). These children spoke about how "at first, we were owned by the British and we had a huge war and then we were free" (Samantha, 3). Another subset of the children equated American freedom with a personal freedom of choice. In the United States, explained Rina (3), "I can do whatever I want. Except not go to school." Similarly, Micah (3) reflected on "how lucky our lives are to be able to go anywhere or do anything." For second and third graders, American freedom often had a single, clearly defined explanation.

By the time the children were in fourth grade, most had come to see the United States as a "free country" (Keren, 4) because it is a place that offers *multiple* forms of freedom to its inhabitants. The children believed that, as U.S. residents, "I have freedom of speech" (Hayim, 4), "freedom of religion" (Avigail, 5), and "freedom of choice" (Tzvi, 4). Many fourth and fifth graders equated freedom with having rights. As Keren (4) explained, "It's a free country because we have lots of rights." In Carly's (4) words, "I'm free to be who I want here. I have rights to do what I want." For these fourth and fifth graders, "To be American is to know that you're free" (Gia, 5) and to know that "we have a free country and a free society" (Tzvi, 4). For them, the United States had become not only a place where "all the U.S. citizens all have rights" (Caleb, 5) but also a country that acts as a beacon of freedom for "all people" (Carly, 4).

These older children did not believe that the United States was flawless in its attempt to exemplify a free society. As Samantha (5) explained, "America is an amazing place, but sometimes we make mistakes." In Rina's words (5): "I'm proud to live free now. But I'm glad I didn't live in the 1960s because people weren't equal. It took so long for whites to believe Blacks to be equal. Why would I want to live in an era where people weren't free when it's the land of the free and the home of the brave?"

As Rina pointed to inequality in the past, she also worried about it in the present. She was especially concerned about efforts to restrict immigration "because if people want to live in America, people should live in America. We had a revolutionary war so that people could live free in the land." Rather than view the story of America as one of expanding and contracting freedoms over time (e.g., Foner, 2005), these children viewed the United States as on a clear path toward increasing freedoms, with some "mistakes" along the way.

If the children viewed freedom as the bedrock of American society, they also viewed other things as quintessentially American: football (David, 2), the Statue of Liberty (Gia, 2), pickup trucks (Seth, 5), and Thanksgiving (Bella, 5). Yet in the children's minds, the most American thing of all was a shared belief that "everybody belongs here" (Maya, 4). Regardless of how many generations their own families had been in the United States, and irrespective of their parents' political beliefs, the children were united in their assertion that "America is a place for all people" (Lailah, 4).

Like children's belief that the United States represents freedom, their conception that the U.S. is "a very diverse country and everyone's welcome" (Hayim, 5) developed over time as the children grew. The seeds of this idea were present as early as first or second grade, as the children made claims like "everybody can come to America" (Gia, 1) or "all kinds of people are part of America" (Dina, 2). At this age, the children tended to conceive of the United States as a geographically "very big place" (Lailah, 2). They assumed that "because it's a big place, a lot of people can go there" (Jacob, 2). America, in their minds, had enough room to welcome any kind of person who wanted to live there.

By fourth grade, the children's thinking had become more abstract, and they began to believe that the United States welcomed "everyone" (Seth, 4) not because it has enough physical space but because it has an explicit ideological commitment to be "a place for all people" (Gia, 5). As Lailah (4) explained, "China is a place for Chinese people. Israel is a place for Jewish people. America is a place for all people." In Brent's (5) words, "To be American means you come from many different people. America is so diverse." The children viewed diversity as an inherent part of the United States and reflected on "how beautiful it can be learning from other people different than myself in the U.S." (Caleb, 5).

In the upper elementary grades, the children frequently discussed how, in the United States, it is possible to be any religion, race, or national origin. They spoke of how "America's not a place for just one religion" (Esther, 4) but rather "you could be any religion in America" (Naomi, 4). Often conflating race and nationality, they believed that "America is a country for every race, like African American, Indian, Israeli, Australian, Chinese, Korean, anything" (Lailah, 5). Many of the children also explicitly framed the U.S. as a place where "we welcome immigrants" (Naomi, 4) because "people in America, they're from a lot of places" (Maya, 4).

As fourth and fifth graders, though not before, the children explicitly tied an American commitment to being "a place for everyone" (Carly, 5) to their own experiences as "a Jew in an American place" (Ryan, 4). Most of the children understood that Jews were a demographic minority in the United States. As Naomi (5) explained, "Americans right now are mostly Christians [although] we do have Jews [because] we have a lot of religions." Nonetheless, they viewed the United States as a "Jewish-friendly" place (Hayim, 4) because a country that would accept all people would be a good place for Jews to live. As Seth (4) explained, "Mexicans could stay here, Jews could stay here, everyone could stay here." Even as these children acknowledged that "some people in America are antisemites" (Keren, 5), they also viewed themselves as living in a country whose commitment to diversity made it safe for them "to be in a Jewish community" (Maya, 5). In their minds, their own Jewish lives were made possible because America is a place in which all people "have the rights and the privileges to be different and unique" (Caleb, 5).

Summary of Children's Ideas about the United States

Throughout their elementary years, the children understood that the United States represents not only a physical place but also a conceptual ideal. From the earliest days of elementary school, the children knew that they lived in the United States, and they self-identified as American. They viewed the United States as a bastion of freedom and as a place that welcomes people of all different religions, races, and national origins. The children's ideas about what it means to call the United States a free place and a place for all people evolved over time, becoming less generic and more specific as the children grew. By the end of elementary school, they began to reflect on what it means to be part of a Jewish minority in a diverse American society.

Israel: The Jewish State

A child's process of learning about the world is often thought of like a pebble dropped in water, creating ripples of understanding that begin in the center and expand outward over time. Many studies of young children have found that children must understand their own local area before expanding their knowledge to include places that are geographically farther away (Arenas, 1999; Gould, 1973; Gould & White, 1986).

Yet a pebble enters a pond in a single location, rippling out from one center; children, on the other hand, may make sense of the world from multiple entry points at once. Especially in an age of digital connectivity when children can access places that are geographically far away (Palfrey & Gasser, 2016), their understanding may be more like a branch than a pebble, entering the water in many places and creating ripples—though differently shaped ones—along multiple edges.

This is certainly the case for the children in this study, who from the earliest days of elementary school knew not only about the country in which they live but also about a faraway Jewish state. Their understanding of the world developed—although in different ways—from both of these places. American Jewish children know about Israel even in preschool (Applebaum et al., 2020), and by the time they enter elementary school, they have a clearly formulated idea that Israel is a distinctly Jewish place.

The children in this study understood, even at age 5, that Israel was a "Jewish state" (Brent, K), a "Jewish place" (Gia, K), and a "Jewish country" (Samantha, K). But what makes Israel Jewish? Why, in the children's minds, is Israel a Jewish state, place, or country? Throughout elementary school, the children offered four different theories[2] about what makes Israel distinctly Jewish: (1) It is home for lots of Jews, (2) it has lots of Judaism, (3) it offers special protections for Jews, and (4) it has a special relationship with God. Most children provided multiple of these explanations, often in a single conversation. And, like the children's ideas about the United States as a free and welcoming country, their overall conceptions of Israel as a Jewish place remained constant over time even though, as the children grew, they developed new explanations for why this was the case. See table 1.1 for the trajectory of children's evolving conceptions of what makes Israel Jewish.

TABLE 1.1. Children's Conceptions of What Makes Israel a Jewish State

Children's Theories	K	1	2	3	4	5
1. "Israel has lots of Jewish people"						
Large number of Jews currently live in Israel	✓	✓	✓	✓	✓	✓
The ancestors of the Jewish people lived in Israel	-	-	✓	✓	✓	✓
2. "Israel has lots of Judaism"						
Synagogues, rabbis, and kosher food are in Israel	✓	✓	✓	-	-	-
Israel is holy for Judaism and other religions	-	-	-	✓	✓	✓
3. "Israel offers special protections for Jews"						
Israel offers protection to Jews who live there	✓	✓	✓	✓	✓	✓
Israel offers protection to Jews around the world	-	-	-	✓	✓	✓
4. "Israel has a special connection to God"						
Israel is God's special place	✓	✓	✓	-	-	-
God promised the land of Israel to the Jewish people	-	-	✓	✓	✓	✓

Theory 1: Israel Is a Jewish State because Lots of Jews Live(d) There

The children's most common explanation for what makes Israel a Jewish state was demographic; lots of Jews, they understood, live in Israel. Younger and older children sounded virtually identical in their explanations that "a lot of Jewish people live there" (Samantha, K; Bella, 5) or "many people [in Israel] are Jewish" (Eli, K; Isaac, 4). Only beginning in fourth grade did children explicitly frame Israel's population as majority Jewish, saying things like "the majority of Israel is Jewish" (Naomi, 4) or "Israel has a majority of Jews" (Samantha, 5). Yet throughout childhood, they spoke about Israel as having "so many Jews" (Brent, K; Tzvi, 5) or "a lot of Jews" (Elliott, 1; Seth, 3). As Gia (5) explained, "Israel is the go-to place for Jewish people."

That many Jewish people live in Israel was, for most children, the primary defining characteristic of the Jewish state. Yet it was also the most complicated of the children's theories about what makes Israel a Jewish state. This is because, in order to think about a state "made of Jewish people" (Avigail, 1), they also had to consider Jews living outside of the state and non-Jews living within its borders.

Throughout elementary school, the children clearly understood that even though "many people" (Tzvi, 2) who live in Israel are Jewish, not all Jews live in Israel. At every grade level they would make claims like, "I live in America, and I'm Jewish" (Kevin, K), "I'm Jewish and I live in Los Angeles" (Gia, 3), or "I live here, in America, and I am also Jewish" (Lailah, 5). They also clearly knew that Jews lived in countries other than the two largest Jewish population centers of Israel and the United States. They spoke of Jews living in Argentina (Seth), the Czech Republic (Maya), England (Caleb), Germany (Lailah), Iran (Brent), Iraq (Lior), Mexico (Hannah), Peru (Olivia), Romania (Lailah), and elsewhere. Thus, throughout childhood, the children understood that many—but by no means all—Jews live in Israel.

If the children clearly understood that Jews both live outside of Israel and constitute "most" (Hayim, K) of Israel's population, did they also understand that there are non-Jews who make their homes in Israel? Approximately half of the children (17 of 35) understood this even at age 5 or 6. For example, Hayim (K) explained that most but not all of the Jews in the world live in Israel and most but not all people in Israel are Jewish. In Bella's words (K), Israel is "a place where Jewish people live . . .

but you can live in Israel if you're not a Jewish person." These children were able to distinguish between "the Jewish and Israeli people" (Samantha, K), understanding that Israeli citizens and Jewish people were overlapping but not identical categories.

Yet for the other half of the children, the idea that there can be non-Jewish Israelis was not conceptually clear in early elementary school. For example, David (K) defined Israel as "a land for Jews" and when asked what that meant, he explained, "It means only Jews can be there." Similarly, Lior (K) insisted that Israel is a place "only for the Jewish people," and Ari (K) defined Israel as a "special country . . . because it's only allowed for Jews." Other children in early elementary school were not convinced that only Jews live in Israel but were generally unclear about who constitutes Israel's population. For example, Hannah (K) spoke confidently about how not all Jews lived in Israel—after all, she herself did not—but when asked if all the people in Israel are Jewish she replied, "Mm, maybe?" Dina (K) expressed similar uncertainty, saying, "I know that Israel is a place that's full of Jewish people. And all of the people in Israel are—wait. All of the people in Israel are Jewish, right? Are they? I don't know." For these young children, it was abundantly clear that Jews can live outside of Israel, but a lot less clear whether non-Jews can live in Israel.

Yet even for these children, uncertainty faded over time so that by second or third grade, the children were unanimous in their understanding that some residents of Israel are not Jewish. At this point, the children were generally clear that non-Jews constitute part of Israel's population, though not all were clear *who* those non-Jews include. At age 8 or 9, some children could identify types of non-Jewish people who live in Israel including Christians (Avigail, 2; Dina, 2; Samantha, 2), Muslims (Carly, 2; Keren, 2; Maya, 2), and Arabs (Hayim, 2; Jacob, 2). Other children at this age had a more generic understanding that "different kinds of people" live in Israel (Bella, 2) but they could not name any specific people other than Jews. These children talked about a generic "Israeli people" (Elliott, 2) or "Hebrew people" (Esther, 2) who were distinct from the "Jewish people" (Ari, 2). However, when they were explicitly asked to identify other populations that live in Israel, these children expressed hesitancy, explaining, in Gia's words, "I think there are other people [but] I don't know what they're called." See table 1.2 for children's developing theories about who constitutes Israel's residents.

TABLE 1.2. Children's Theories about Who Lives in Israel

Children's Theories	K-1	2–3	4–5
Jews live in Israel	✓	✓	✓
Jews live outside of Israel	✓	✓	✓
Non-Jews live in Israel	Clear for some children, unclear for others	Clear *that* non-Jews live in Israel, unclear *who* those non-Jews are	Clear that Christians and Muslims live in Israel, unclear whether Arabs live in Israel

By the end of elementary school, the idea that other religious traditions—especially Christianity and Islam—had strong ties to Israel was clear to the children. Even the children who had struggled with this idea in second and third grade understood by fourth or fifth grade that "Christian people, Muslim people, Jewish people, and all sorts of people" can live in Israel (Gia, 4). These children recognized that even though Israel is "mostly a Jewish state where Jews live," it is also true that "many different kinds of religions live in Israel" (Tzvi, 4).

Less clear for children at the fourth- and fifth-grade level was the role that Arabs played in the Jewish state, in part because the children had a fuzzy conceptual understanding of what "Arab" meant. The children all understood that Israel can be "a home to a lot of religions" (Gia, 5), but approximately half of the fourth and fifth graders did not view "Arab" as an overlapping category with "Christian" or "Muslim." This is evident by their talk of "Muslims *and* Arabs" (Keren, 5) or "Arabs *or* Muslims" (Lailah, 5) rather than "Muslim Arabs." Many of these children also delineated between Arabs and Jews, explaining that "Arabs and Jewish people are different" (Hannah, 5). Others, however, believed it was possible to be a Jewish Arab, which they defined as a Jew who was born in an Arab country. For example, Avigail (5) explained that "you could be Arabic and still be Jewish," and Lior (5) spoke about a child he identified as "Arab-Jewish." These children knew that there are people—including Jewish people—who live in or were born in "Arab countries" (Dina, 4), but they had little sense of either the possibility that Arabs could live in Israel or that one could be simultaneously Muslim and Arab.

The other half of the children clearly understood by fourth or fifth grade that "some Arab people live in Israel" (Carly, 4). Yet while these children could offer rudimentary explanations as to why Christians

("Jesus was born there," Gia, 4) or Muslims ("the Dome of the Rock is there," Rina, 5) might have deep ties to the land of Israel, they were unable to explain why Arabs living in Israel might have a connection to it. Why did some Arabs live in Israel? Even those children who clearly knew that a sizable part of the Israeli population identifies as Arab offered either surface-level explanations like "they like the weather" (Elliott, 4) or admitted ignorance, explaining "I don't know. Maybe they just come and live" (Seth, 5). These children believed that Jews live in Israel because "that's where their home country is" (Jacob, 4) but when asked why Arabs live in Israel they replied, "I don't know" (Jacob, 4).

The children spent a great deal of intellectual effort trying to sort through—with varying degrees of conceptual clarity—how to think about Israel as a demographically Jewish state given the fact that not all Jews live there and that some people who live there are not Jewish. In the younger grades (K–1) the children focused exclusively on contemporary Israel, thinking about current-day demographics of the Jewish state. But as they grew, the children also began to regard Israel as a Jewish state because "Jewish people's ancestors lived there" (Gia, 3). In second grade, only two children considered Israel a Jewish state because "it's where my family's ancestors lived" (Gia, 2) and "our grand-grandfather, our ancestor" lived there (Olivia, 2). Beginning in third grade, and continuing through the rest of elementary school, it was a common refrain in children's reflections that Israel is a Jewish state because "it's where Jews' ancestors were" (Hayim, 3) or "our ancestors were buried there" (Olivia, 3). Using both collective (e.g., "We're Jews and our ancestors lived there," Keren, 4) and personal language (e.g., a "country that my ancestors lived in," Lior, 4), children in the upper grades insisted that Israel is a Jewish state not only because of its demographic Jewish majority today but also because it is where "Jewish ancestors came from" (Pearl, 4).

Theory 2: Israel Is a Jewish State because Lots of Judaism Exists There

Israel is Jewish, the children explained, not only because of Jewish people but also because of the expressions of Judaism that can be found there. In Bella's (1) words, Israel is Jewish because it has "a lot of Jewish things." In the early grades (K–3), this was children's second most common explanation of what makes Israel Jewish.

What "Jewish things" did the young children expect to find in Israel? They described Israel as a place with "a lot of rabbis" (Samantha, K) and "people who pray and go to temple" (Brent, 1). Several children viewed Israel as a place that encouraged "kosher eating" (Hayim, 3) because "there's no shrimp [and] they don't catch squid, they don't catch crab, they don't catch lobster, no pig" (Hayim, K). Others discussed the fact that in Israel it is common to find Jewish ritual objects such as *kippot* (religious head coverings) (Avigail, K), Torah scrolls (Isaac, K), menorahs (Jacob, 1), and mezuzahs (Olivia, 3).

While in the early grades (K–3) the children believed that these visible identifiers of Jewishness were both common in Israel and a substantive part of what makes Israel Jewish, in the later grades (4–6) this kind of framing dropped from children's explanations of what makes Israel Jewish. As the children grew, they continued to believe that Israel was a place for "practicing Judaism" (Gabe, 4), but they focused less on Jewish ritual items and more on a belief that Israel is a "holy place" (Gia, 4).

As the children neared the end of elementary school and were more acutely aware of non-Jewish presence in Israel, they were much more likely to talk about "our religion and other people's religions" (Avigail, 4) than they were to talk only about the symbols of Jewish life that could be found in Israel. Although children in the upper grades continued to acknowledge that Israel has "temples and Jewish places like kosher markets" (Dina, 4), they did so not as a way of explaining what is distinctly *Jewish* about Israel, but rather as a way of explaining that one of the hallmarks of Israel is that it is a place where all kinds of "people are visiting temples" (Seth, 4). They spoke of Jewish ritual markers as they also explained sites of other religions including "Muslim[s'] own synagogue or temple" (Brent, 5) and "Armenian temples and churches for the Catholics" (Lailah, 5). Thus discussions of "Jewish places" (Olivia, 1) and "Jewish things" (Bella, 1) had a different resonance in the early and later grades, starting as a way of explaining Israel's Jewish character and transforming into a way of discussing the ways that Israel is a "holy land" (Naomi, 4) for multiple religious traditions.

Theory 3: Israel Is a Jewish State because It Offers Special Protections for Jews

Most of the children spoke, at each grade level, about the ways that they viewed Israel as offering special protections for the Jews who live(d) there. For example, in identical language, Ari (K) and Bella (4) described the Israeli army as "protecting Jews in Israel." In the early grades (K–2), the children used generic language of "protecting Israel" (Caleb, K; Gabe, 2) to reflect their belief that Israeli soldiers, the Israeli government, and/or God "protects Israel and the Jews there" (Avigail, 2). At this point in their development, the children emphasized the ways that "Israel is trying to protect *their* country" (Lior, 2, emphasis added), envisioning Israeli Jews as the primary recipients of protection.

In the later grades (3–5), by contrast, the children explicitly spoke of Israel as providing protections to Jews around the world, not only Jews living in Israel. Consider, for example, the transformations of two children, Gia and Brent, whose shifts over time were typical of the children as a whole. In early elementary school, Gia (2) spoke repeatedly about how the Israeli army "is working to protect Israel" and Brent (K) discussed how Israeli soldiers "protect people that are Jewish in Israel." But by late elementary school, both children had expanded their conception of the scope of Israel's protections to include not only "people that are Jewish in Israel" but also Jews around the world, including themselves and their immediate families. In Brent's (5) words, "I feel protected because I know these men or these women are fighting for us, and it just makes me feel good because I know I'm safe." As Gia (4) explained, it "makes me feel like I'm protected all the way here [in the United States]."

As they reached the upper grades of elementary school, most of the children repeatedly insisted that Israel protected not only its citizens but also their own families in the United States. Pearl (5) believed that Israel protects not only Israelis but also "everyone" who is Jewish. In her words, "I know we are safe because we have these people protecting us. They're protecting all the Jews." Hannah (4) explained, "Even in the United States Jewish people are protected because Israel is a strong country," and Caleb (5) insisted that Israel "work[s] to keep us safe and to keep the Jewish religion alive." These children's conceptions of what makes Israel a Jewish state had expanded to encompass a notion that

Israel—through its military might and its mere existence—offered protections to Jewish populations outside of its borders. In Hannah's (5) words, "Israel has power, so I also have power too." This extension of power, stretching from Israel to Jews around the world, was part of how these older children conceived of what makes Israel a Jewish state.

Theory 4: Israel Is a Jewish State because It Has a Special Relationship with God

Many of the children also spoke of Israel as a place with a special relationship with God, though—like their understanding of Israel's population, Israel's relationship to Judaism, and the protection Israel offers to Jews—children's ideas about this shifted over time. In the early grades (K–2), children spoke frequently about Israel as being "God's favorite state" (Jacob, K). At this phase in their development, many children believed that "God made Israel" (Esther, 1) and "God lives there" (David, 2). They spoke of Israel as "important" to God (Gia, 1) and the place that "God picked to be His" (Naomi, 1). Most important in the children's telling, they trusted that "God is always with Israel" (Avigail, 2). They believed that "God made Israel and then He made it safe" (Caleb, K) and "God is surrounding it with a big bubble" (Naomi, K).

How, in the children's mind, was the idea that "God made Israel" (David, 2) related to the fact that Israel is a Jewish state? Kids offered three different explanations about the relationship between God and the Jewishness of Israel. Some children thought that God *is* Jewish. As Brent (1) explained, "God wanted to create that place because He was Jewish." Some believed that God made Israel especially *for* Jews. Dina (1) explained that "God made it specially for [my family in Israel] and all the Jewish people that live there." Other children believed that Israel is a place where Jews can best communicate *with* God. These children framed Israel as a place where Jews "pray to God" (Carly, 2), "talk to God" (Rina, 2), and where it is most likely that "God hears Jews" (David, 1). Regardless of which explanation the children offered, it was clear that in their minds, Israel is a Jewish place in part because of God's special relationship to it.

As they grew, the children continued to believe in a special connection between Israel and God, but they spoke less about Israel as a place where "God's there" (Samantha, 2) and more about Israel as a promise that God made to the Jewish people (and others). In kindergarten and first grade, not a single child referred to Israel as "the Promised Land," but in second grade several children began to speak about it as "the land that God gave us [Jews]" (Hayim, 2) or the land that "God gave them [Jews in Israel]" (Samantha, 2). By third grade, approximately one quarter of the children (8 of 35) had begun to explicitly refer to Israel as "the Promised Land."

To whom did the children believe the land had been promised? Children offered five different explanations, believing that God promised the land to Abraham (e.g., Tzvi, 3), to the Israelites (e.g., Dina, 3), to all Jews living in Israel (e.g., Samantha, 3), to the Jewish people more broadly (e.g. Gabe, 3), or to all of the people who claim it and "not only the Jewish people" (Gia, 3). Many children offered shifting answers in a single conversation, speaking alternately of "how God promised us [Jews] the land of Israel" (Keren, 3) and how "God promised them [ancestors of the Jewish people] the land" (Keren, 3).

In fourth and fifth grade, approximately one third of the children (12 of 35) spoke of Israel as "the Promised Land," often listing this description as one of many ways to conceive of Israel. For example, Naomi (4) explained, "Israel is a country of the Jewish people, and Israel is above Africa, and it's the Promised Land." Rina (5) offered, "Israel is a country that was the Promised Land [given] by God in the Torah, and it's the modern country, and it's awesome." Although the majority of the children never described Israel as "the Promised Land," the sizable minority who did developed this conception only over time as they traversed elementary school.

Summary of Children's Ideas about Israel

From the time they began elementary school, the children already had in their minds the idea that Israel is a Jewish state or a Jewish country. As they grew, they voiced multiple explanations about what makes Israel Jewish. They viewed Israel as a Jewish place because it offers special protections for the Jews who live there and to Jews around the world. The children believed that Jewish symbols and rituals were prevalent in Israeli society, and they imagined that God—whom the children viewed as either Jewish or as having a special relationship to Jews—lived in Israel. Most of all, the children viewed Israel as Jewish because of its demographic Jewish majority. Slowly over time, the children sorted through what it means to call Israel a Jewish state even though not all Jews—including themselves—live there, and not all those who live there are Jewish. Over the course of elementary school, the children came to embrace Israel as a place that carries symbolic importance for Muslims and Christians as well as Jews, yet they struggled to understand the role that Arabs play in the Jewish state.

Developing a Conception of Homeland

As children work to understand the world, they attempt to make sense of the fact that countries are not only geographic places but also hold societies that set forth particular values and ideals. This is a complex notion that children begin to think about from a very early age, and it develops in tandem with another abstract idea: the concept of homeland. At its most basic level, the idea of homeland connotes connections between people and place, recognizing that some places hold special symbolic resonance for particular communities.

From the earliest research focused on children's understandings of countries, the idea of homeland has been considered important in demonstrating that children can understand not only how countries function in the world but also that they personally "belong to a particular country" (Piaget & Weil, 1951, p. 563); cognitive understanding and communal affiliation both play a role in children's development. More recent studies have shown how children view the homelands in which they and/or their parents were born (e.g., González et al., 2016; Nugent, 1994; Wilberg, 2002), demonstrating that even elementary school children can recognize the complex and multilayered nature of national identity, reflecting on the relationships among birthplace, citizenship, residence, and family ties (Murphy & Laugharne, 2013).

Children's understanding of homeland is also often deeply personal even as it is rooted in an understanding of the collective (Coles, 1986b), and there is considerable cultural variation in the ways that children of different communities conceive of home and homeland (H. Lee, 2009). How, then, do American Jewish children develop a conception of homeland? And how do their ideas about the relationships between people and place develop over time?

To understand how American Jewish children view these questions, it is first necessary to understand how Israel functions as a symbolic homeland in the American Jewish community writ large. Most American Jews have not migrated to the United States from Israel, and neither they nor their immediate families have ever lived there. As sociologist Shaul Kelner explains, the vast majority of "Jews living outside of Israel tend to be . . . non-migrants whose ties with the country, if any, are based on its status as a *symbolic* homeland" (2010, p. 13). While the country once represented the dreams rather than the lived experiences of American Jews (Sarna, 1994), contemporary American Jews are more likely than ever to visit Israel, consume its news and entertainment, and invest time and money in influencing its internal policies. As they do so, they are "increasingly behaving like other contemporary diaspora communities" who participate from afar in cultural practices of the homeland (Sasson, 2014). Thus children growing up within the American Jewish community might be thought of as having a "diasporic birthright" (Tsolidis & Pollard, 2010), a phrase used to describe children's connections to a country in which they have not personally lived but that nonetheless serves as a symbolic touchstone for their families and communities.

For the children in this study, attempting to make sense of the fact that Israel functions as a symbolic homeland of the Jewish people was a cognitive process that unfolded in three distinct phases. Although these phases did not occur at the same time for each child, they did occur in sequence. The children first situated Israel as a physical place in the world, then distinguished between its geographic location and its symbolic import, and only then began to conceive of Israel as a homeland for the Jewish people.

The first phase of the children's development was marked by two concomitant trends: It was clear to the children that Israel is a geographic place that exists both in the world and on a map, and that Israel is far away from their own lives. Israel's physical distance was one of the first things that the children understood.[3] At this phase, the children described Israel as "far away from here" (Jacob, 1) and "across the sea from here" (Avigail, 1). Most of the children's descriptions highlighted Israel's distance in relation to their own home communities. For example, Naomi (1) depicted Israel as on "the other side of the earth from America" and Samantha (1) explained that "Israel is on the other side [of the globe], so we're here and then Israel is over there." Some children also described Israel in terms of the length of time it might take for them to travel to it—whether or not they themselves had actually ever been there. For example, Carly (2), who had never been to Israel, recounted that "Israel is about 15 hours away from here, all the way across from here." Similarly, Micah (2) explained, "It's 14 or 13 hours away from LA. It's probably the longest plane ride I've ever took in my whole life."

This initial phase occurred for most children in kindergarten and first grade, though for some it continued in second and third as well. This phase of children's conceptual development roughly corresponds with a Piagetian framework, which understands 5- to 8-year-olds as viewing countries primarily as geographic units rather than particular forms of collective affiliation (Piaget, 1928; Piaget & Weil, 1951).

As the children neared the end of this phase, they also began to describe Israel in geographic terms. They began to explain that it is "in the Middle East" (Seth, 2) or "right next to Egypt" (Rina, 2) or "in the continent Africa but some people say it's in Asia" (Samantha, 2). Although most children did not have the language to describe Israel in this way until second grade at the earliest, these descriptions are part of the first phase of children's development because they characterize Israel in relation to geography.

In the second phase, the children began to distinguish between Israel as a physical place in the world and Israel as a symbolic place in the collective consciousness of the Jewish people. It is only at this point that children begin to develop a sense of "place attachment," viewing Israel not only as a place existing in the world but also as a culturally important place to them and their community (Low, 1992).

For most of the children this additional symbolic layer began to arise in third grade, although some children thought this way as early as second grade and some not until fourth or fifth grade. Children in this phase can most clearly be identified by their answer to the question "Where is Israel?" Whereas their younger selves answered with responses like "far away" or "on the other side of the earth," in this phase the children offered a two-layer explanation, simultaneously physical and symbolic. For example, Gabe (3) said that Israel is "far from the state of California, but near because it is special to me" and Hayim (3) explained that "it's close to my life but it is pretty far from me." Samantha (2) described the distinction like this: "Well, I'm close to Israel. I mean I love Israel. But if you're counting where we are and where Israel is, it's like a 15-hour plane ride."

The children's sense of Israel as a geographically remote place did not fade away, but many children began to describe Israel as *also* existing "in my heart" (Hannah, 3) or "in my soul" (Ryan, 3). Rina (3) explained, "It's far in the actual world, but it's near when you think about it. Because when you're Jewish, you think about Israel. [So it's] far in the world, but close to my heart." Similarly, Hannah (2) said, "It's far because you have to take a lot of transportation to get there, but since I'm Jewish I feel that it's near my heart." Naomi (4) explained, "I've never been to Israel and physically it's far away, but emotionally it's right in my heart." Carly (4) made the distinction, "Literally it's far away, but it feels close to my heart." Mirroring this language, Tzvi (4) described Israel as "physically, it's very far. But figuratively, it is right next to us in our hearts." While only beginning in fourth grade did the children have the linguistic repertoire to identify this distinction as "literal" and "figurative," even before then most had the ability to describe Israel as both a literal place and a place with symbolic resonance for Jews.

The third stage in the children's thinking built upon the idea that Israel had symbolic meaning, explicitly framing Israel as the homeland of the Jewish people. Some children used the word "homeland" as early as third grade, but for most children it was only in fourth or fifth grade that the concept of homeland had solidified into a tripart idea encompassing the Jewish past, the global Jewish present, and their own Jewish lives. If in early elementary school children thought about Israel as a geographically rooted place, and in middle elementary school they began to think about it as a place also "in my heart," by late elementary school they spoke of Israel as both a real place and a place with symbolic meaning for the Jewish people across time and space. In the words of Keren (5), "Israel is a country in the Middle East and it's the homeland of the Jewish people."

For the children who had developed a multilayered understanding of the idea of homeland, Israel was—at once—a place of origin for the Jewish people, a place where contemporary Jews gathered, and a place that they found to be personally significant as a Jew. This did not deny that Israel could also be significant for non-Jews even as it did highlight Israel's ongoing significance to the Jewish people. Consider, for example, the words of fourth-grader Tzvi and fifth-grader Naomi in table 1.3. Each of these children spoke of Israel as a homeland, weaving together ideas about collective and personal meaning in the Jewish past and present.

TABLE 1.3. Children's Conceptions of Homeland

Child	Reflections on Homeland
Tzvi (4th grade)	"Israel is the first Jewish state, the Jews' **homeland**. Jews have been wandering around for centuries, because first they built the First Temple [in Israel] (1). And the Greeks took it, the Second Temple and the Romans took it, and so they were kind of all over the place for a bit. And then, in 1948, they made a Jewish state, and now Jews are happy living there (2). Well, most Jews are happy living there. It's now their homeland. So, we, the Jews, are connected emotionally to Israel (3) even though other people are too, even if they're not Jewish (4). It makes me feel good inside (5) because Israel is our homeland."
Naomi (5th grade)	"Israel is special to a lot of people (4) and a lot of Jewish people (3). It's our original place from Abraham and Isaac and Jacob and their wives, where our ancestors were a thousand years ago (1). But then it got taken over by a different people. [Today it's] a **homeland** for Jews to gather and for Jews to meet up with family, but distant family they didn't even know they had (2). It's physically far, but it's also near, because it's in my heart (5), and it's in everybody who comes to Israel's heart (3 & 4)."

Key: (1) a place of origin for the Jewish people; (2) a place where Jews gather today; (3) a place with collective Jewish meaning; (4) a place that has meaning to others (not only Jews); (5) a place with personal resonance.

As they traversed elementary school, the children's ideas shifted from viewing Israel as a faraway place, to seeing Israel as a place both physically remote and emotionally close, to describing Israel as a place with layers of symbolic resonance. As Samantha (4) explained, Israel may be "a very small state, [but] it holds so much meaning that it doesn't matter the size." For the children, this meaning was both collective, "uniting the Jewish people" (Gia, 4), and personal, "like a chant in my heart" (Ryan, 5).

Summary of Children's Conceptions of Homeland

The idea of homeland is an abstract one, signifying the symbolic import of a physical place. For the children in this study, the idea that Israel is often considered the homeland of the Jewish people developed over time in three distinct phases, each of which built upon the previous one. First, children understood that Israel is a real place—existing both in the world and on a map—that is geographically remote from where they live. Next, children began to view Israel as both literal and symbolic, simultaneously "far" from their homes and "near" their hearts. Then and only then did the children begin to describe Israel as a "homeland," an idea that tied together the Jewish past, the global Jewish present, and their own Jewish selves.

Developing a Sense of Belonging

By the end of elementary school, the children had developed a multi-layered conception of Israel as a Jewish state, and they viewed Israel as a place with symbolic meaning for the Jewish people. Yet just because a child *knows* about a country does not mean that a child *feels* an affective connection to that country (Barrett, 2007). Feeling association or attachment—a sense of belonging—requires children to consider not "What are countries?" but rather "What am I?" (Lambert & Klineberg, 1967). Children's attempts to make sense of "the place where I belong" (Dina, 2) are not a cognitive process but an emotional one.

Cognitively, children from a wide variety of national and ethnic backgrounds are aware of their own memberships in one or more national groups by the age of 6 (Barrett, 2007). Affectively, as children reflect on what their national affiliation(s) mean in their own lives, subjective identification varies considerably among children from different national, ethnic, and geographic contexts (Barrett et al. 1997; Barrett et al. 2001). How, then, do American Jewish children view their own national affiliation? As they live in the United States and look to Israel from afar, where do they see themselves as belonging?

While the children in this study shared a cognitive trajectory as they developed a conceptual understanding of homeland, their affective beliefs about what constitutes home were much more idiosyncratic. By the end of elementary school, the children all understood intellectually that Israel is often called the "homeland of the Jewish people" (Keren, 5), but some children believed that Israel was their own personal "second home" (Carly, 5) whereas others viewed only the United States as home.

Like American Jewish adults, American Jewish children do not all share a common relationship to Israel. Even so, none of the children in this study felt entirely "detached" (S. M. Cohen & Kelman, 2010) or "disengaged" (Pomson, 2018) from Israel. This may be the result of the study sample, which included only children who actively receive a Jewish education of some form and who live in a metropolitan area with a substantive and highly visible Jewish population. But it also may be a result of participating in the study itself. The very act of sitting down, on a regular basis, to talk about Israel with adult researchers may have led the children to take more seriously their own developing relationship to Israel.

Regardless of the reason, it is clear that all of these children were engaged in an ongoing process of attempting to make sense of their own relationships to the two countries that mattered most to them: the United States and Israel. Although each individual child's beliefs and feelings about what makes a place home developed over time, the children as a whole did not develop along any common path. The reflections of three children, Hannah, Tzvi, and Avigail, demonstrate some of the many different ways that American Jewish children feel about home and belonging.

Hannah: My Home and a Place for Jewish People

Of all the children in the study, kindergartener Hannah was the most interested in learning about Israel. Hannah had never been to Israel and has no Israeli relatives, but as a loquacious 6-year-old, she declared, "I'm ready to learn about Israel because it's exciting to learn new things!" Despite her enthusiasm, Hannah had no interest in visiting Israel. She explained, "To go to new places sometimes I feel worried inside a little bit," but she wanted to learn to speak Hebrew and better understand the place "where Hebrew people live." She described herself as firmly planted on American soil, a place where all her grandparents and some of her great-grandparents were born. Even so, she was enthusiastic about learning about a place that was "far away" and therefore "exciting."

By the end of first grade, Hannah began to express what would become a theme throughout her childhood: pride in who she was. "I'm happy that I'm a Jew," she explained, "and I'm proud to be an American in America." These two primary identities—Jewish and American—stood at the core of her expressions of self. In second grade, she reiterated that she was "proud to be Jewish" as well as "proud to be an American and to live in the U.S." Hannah echoed this language at every grade level, speaking of being "proud to be a Jewish person" and "proud to be American" (3), "proud to be a Jew" and "proud to be American" (4), and "proud to be Jewish" and "proud to live in America and be American" (5). From first grade onward, corresponding to when children's understanding of nationality generally becomes less idiosyncratic and more patriotic (Barrett, 2007), Hannah expressed clear and consistent "patriotism" for being both American and Jewish. She viewed the United States as "my country" (2) and Judaism as "my religion" (4), and she was exceedingly proud of both.

Where, then, did Israel fit into her self-conception? Hannah never once mentioned the word "pride" when speaking of Israel, but she did express feeling "connected to Israel" (2), "love [for] Israel" (3, 4), and "close to Israel" (5). Why did she express these feelings about a place to which she had never been and was reticent to visit? Beginning in second grade, she used transitive inference to explain this connection. As a proud Jew, second-grader Hannah believed that she was "connected to Jewish people" wherever they lived. Because she knew that "a lot of people that are Jewish live in Israel," she therefore felt connected to the place where so many Jewish people live. "Israel is a big part of Judaism," she explained in third grade, and "I'm proud to be a Jew, so it makes me feel close to Israel."

Although Hannah felt "close to" Israel, at no point did she view herself as Israeli. Like other American children who tend to equate national identity with birthplace (Carrington & Short, 2000), Hannah defined an Israeli as someone "born in Israel" (5). She was clear and consistent over time in explaining that she is "someone who is in the United States of America" (3). She viewed being American as "who I am" (4) and "part of my family" (4), and she described the United States as "my home, where I was born, and where I grew up" (5). While Hannah viewed both the United States and Israel as offering "religious freedom" (5) to Jews, only the United States was "my home." She described the United States as "my homeland" (5) and Israel as the "number one homeland" for Israeli citizens.

Hannah's sense of her own relationships to the United States, Israel, and Judaism remained largely stable over time. From first grade onward, she was consistent in explaining that she was proudly American and that the United States was "my home." She also repeatedly described herself as a "proud Jew," and as such she felt an emotional connection to Israel, which she viewed as "a Jewish state, a place for Jewish people" (3). The distinction Hannah made was clear and unwavering: Only the United States was "home," but Israel was a "place for Jewish people" and thus held significance in her own life as an American Jew.

Tzvi: Our Country and Our Land

Tzvi has no memories of a time before he started flying back and forth between the United States and Israel. "I have a lot of family there," second-grader Tzvi explained, "and I go every two years. So I have been there when I was 2, when I was 4, when I was 6 and now when I'm 8. I just really like Israel." He viewed Israel as a place where he got to visit with his extended family and one that offered exciting opportunities for pursuing his hobby of coin collecting.

When Tzvi started thinking about nationality as a second grader, he described the United States as "our country," referring not only to himself but also to his parents in his descriptions of "our community." Even at age 8, Tzvi was aware that he is an American citizen not by happenstance but as a result of a deliberate choice that his parents made to leave Israel before he was born. He explained, "My mom and dad chose to live in a really free and good place, which means a lot to me." He felt "good and proud of America."

Yet in third grade, he also began calling Israel "our home," referring in the plural not to his immediate family but to the "Jewish people." He described Israel as "the Jews' homeland" and "the Jewish people's land," and he viewed Israel as a place where Jews "can live their lives Jewish." In his view, "Israel is a country that's meant for Jewish people, where they can be free to be Jews." He believed that God gave the land to Abraham and "to the Jewish people."

Over the course of his fourth- and fifth-grade years, Tzvi began to refine his conception of his relationships to Israel and the United States. Whereas Hannah believed that Israel was connected to her because it was "part of Judaism" but in no way viewed Israel as "my home," Tzvi insisted that he had "two homes." Despite having lived only in the United States, he called both the U.S. and Israel "home."

"I have Israel and I have America," he explained, and both places held important—though different—significance in his own life. For Tzvi, the United States was his "physical home." In his words, "America is where I live, it's where I was born. I love America." He added, "This place provides me a home and food and shelter." Despite feeling protected in, and connected to, the United States, he referred to the U.S. as "our home, but not our land." Only Israel, in Tzvi's mind, was "our land" and "the land of the Jews." If he called the U.S. his "physical home" and his "country," then he considered Israel the "home in my heart" and the "land of the Jewish people."

For Tzvi, there was no contradiction or tension between these two ways of framing the countries to which he "feel[s] connected." In fact, for him it was clear that "two places" were important because he had "two homes . . . a home here and home for the Jewish people." Even though his actual home and life were in the United States, he viewed himself as metaphorically living "in Israel as well as living here at the same time," an idea he voiced in nascent form as early as third grade and that had crystallized for him by fifth grade. "Israel is the land, the home of the Jews," he explained, and as such he "feels loyal" to it. At the same time, "My home [is] here in America" and he felt "connected to America."

Avigail: Two Homes, Fitting Nowhere

"I really, really, really want to be in Israel," declared kindergartener Avigail, "because Israel is meant for me." Avigail's mother and primary caretaker, Roni, was born and raised in Israel, so Avigail grew up hearing stories about her mother's youth there. "My family's there, and I really care about my family," Avigail (K) explained. "I just wish that I could go to Israel."

As a kindergartener and first grader, Avigail considered Los Angeles her home, but she longed to visit Israel. "When am I going to be there?" she wondered repeatedly. "I've been to Israel when I was a baby," Avigail (1) explained, and she imagined it as "a really nice country to be in." But she also had a lot of questions about a place about which she had no personal memories. "What does Israel look like?" she wondered. "What places are in Israel? What kind of houses, what kind of animals, how does the place look? And how does the food look?"

Avigail's questions were answered in second grade, when she visited Israel for her cousin's bar mitzvah. By the time she returned home, Avigail was able to point to a map of Israel and, with some degree of accuracy, locate different places where her relatives lived and tell stories about their homes and cities. Avigail continued to call the United States her home "because my cousins are here, my friends are here, my mom is here," but she also experienced Israel as a place that "makes me feel very comfortable." If she called the U.S. home, she considered Israel "like my home." She explained, "I feel that I belong there."

Yet Avigail's sense of comfort in her "two homes" quickly dissipated when, in third grade, she and her mother moved to Israel. Avigail framed her move as a "big transition." She "really, really missed" her old life, especially her friends, visits to Starbucks, and shopping at Target. Even after a full school year in Israel, she continued to describe herself as "new around here." An excerpt of an interview transcript with Avigail and her mother, Roni, reveals how she thought about her own place in the world at the end of third grade.

> RONI: Where do you feel like home is?
> AVIGAIL: Home is America. It's probably my home.
> INTERVIEWER: Why?
> AVIGAIL: I belong more in America than here because here people are kind of rude to me and . . . don't really like Americans.
> RONI: Where do you feel most at home, Avigail?
> AVIGAIL: [Long pause.]
> INTERVIEWER: That's okay. You can say, "I don't know."
> AVIGAIL: Like America? I don't know.
> RONI: Where do you feel most at home? In America or in Israel?
> AVIGAIL: America!

In Israel, Avigail viewed herself as an American transplant, yet when Avigail and her mother moved back to California in time for Avigail to start fourth grade at a new public school, she felt even more confused about where she belonged. When she was in Israel, it had been clear to her that she was American, but now that she was back in the U.S., she felt "a little bit Israeli." She missed her Israeli friends and family, and she yearned for a return to the life of an Israeli child, which she characterized as "just getting to go outside, be free." Where did she belong? She explained:

> People ask me that question all the time. And I say I don't know. I either say, "Israel is a place to visit and America is a place to live" or "Israel is a place to live in and America is a place to visit." There's no answer for

that one because it's one of the most toughest questions I've ever had in my lifetime. If it were to be on a test, I'd probably get a zero on it 'cause I cannot answer it.

Like other children who have moved from country to country and have difficulty identifying a place of belonging (Nette & Hayden, 2007), Avigail described herself as having "two homes" and, at the same time, as fully belonging in neither. In the U.S. and in Israel, she felt like "a part of me is missing." Unlike Tzvi, who lived only in the U.S. but considered both the U.S. and Israel "home," Avigail had lived in both countries. Yet no matter where she was at any given time, she always looked to the other place from afar, constantly dissatisfied by navigating between "my second home and/or my first home" at every moment.

Summary of Children's Sense of Belonging

As children reflect on where—and to whom—they feel they belong, they express their deepest sense of self. Children's understanding of the *idea* of a homeland is cognitive, and the children in this study built that idea in a shared developmental sequence. But how children *feel* about what constitutes home is much more idiosyncratic. Some of the children in this study view themselves "at home" only in the United States even as they recognize that Israel plays a special role in the past and present of the Jewish people. Other children believe they have multiple homes— including the United States, Israel, and their own family's country of origin before immigrating to the United States. These children under- stand that they live only in the United States, but they believe other places are so symbolically resonant as to be considered "second homes." In developing a sense of belonging, children do change over time as they understand and experience more about the world. But the ways that they shift as they grow are as much about their family narratives and their personal experiences of the world as they are about child develop- ment, so that the more kids mature, the more textured and varied their feelings are about the place(s) they call home.

Conclusion

As children develop an understanding of the world and the countries that comprise it, they draw from a number of resources at their disposal: schools and media, family and peers, and the larger communal and national contexts in which they operate (Barrett, 2007). For the children in this study, any attempt to make sense of countries and nations includes a special place for the "countries I care about" (Rina, K): both the United States and Israel.

From the earliest days of elementary school, these Jewish children worked to understand not only the geographic boundaries of their "favorite" and "second favorite" countries, but—more important to the children's ways of thinking—their *conceptual* boundaries. The children invested a great deal of intellectual effort in making sense of the ideals and values that they believe each of these countries represents to the world and to the Jewish people. As the children attempted to make sense of the United States as a free and open society, and Israel as a Jewish state and a Jewish homeland, their ideas developed in relative lockstep. Children who attended different schools and whose families come from a range of ethnic Jewish backgrounds and countries of origin sounded alike as they developed initial theories about what the United States and Israel are and what they represent. Over time, children's ideas became both more abstract and more specific as they were able to better understand—and articulate—symbolic thought and concrete manifestations of national ideals. Although there was some variance in the ages at which they made shifts in their thinking, their overall intellectual trajectories were remarkably similar to one another.

Yet cognitive understanding about nations, countries, and their values is only a small part of what children are working to make sense of as they build an understanding of the world. As developmental psychologist Martyn Barrett (2007) explains:

> National enculturation is not only a process through which children are inducted into particular cognitive representations of their own nation and state and into particular cultural practices. It is also a process that generates a subjective sense of personal affiliation and belonging, and an emotional attachment to the history, culture, and territory of the child's

own nation and state, engendering in children a sense of who they are, influencing how they see themselves, and impacting on how they locate themselves in the wider world. (p. 17)

That process of self-location is both idiosyncratic and fluid over time, so that children follow multiple and winding paths as they consider where, to what, and to whom they belong.

As children reflect on their own sense of national and communal affiliation, they take a multitude of positions and pathways. Some children in this study, at some moments, felt an expansive sense of belonging, believing themselves to be part of both U.S. and Israeli life regardless of whether or not they are dual citizens. Others felt firmly rooted in the United States, proud and patriotic Americans even as they cognitively understood that Israel is an important place for Judaism and the Jewish people. Others still felt like the perpetual outsider, part of a Jewish minority in the United States and an American minority in Israel. All of the children, regardless of how they viewed their own affiliation(s), expressed both interest in and ability to participate in deeply reflective conversations about attachment and belonging.

Any attempt to honor the experiences of children must account for *both* what unites children developmentally *and* what allows them to thrive as their own unique selves. Understanding the common developmental stages of children is necessary for creating experiences that allow them to learn. Just like the "Goldilocks Zone" that scientists use to refer to the region around a star where the temperature is just right— not too hot and not too cold—for liquid water and thus habitability, so too is there a "Goldilocks Zone" for engaging children in learning about the world.[4] It is in this just-right zone, which neither underestimates the complexities of children's emerging theories nor overshoots their conceptual and linguistic repertoire, that meaningful learning and growth can happen. Yet for children to exist within this zone requires adults to listen carefully and respectfully to children's developing ideas and theories, a process that is all too often obscured in educational attempts to help kids understand the ideas and theories of adults.

Equally important is for adults to recognize that children's sense of affiliation and collective belonging is both deeply personal and highly variable. Children do not all feel one way about national and collective identity, and though they do shift over time, their changes reflect their own particular viewpoints and experiences rather than shared developmental stages. The multiplicity of children's experiences and beliefs about belonging reinforces the need for elementary education to honor what early childhood expert Patricia M. Cooper calls an "N of many" (2009, p. 155), providing classrooms in which children—with all their various beliefs and ideas—are respected and appreciated just the way they are.

Children's idiosyncratic reflections on their own sense of belonging pose a particularly profound challenge to Jewish education. As the education of young American Jews has increasingly come to include education about Israel, scholars and field leaders who agree on little else are virtually united in their belief that one "main purpose" (Horowitz, 2012, p. 3) of Israel education is to "nurture an individual's connection" (L. Grant & Kopelowitz, 2012, p. 114) and/or "personal relationship with Israel" (Chazan, 2016, p. 17). In fact, feelings of connectedness to something greater than the self are essential for children's development, helping children build resilience (K. R. Ginsburg & Jablow, 2005; Jordan, 2013) and spiritual meaning (Hyde, 2008; Kessler, 2000). Yet the goal of connecting American Jewish children to Israel in particular is a complex one, as it must be situated in a much larger process of offering children opportunities to build for themselves a sense of connectedness.

To what, and to whom, ought American Jewish children feel connected? To their families and friends? To their schools and/or local communities? To the United States and/or the principles of American democracy? To the American Jewish community? To the global Jewish people? To Israel and/or Israelis? To Zionist ideas? To the Jewish past and/or the Jewish present?

American Jewish children can—and do—express some emotional attachment to each of these. Yet the particular forms of connection and the relative weight of each are—and ought to remain—varied. Elliot Eisner (2005), renowned scholar of arts education, calls this idea "productive variance," suggesting that good education ought to help children amplify their differences rather than smooth them out. If taken seriously, a commitment to productive variance undercuts the notion that there is an "ideal product of thoughtful Israel education" (Sinclair, 2009, p. 84). Instead, it honors *multiple* forms of connectedness and respects the varied and idiosyncratic paths that children take as they attempt to situate themselves in the broader world.

Children think deeply—often in shared developmental stages—and they feel passionately—in ways that are personal and idiosyncratic—about homeland and home. Doing so requires children to reflect on how countries and societies function—what they are, the values they cherish, and who belongs where. Children's ideas and beliefs about countries and societies are rooted in their present-day experiences, yet even as children attempt to make sense of how the world functions today, they also develop foundational ideas about the past. The origin stories that children tell about that past—like the reflections they share about the present—reveal both the complexity of children's thinking and the care with which they consider the world. These origin stories, and how children tell them as they develop during elementary school, are the subject of the next chapter.

2

"Once Upon a Time God Made Israel"

Children's Narrations of Israel's History

What is Israel's origin story? "God created the world," explained second-grader Seth, "so God made Israel. He made the whole world, every continent put together. First, [the continents] were like a rubber band, like this," he explained, clasping his hands tightly together. "And then," Seth made the sound of a small explosion and flung his hands apart, "they stretched out. And Israel did not get stretched out. It was in the middle."

In third grade, Seth offered a different explanation of Israel's origin. "Israel was first called Canaan. The three fathers of the Jewish nation are Abraham, Isaac, and Jacob. The three of them, along with a lot of other Jewish leaders like Moses, Joshua, Joseph, Sarah, Rachel, Rebecca, and King Solomon made Israel. They were in the Torah and Bible," he explained, and those books are the story of the creation of Israel.

By the time Seth reached fifth grade, he crafted a story quite different from those told by his younger self. "Theodor Herzl made Israel," Seth explained. "Also there's Ben-Gurion and Weizmann. They made Israel because most countries don't really like [Jews], and they needed to have a home." He paused before continuing, "Theodor Herzl published a pamphlet that explained the reason why Jews need a home. But sadly, he couldn't see his creation of what he made because he had pneumonia."

Starting when the children were in first grade, we began asking them to tell us a story about how Israel was created. *Who made Israel*, we asked, *when, and why?* Origin stories offer a glimpse into how people conceptualize national identity (J. H. Wright, 2004) and collective belonging (Nash, 2008). Thus the children's narrations of Israel's origins offer an important window into how they think about Israel,[1] and this is true regardless of whether they tell "Jewish myths of origin" (Kurtzer, 2012, p. 2) or narrate "towards a more critical and interpretive encounter with the past" (Levstik & Barton, 2011, p. 42). Like Seth, all the children took on the role of historical narrator, crafting their own shifting interpretations of the origins of Israel.

How do children make sense of the past, and how do they narrate it? Even when children do not know the word "history," they can understand that life in the past was different than it is today (Barton, 1997a). Even when children underestimate just how much has changed over time (Brophy & Alleman, 2006), they can understand that history is not merely a chronicle of past events but a narrative about them (Levstik & Barton, 2011). And even though children often struggle to understand how historians use evidence to craft historical narratives (Barton, 1997b), they can interpret information about the past and communicate their interpretation to others through stories (Fertig, 2005).

In fact, hearing and telling stories about the past has long been understood as central to the way that children make sense of history (e.g., Barton, 1996; Brophy et al., 1992; Levstik, 1989; Levstik & Pappas, 1987). Children, and especially those in the early elementary grades, have an "orientation towards narrative" (Brophy & Alleman, 2006, p. 419) and are able to craft stories about the past long before they can engage in other forms of historical analysis.

Clearly, elementary students' narratives of history differ in substantive ways from the historical narratives of adults. Children's stories about the past are marked by what scholar of social studies education Keith Barton (2008) calls "narrative simplifications," as children often tell history as a straightforward and linear story even when many adults understand that history is more ambiguous. Nonetheless, even very young children can express both interest in and ideas about historical narratives (Levstik, 2008a).

Inviting children to tell origin stories offers an important glimpse into the ways that children understand the past and build foundational ideas about both the discipline of history and the concepts of country and nation. It draws upon a methodological approach that recognizes that children are capable of some historical understanding (Levstik & Barton, 2008) and can construct coherent narratives of past events even when they mix up, conflate, or imagine particular details (S. G. Grant & VanSledright, 2014; VanSledright & Brophy, 1992). In other words, children's narrations may be "technically inaccurate but understandable"

(Brophy & Alleman, 2006, p. 335), revealing important insights into children's thinking even when they offer mistaken or impartial information.

This approach asks not *What do children get right and what do they get wrong about history?* but rather *When children think about a collective past, what do they think about? How do they understand and make sense of historical origin stories?* Longitudinal research affords an opportunity to understand how children narrate the "same" story in different ways at different ages.

Using the terms "stories" and "narratives" interchangeably (Polletta et al., 2011), this chapter examines the children's narrations of the founding of the state of Israel as one example of how children build foundational ideas and theories about the world. I argue that children can craft and reflect on multiple kinds of origin stories, demonstrating that children can think deeply about historical narratives even when their stories are not chronological or evidentiary. To make this argument, I examine four distinct kinds of stories that the children in this study told about Israel's past: stories that frame Israel's founding as a divine act of creation, as part of a larger biblical narrative, as a tale about the Jewish people's wandering in search of a home, and as a distinctly modern Zionist phenomenon. As the children developed greater historical understanding over time, some children replaced their initial historical narratives with new ones, while other children began to layer narratives in order to offer multiple explanations of historical events. The evolution of the children's origin stories, and their reflections on those stories, illuminate their thinking not only about history but also about how communities in the present hear and tell stories about a collective past.

Four Types of Children's Narratives

As the children in this study narrated the history of Israel's founding, they primarily told four different kinds of stories about it: theological narratives, biblical narratives, Jewish heritage narratives, and Zionist narratives. Children's theological narratives framed the founding of Israel as a divine act. Biblical narratives situated the founding of Israel as part of a larger biblical story. Jewish heritage narratives positioned the founding of Israel as part of an ongoing tale about the oppression and redemption of the Jewish people over time. And Zionist narratives located the founding of Israel as a modern phenomenon brought about by the ideas and actions of famous Zionist figures.

Each of these kinds of narratives had its own internal logic and storyline, and each offered different answers to the questions *when, why, and by whom was Israel created?* See table 2.1 for an overview. Some of the children, at some moments, told a single kind of narrative; others wove together different kinds of narratives in a single story.

TABLE 2.1. An Overview of Children's Historical Narratives

Narrative Type	Narrative Orientation	When, Why, and by Whom Was Israel Created?
Theological	Frame the founding of Israel as a divine act.	God created Israel when God created the world.
Biblical	Situate the founding of Israel as part of a larger biblical story.	Biblical characters made Israel, often in partnership with or in response to God.
Jewish Heritage	Position the founding of Israel as part of an ongoing story about the oppression and redemption of the Jewish people over time.	At various points in time, the Jewish people were not safe. They needed a place to go, so they went to Israel.
Zionist	Locate the founding of Israel as a modern phenomenon, the result of the ideas and actions of famous Zionist figures.	In 1948, after the Holocaust, famous Zionists created a Jewish state and the United Nations voted to allow it.

The narratives that children tell about the past are distinct from those told by adults, especially adults with knowledge and training in the discipline of history. Children's stories about the past do not necessarily offer a chronological structure, nor do they provide an explanatory framework for how disparate events might be part of larger historical processes (cf. J. Hassenfeld, 2016; White, 1975). Many of the hallmarks of historical analysis, including serious thinking about evidence and intertextual corroboration (Wineburg, 1991), are well beyond the reach of most elementary school children. Nonetheless, children can and do tell stories about the past that have a clear sense of structure and storyline, and these narratives reveal both how children think about times that predated their own lives and how they locate themselves in the present (Barton, 2001a). It is a deliberate choice to view these stories not as "surface narratives" that reflect a shallow understanding of history (McKeown & Beck, 1994, p. 9) but instead as children's narratives that reveal a deep sense of how children, in their own way, make sense of the past.

Theological Narratives

"The whole world started as a big blob," explained first-grader Naomi. "Then God made things. And He made the parts of land, and Israel was one of them."

Second-grader Ari's story began, "Once upon a time, God made Israel." Ari continued, "God created Israel and He created everyone that started living in Israel."

Children like Naomi and Ari told Israel's origin story as a theological narrative. Situating God as the story's protagonist, and attributing the creation of Israel to God and God alone, children who told theological narratives began their stories with the creation of the world and framed the creation of Israel as an extension of the world's creation.

While children, and especially Jewish children, often believe that God is part of history (Heller, 1988), a belief that God acts in human history does not belong to children alone (Cracraft, 2007; Fackenheim, 1970). In fact, even trained historians can be religious believers, and while the *tools* of the historian and the theologian are distinct, one can be both a sophisticated historical thinker and a believer in the divine (Gottlieb & Wineburg, 2012). Therefore, children's stories about God should not be mistaken for naivete and must instead be understood as one way of framing tales about bygone times. As these children crafted stories that placed God at the center of Israeli history, the structure and the storyline of these narratives were the most simple and straightforward of the stories that the children told about the Israeli past, but their *function* was the same as any other kind of child's narrative: a serious attempt—albeit one very different than that of adult historians—at making sense of the past.

THE STORY AND LOGIC OF THEOLOGICAL NARRATIVES
The story of the founding of Israel was simple and clear to the children who told these theological narratives: God made Israel when God created the world. The logic of this story was straightforward: "God made everything" (Micah, 1), so therefore it follows that "God made Israel" (Esther, 1). As Avigail (1) explained, "Israel was created by God, because He created lots of things."

Why, in the children's minds, did God create Israel? Some of the children believed that God *is* Jewish and therefore chose to make a Jewish place, Israel. For example, Brent (1) explained, "God made Israel. God was mostly kind of Jewish, and He wanted a Jewish place to make up." Other children believed that God created Israel *for* the Jewish people because of God's special relationship with Jews. In Carly's (3) words, "God is close to the Jewish people, so He helped the Jewish people make this land for the Jewish people because the Jewish people didn't have a land for themselves, so He made it for the Jewish people." In both of these versions, children told stories in which God created Israel as a special Jewish place. As Ari (5) explained, "God made Israel for a place for Jews."

Drawing upon a common childhood belief that "everything in the world was created *by* someone *for* some purpose" (Kushner, 1989, p. 60), the children who told theological stories were united in their belief that Israel was created *by* God (and God alone) even as they differed in their explanations about the purpose *for* which God created it. With shades of difference, their theological narratives were united by a common storyline that situated God as the sole creator of the world and, by extension, of Israel.

While some children's stories situated God as the sole creator of Israel, other children's stories framed God as acting alongside human beings to create it. These stories focused not on the moment of God's creation of the world but rather on a larger narrative that wove together elements of the books of Genesis and Exodus. These biblical narratives were distinct from theological narratives in both their scope and their positioning of God's role in history.

Biblical Narratives

"Israel came to be when God told Abraham to go," began third-grader Rina. "[God said to] leave Haran and go to Israel, and that's how Israel was really born because if God didn't have the urge to tell Abraham to go out of Haran, then Israel wouldn't really be. When God told Abraham to go, Israel was born! [Before then] it was called Canaan, and it wasn't really Israel. It was more like a desert with no greens, just nothing there. So Abraham, Isaac, Jacob, Moses, all those people made Israel happen."

"It all started during Passover," explained fourth-grader Avigail. "Moses was leading all the Jews from Egypt to Israel. God told Moses, and it took 40 years for him to actually arrive. And before they called it Israel they called it the land of milk and honey. So it came to be. A lot of years went by and it became the Israel that it is now. So that's how it all started: with Moses leading the Jews to Israel, because God helped Moses, and Moses led them to Israel."

Children like Rina and Avigail told Israel's origin story as part of a larger biblical narrative. Recounting parts of the books of Genesis and Exodus in their own words, they wove tales that cast important biblical characters, acting in conjunction with or at the direction of God, as the creators of Israel.

Many of the children's biblical stories, like those of Rina and Avigail, attributed the creation of Israel to human action, not a divine act of creation. In their accounts, the land that is Israel had previously existed, often with a different name such as Canaan, the land of milk and honey, or the Promised Land. This land, according to the children's biblical narratives, became Israel only when the biblical characters took some kind of action to transform it. Children who told biblical narratives often equated Israeli history with biblical stories. As Isabelle (4) explained, "The history of Israel *is* the Torah" (emphasis added).

PIVOTAL MOMENTS IN CHILDREN'S BIBLICAL NARRATIVES

The children populated their stories about the creation of Israel with a cast of biblical and apocryphal characters stretching from Adam and Eve (Maya, 3) to Judah the Maccabee (Ryan, 4). Some children began their stories with the Jewish patriarchs Abraham (Samantha, 2), Isaac (Gabe, 5), and Jacob (Lior, 2) and the Jewish matriarchs Sarah (Tzvi, 5), Rebecca (Seth, 3), Rachel (Brent, 5) and Leah (Samantha, 4). Others started later in the biblical story, focusing on Moses (Avigail, 2), Aaron and Miriam (Gabe, 3), Joshua (Seth, 2), Pharaoh (Gia, 1), and Pharaoh's daughter (Isabelle, 5). The biblical kings David (Carly, 2) and Solomon (Keren, 5) along with the armies of the Egyptians from the Passover story (Hayim, 3) and the Greeks from the Hanukkah story (Olivia, 1) were also present in some children's narratives.

Two parts of the biblical story were most common in the children's narrations: God's directive to Abraham to travel to a new land, and the

Israelites' exodus from Egypt. Even when children told other parts of the biblical story, they often highlighted one or both of these points as the defining pivotal moment when Israel became Israel.

GOD DIRECTS ABRAHAM TO ISRAEL

In many of the children's stories, Israel was created as the result of an interaction between Abraham and God, in which "God told Abraham to go [to] Israel" (Lior, 2) and Abraham "became the father of a new nation [and] led the people to Israel" (Ryan, 3). As these children told tales focused on "the story of Abraham" (Isabelle 3), they framed a two-part story in which God's directive and Abraham's response together led to the creation of Israel. These stories are similar to the kinds of "divine providence" narratives that Jewish teenagers tell, situating God's promise to Abraham as a central moment in Israeli history (J. Hassenfeld, 2016).

Consider, for example, the stories of Samantha, who year after year located Abraham's journey as the pivotal moment in the creation of Israel. As a first grader, Samantha explained that Israel was created "when Abraham came along. [God] said, 'Come with me to the Promised Land,' and Abraham followed, and he found Israel. But back then it was called Canaan."

By third grade, Samantha's narration of Israel's creation had come to include additional language—both in English and in Hebrew—that more closely mirrored the biblical text even as it remained similar in its overall framing of the events that brought Israel into being. In her third-grade words:

> God told Abraham from Haran, "*Lech l'cha*" [Go forth], and a few other words but I can't remember them, which is, "Leave your land, your father's house, and go to the land I will show you." So Abraham left from Haran, not asking why he was [going], and he just went. And God promised him a land, and He promised him to have as many children as stars and the sand. So Abraham went on a journey, and even though at times it was tough, he managed to get to Israel, and that's why we're here in Israel today.

Again in fourth grade, Samantha framed Israel's creation as a story focused on Abraham. Her narration contained additional Hebrew words from the Bible as well as details not contained in the biblical text itself. According to fourth-grader Samantha:

Way, way back in the days of Abraham, God said *"Lech l'cha m'artzecha"* [Go forth from your land]. And He said, "I will take you. Follow me to the land where I will show you." So God brought Abraham to Beer Sheva in Canaan, which wasn't Israel yet. And He said, "You will have many offspring, as many children as the grains in the sand and the stars in the sky." That was really the beginning [of Israel].

In each of these narrations, Samantha enacts two different interpretive processes: she frames the biblical story of Abraham in her own words, and she locates this story—a directive from God and a journey of Abraham—as foundational to the creation of Israel.

Samantha was far from the only child who framed an interaction between God and Abraham as the defining moment in Israel's formation. Isabelle (3) asserted that "it became Israel because long, long ago, God told Abraham that Israel is a place where the Jews [should] live." In Gabe's (3) story, Israel "started out with Abraham, the first Jew. He was promised land by God." In Keren's (5) narration, "God promised Abraham that his descendants would live in the land of Israel. . . . It was the covenant with the Jews and Abraham, that God made. God told Abraham that his descendants would be numerous in the land of Israel, and that his name would be great, and the Jewish people would be safe in Israel." Tzvi (5) explained that Israel "started out with Abraham. . . . He belonged to a religion where they prayed to idols . . . so God said 'Lech l'cha [Go forth], go to the land where I will show you. Go from the land of your birthplace, the land of your father.' And so he took cattle and sheep and livestock with his wife Sarah, and they found Canaan."

In their own words, each of these children recounted a biblical story about God's instructions to Abraham in response to a prompt about the founding of Israel. In doing so, the children were engaging not only in an act of storytelling but also in an act of interpretation; they located the interaction between God and Abraham in the biblical story as a formative moment that led to the creation of Israel.

THE ISRAELITES LEAVE EGYPT AND TRAVEL TO ISRAEL

As the children told biblical narratives, many of them located the Israelites' exodus from Egypt and subsequent journey through the desert as the story of Israel's founding. In these children's stories, "The Jewish people escaped from Egypt, and they moved to Israel, and that's how it became Israel" (Bella, 2). The children's exodus stories focused on how the Israelites, under the leadership of Moses and with the guidance of God, traveled from slavery in Egypt to freedom in Israel.

Some of the children told brief and straightforward narratives in which they traced the Israelites' journey from Egypt to Israel. Gia (3) explained that "Moses took us out of Egypt to Israel, which we called the Promised Land." According to Bella (4), "The Jews were slaves in Egypt, and when they finally escaped, they went in the desert. And they traveled for a long time and then they finally got to Israel." These stories followed a sequential and linear timeline, taking the Israelites directly from Egypt, through the desert, and to Israel.

Other children's stories started earlier in the exodus narrative, beginning with the birth of Moses and then "skipping ahead" (Isabelle, 5) to the slaves leaving Egypt. In these stories, the children often offered both more details from the biblical story and a less linear narrative that jumped back and forth in time and space. For example, Hayim (3) recounted:

> First, Pharaoh wanted to kill the firstborn of a Jewish boy. And there was this mom. We don't really know her name. And she wanted her little baby to live. So she put him in a basket and his sister Miriam watched him float to make sure that he's safe. And an Egyptian princess found him and named him Moses. And then years later . . . God said, "Go down to Egypt and tell Pharaoh to let my people go, and if you don't there shall be 10 plagues." And Pharaoh kept on saying no. After the first nine, Moses warned, "This plague will be the worst of all." And Pharaoh still said, "I won't let your people go." And by then Pharaoh had a child, a boy, his firstborn. And God said, "Every Egyptian firstborn shall die," and they all died. And that's when the [Israelites] all walked on a journey to Israel. And that's the story of how Israel was born.

Isabelle's fifth-grade narration, like Hayim's third-grade one, began with Moses's early life and then jumped to the slaves' exodus from Egypt. In her telling:

> So there was a long, long time ago. This woman had her child in Egypt. Pharaoh didn't want families to have more boys, 'cause he knew that when

the baby boys will grow up, they'll wanna go against him and they will be strong. So he decided to take all the baby newborns and drown them in the river. And so the woman didn't want Pharaoh to take her child, so she made a basket and put him in the basket into the river. Then Pharaoh's daughter found him and took care of him as her son. He grew up to be an Egyptian, and then when he grew up he knew that he was actually Jewish. And, I'm skipping ahead, and then he took out the slaves of Egypt. It took about 40 years to get to the land of Israel. God promised the Jewish slaves to take them to the Promised Land, Israel.

She situated the founding of Israel not as a single discrete moment in time but as an extended story involving Moses, Pharaoh, and the Israelites' 40-year journey through the dessert.

As these children reflected on the events that led to Israel's founding, they often claimed that "it started with Pesach [Passover]" (Avigail, 5). "When I think of how Israel was created," explained Olivia (3), "I think Passover. God told Moses to go to the land and it was Israel." Israel, in these children's narratives, was framed as the pinnacle of the Passover story and endpoint in a journey in which the Israelites "traveled for a long time and then they finally got to Israel" (Bella, 4).

In several of the children's narratives, two journeys—Abraham's travels to Israel and the Israelites' subsequent return to Israel—functioned as bookends to a larger biblical narrative that, in these children's minds, told the story of how Israel came to be. For example, Seth (4) explained that Israel was created when

God told Abraham to go to Canaan, which was Israel back then. Then he had his son Isaac, and then Abraham's wife, Sarah, died and then Abraham died. And then Isaac got Jacob and Esau. Then Jacob wrestled with an angel. And then [Jacob's son] Joseph had a dream that he was a leader, and the brothers buried him in a hole and took him to Egypt. And then Joseph became [a helper to] Pharaoh, and then Jacob died and then Joseph died. And then a couple years later, Moses goes out of Egypt, crossing the Red Sea.

In Seth's abridged version of the stories of Genesis and Exodus, Abraham, his descendants, and Moses are all part of a larger story that explains the creation of Israel.

The children's biblical narratives—whether they focused on Abraham and God, Moses and the Israelites, or both—framed the creation of Israel not as a single moment in time but rather as a process. It is typical for elementary school students to present history not as gradual shifts over time but as large moments of epiphany (Barton, 1996). Yet in these children's narrations of biblical stories, they highlighted *both* pivotal moments of change in the stories of Abraham and Moses *and* an ongoing narrative that located the creation of Israel not as a single event but as a series of journeys over time.

The Distinction between Theological and Biblical Narratives

God appeared in both the children's theological and biblical narratives. What, then, was the difference between the two types of origin stories, and how distinct were they? Two defining features distinguished between these types of narratives: the scope of the story, and the role that God played in it.

The children's theological stories started and ended with an act of creation. Like Naomi's (1) story that "God made things . . . and Israel was one of them," the stories that I have classified as theological never extended beyond that moment. The children's biblical stories, by contrast, contained a much broader register of time. Even when these narratives included elements of the creation stories from Genesis 1 and 2, they also incorporated other parts of the books of Genesis and/or Exodus, and not all of the children's biblical narratives included any mention of creation.

The two types of stories also differed in the ways that they presented God's role. The children's theological narratives cast God as the sole creator of the universe and everything in it, including Israel. Their biblical narratives, by contrast, typically framed God as a partner with human beings in the creation of Israel. In the former, the children told stories in which "God created Israel because He's the only one that really created this world" (Lailah, 5). In the latter, "God and the Jewish people all worked together to make Israel" (Bella, 5).

In the children's biblical narratives, God sometimes took the lead and at other times played a supporting role in an otherwise human-driven story. Many children who told biblical narratives framed God as responsible for leading or directing human beings to Israel. For example, Olivia

(2) explained that "God led [the Israelites] into the land of Israel." In these stories, human beings were God's helpers. The children explained that "Israel started because God led the Jews out of Egypt with the help of Moses" (Esther, 5), or God directed the Jewish people and "Abraham helped God and he did what He said" (Lailah, 5). In other stories, the primary and secondary roles were reversed, with the biblical characters doing most of the work and God acting as supporter. In these stories, "God helped Moses" (Avigail, 4) or "God helped the Jews" (Keren, 3). In both instances—God supporting humans or people helping God— children who told biblical narratives viewed human and divine action as jointly responsible for creating Israel.

Yet while God appeared as a primary agent of history in both the children's theological and biblical narratives, not all of the children's stories about Israeli history included God, and not all were tied to stories that can be found in the Bible. The children also told a third type of narrative, a Jewish heritage story that focused on the Jewish people's ongoing quest for belonging and a sense of home.

Jewish Heritage Narratives

"A long time ago," began fifth-grader Gia, "the Jewish people needed an actual place to call home because they were wandering around. The Jewish people needed a place, and they needed somewhere to live and be safe and protect and raise families. So they made Israel their own country."

"It was a long time ago," explained fifth-grader Hannah. "The Jewish people created Israel because they wanted a place for [Jewish] people to express themselves and to follow their own religion without being judged."

Children like Gia and Hannah told Israel's origin story as a tale about the collective Jewish people wandering, unmoored, in foreign lands. These Jews were in need of a place to call their own, and thus they went to Israel and made it their home.

The children's Jewish heritage narratives stretched across time and space, framing the Jewish story as one of persecution in foreign lands and safety in building or returning to the Jewish land, Israel. Jewish heritage narratives, like other heritage narratives, are a form of collective memory (Funkenstein, 1989; Halbwachs, 1980/1950; Yerushalmi, 1989), a cultural expression linking people to a collective past (e.g., Davies, 2013; Lowenthal, 1985). They rely not on any particular forms of historical evidence or argumentation but rather on broad tropes that offer collective meaning. As the children told Jewish heritage narratives, they crafted stories that framed the founding of Israel in terms of the Jewish people's ongoing quest to find a place where they belonged.

These heritage narratives were the only kind of historical stories the children told that transcended time and place. Many of the children's heritage narratives, like those of Gia and Hannah, situated the Jewish people in an indeterminate "place that they were living before" (Elliott, 1) and ended with the Jews going to Israel so they "could have their own place" (Carly, 5). Others specifically located the Jewish people as foreigners in a variety of specific places, from Germany and Romania (Lailah, 5) to Iran and Syria (Hayim, 5), where, according to the children's stories, it was "not very safe for Jewish people" (Hayim, 5).

Whether these narratives were set in a particular place or an unspecified one, they always occurred at an indeterminate time: "a long time ago" (Hannah, 5) or "back, back, back in the olden times" (Olivia, 5). Like other elementary-school-age children, these children used the language "a long time ago" to distinguish the present from the past (Foster et al., 1999; Levstik & Pappas, 1987). Yet while fourth and fifth graders are developmentally capable of more nuanced ways of understanding historical time—including some forms of dating and sequencing (Barton & Levstik, 1996)—the children who told Jewish heritage narratives presented stories with an indeterminate conception of historical time. In their stories, the events that occurred in the Jewish past could have happened at any time, or perhaps even at every moment in time before the creation of Israel.

THE TWO-PART STRUCTURE OF JEWISH HERITAGE NARRATIVES

The children's Jewish heritage narratives always contained a two-part structure. In the first part of these children's stories, "The Jewish people didn't have a land for themselves" (Carly, 3). This was either because Jews had "no state to live in" (Jacob, 1) or because Jews lived in a place where the other people who lived there "didn't like them" (Dina, 4). Regardless of whether the Jewish people were stateless or living in a hostile place, "The Jewish people didn't really have a place where they could just live" (Carly, 5) and they often felt "scared and pushed around" (Rina, 4).

In the second part of the children's heritage narratives, the Jewish people "got their own country" (Esther, 5) called Israel and "finally established that country as their homeland" (Olivia, 5). At this point in the children's stories, the Jews no longer needed to "wander around" (Naomi, 5), and they felt "safe" and "protected" (Dina, 4).

These two parts of the children's heritage narratives functioned as a dyad, situating the Jewish people both before and after the creation of Israel. What, specifically, happened to bring about this change? What, in the children's minds, caused or allowed the Jewish people to move from a stateless people wandering around to a people with a homeland in Israel? Even with additional prompting, none of the children addressed these questions. Their heritage narratives offered no specific details about events or actions that could account for this change. Bella's fifth-grade story clearly illuminates the two-part structure typical of the children's Jewish heritage narratives. In her telling, "The Jewish people didn't have a place to live, but then they found Israel!" As to what allowed or propelled the Jewish people to "find Israel," Bella and the other children who told these stories remained silent.

Although the children who told heritage narratives did not offer any specific details about how or when a transformation between statelessness and "home in Israel" (Naomi, 5) occurred, the children were consistent about who was responsible for this change. If children's theological narratives cast God as Israel's creator and children's biblical narratives framed a divine–human partnership as responsible for Israel's creation, in children's Jewish heritage narratives Jews created Israel. God was generally absent from these stories, and, in the words of Ryan (5), "Israel was created as a land by the Jewish people."

Children who told heritage narratives situated the story of Israel's founding as part of a larger tale about the Jewish past. As Naomi (3) explained, "Israel is part of Jewish history." By framing Israel's founding as an extension of Jewish experiences over time (Biale, 1986)—rather than an opposition to a previous way of Jewish life (Laqueur, 2003/1972)—these children suggested that Judaism itself is intertwined with an ongoing story of wandering in search of home. Yet other children told stories that more closely resembled classic Zionist history, situating Israel's founding as a distinctly modern phenomenon and a vast "improvement" (Gabe, 5) over prior Jewish experiences.

Zionist Narratives

"Theodor Herzl thought of the idea that the Jewish people should be in their own place," began fifth-grader Maya.

> And then many years after he died, somebody said, "Why not try it?" And so they started to make Israel, and it was a big, big thing. David Ben-Gurion was the first prime minister of Israel, and Israel became the country. And then they even got a first woman prime minister, Golda Meir. And then a lot of things happened that were big, big accomplishments. Israel made a lot of inventions like Waze. They even made this cool pill that you can take and there's a camera in it to see how your body is. And they've accomplished a lot in their 70 years. That's how it happened.

"After the Holocaust," explained fifth-grader Tzvi,

> the Jews were scattered all over the world, specifically in Europe. And they were searching for a home. And they were offered a place in Palestine. At first it was a little part of what Israel is today, and then it started growing, and after a few years it became a country. In 1948 it became the state of Israel, which is the home of the Jewish people.

Children like Maya and Tzvi told Israel's origin story as a modern "progress narrative" (Zerubavel, 2002) that framed the establishment of Israel in 1948 as the pinnacle of Jewish history. Like the children's Jewish heritage narratives, the children's Zionist narratives often had a storyline that began in the Diaspora and ended in Israel. Yet unlike Jewish heritage narratives, these Zionist narratives also contained specific (though not always historically accurate) details about the time and chronology of historical events, and children who told them typically named specific moments and/or figures from modern Jewish history.

THE TIMING AND KEY EVENTS OF ZIONIST NARRATIVES
Children's Zionist narratives dated the creation of Israel to a specific year: 1948. If children's Jewish heritage narratives began "a long time ago" and children's biblical narratives occurred "in the time of the Torah" (Rina, 5), then children's Zionist narratives clearly stated that "Israel was founded in 1948" (Tzvi, 5) or "was established in 1948" (Keren, 4). As Carly (4) explained, "Israel was made . . . so it's been 70 years about. Right now it's 2018, so that would be . . . let's see. Minus 70. That would be 1948."

In addition to being rooted in the temporal, children's Zionist narratives were distinct from other kinds of children's narratives in that they alluded to specific events in modern Jewish history. As children told these Zionist narratives, they populated their stories with specific details about particular moments in time. These children spoke about events such as the First Zionist Congress (Tzvi, 4), David Ben-Gurion's proclamation of statehood (Seth, 4), and the 1948 War of Independence (Naomi, 4), telling broad-brushstrokes stories about them. The most common historical events that the children discussed in relation to Israel's founding were the Holocaust and the 1947 UN partition vote, each of which featured prominently in the stories of multiple children.

THE HOLOCAUST
Children who told Zionist narratives clearly had a basic understanding of chronology; the foundation of the state of Israel occurred after the Holocaust. In Keren's (5) words, when Israel was established "the Holocaust happened recently." Why did World War II and the Holocaust figure into these children's stories about Israel? What, in the children's minds, was the relationship between the destruction of Europe's Jewish community and the establishment of Israel? There were three different ways that children's stories situated the Holocaust in relationship to Israel.

In some children's stories, the relationship was *causal*: Israel, in their minds, was created because of the Holocaust. In Seth's (4) story, the Jews "got Israel, they got independence, from defeating the Nazis in World War II." According to Micah (5), "A lot of people in the Holocaust, like Mordechai Anielewicz, stood up for Jews, and without them Israel wouldn't have been here." These children believed that the actions of Jews in Europe, and particularly Jewish resistance, directly led to the establishment of Israel.

In other children's stories, the relationship was *sequential*: the establishment of a Jewish state in Israel happened after, though not necessarily as a result of, the Holocaust. According to Pearl (5), "After the Holocaust, everyone found their way to Israel." In Gia's (4) telling, "The survivors of the Holocaust wanted their own country." For these children, the Holocaust was part of the story of Israel not because of any direct link between the two events but because they believed that the Jews who survived the Holocaust were the same Jews who later built Israel as a Jewish state.

For another group of children, the relationship was *aphoristic*; in their telling, Israel is what it is today because of the larger lessons that Jews learn from the Holocaust. For example, Lailah (5) explained, "The Holocaust happened, and many Jews were forced to work in concentration camps, and they were forced to do many things. And that's why today, the Israeli army is really strong, because they will never want the Holocaust to happen again." The children who looked to the Holocaust to draw lessons from it believed in some version of what Jewish philosopher Emil Fackenheim (1970) calls the Voice of Auschwitz, a post-Holocaust command for Jews to survive.

Children from Ashkenazi and Sephardi backgrounds alike situated the Holocaust as an important part of the story of Israel's creation. Regardless of whether the children saw a direct causal link, a sequence in timing, or broad moral lessons from the Holocaust that shaped Israel, they viewed Israel as "a safe place for the Jews" (Keren, 5) after a period of profound danger and uncertainty in Jewish history.

THE UN VOTE ON THE PARTITION OF PALESTINE

Many of the children who told Zionist narratives distinguished between the declaration of the modern state in 1948 and the time "before Israel when it was still Palestine" (Keren, 4). In their telling, Israel became a state "because the UN allowed it" (Seth, 5).

Consider, for example, Gia's stories about the 1947 United Nations vote to partition Palestine into a Jewish state and an Arab state. In fourth grade, Gia explained that "the United Nations had that vote, and each country in the world would say 'yes' or 'no' or abstained. Most of the countries said yes, but the Arab states obviously said no." In fifth grade, she offered a similar explanation in different words. "The United Nations, United States, and all the countries had a vote on should we make Israel a state," she said. "Then the majority voted that Israel should be a free nation, so then they became free and independent."

Other children also highlighted the United Nations vote as the pivotal moment of transformation that turned the area "to Israel from Palestine" (Tzvi, 4). According to Keren (4), "David Ben-Gurion asked. They had a meeting with some people and he asked them if the Jews, who did not have a place to live, could stay in Israel and live there. And they said 'sure.'" As Naomi (5) explained, "Who decided to make Israel? Well, there was a whole bunch of countries, and then the people who represent them, like our president and the prime ministers and the kings. And most of them voted for Israel, and so Israel was a state."

If children who told biblical narratives framed the creation of Israel as the result of a divine–human partnership and children who told Jewish heritage narratives framed the Jewish people as the creators of Israel, then children who told Zionist narratives typically framed important Zionist leaders, in conjunction with the United Nations, as responsible for creating Israel.

"THAT GUY WAS A VISIONARY": HERZL AND OTHER HISTORICAL FIGURES IN CHILDREN'S NARRATIVES

One of the key features that distinguished children's Zionist narratives from the other kinds of stories that they told about the Jewish and Israeli pasts was the inclusion of specific men and women from modern Jewish history. Some children crafted narratives that framed key figures from Holocaust history, like Hannah Szenes (Rina, 5) and Mordechai Anielewicz (Micah, 5), as an important part of the story of Israel's creation. Some children spoke of key cultural figures like Hayim Nachman Bialik (Rina, 5) or Eliezer Ben Yehuda (Naomi, 5), and others spoke of Israeli prime ministers like David Ben-Gurion (Keren, 3) or Golda Meir (Rina, 5). No children who told modern Zionist narratives spoke of Israeli figures most famous for their military prowess, such as Moshe Dayan or Motta Gur, and none mentioned God as an actor in modern Jewish history.

By far the most common historical figure to appear in children's Zionist narratives was Theodor Herzl. Many of the children credited Herzl with being the "one guy" (Brent, 5) solely responsible for thinking up the idea of Israel. In Keren's (4) telling, Israel was founded because "Theodor Herzl wanted to have a Jewish place, a safe place for Jews." In Tzvi's (5) story, "It all started with Herzl's idea to make a Zionist state, to make a Jewish state." "That guy," explained Rina (5), "was a visionary! He created—well, he didn't really create it, because he didn't ever get to see Israel, but he had so many ideas of what Israel should be like: a homeland for the Jewish people." According to Lior (5), Israel was created because "Herzl imagined it all. . . . He just imagined it, and then he said, 'I imagine that there will be a country just for Jews.'" In Micah's (5) estimation, "Without Theodor Herzl, I don't think Israel would have been Israel."

As children think about the past, it is common for them to attribute to a small number of famous people responsibility for large-scale historical change that actually occurred over time and in response to the actions of many (Barton, 1996, 2008; Brophy et al., 1992). When these children told Zionist narratives, they typically wove stories that cast a small number of famous Jews like Herzl or Ben-Gurion as singlehandedly responsible for the creation of a modern Jewish state.

Summary of Children's Narrative Types

The children told four distinct kinds of narratives about Israel's origins. Theological stories, rooted in the moment of creation, framed God as the creator of the world and therefore Israel. Biblical narratives drew from a broader retelling of the books of Genesis and Exodus, framing Israel's creation as a process of transformation involving divine–human cooperation. Jewish heritage narratives transcended time and place, framing a story of the collective Jewish people's perpetual wandering in search of a home. Zionist narratives were distinctly modern stories that focused on the creation of the state and the heroic actions of famous Jews. Each of these types of narratives offered distinct explanations about when, why, and by whom Israel was made.

The Developmental Trajectories of Children's Historical Storytelling

All four types of narratives that the children told about the origins of Israel—theological, biblical, Jewish heritage, and Zionist—were told by multiple children over the course of multiple years. Yet these kinds of narratives were not told uniformly by the children at every grade level. See table 2.2 for a summary of the grade levels in which the children typically told each of these kinds of stories.

TABLE 2.2. Historical Narratives Commonly Told by Grade Level

Grade Level	Theological	Biblical	Jewish Heritage	Zionist
1	✓			
2	✓	✓		
3	✓	✓		
4	✓	✓	✓	✓
5	✓	✓	✓	✓

Children at every grade level told theological narratives. First graders and fifth graders alike told stories focused on the idea that "God created Israel" (Gabe, 1; Esther, 5). In the younger grades of elementary school (1–3), these stories were often one sentence long and contained no story elements beyond the act of God's creation. For example, Esther's (1) entire story was "God made Israel" and Gabe's (1) was "God created Israel." As the children reached the upper grades (4–5), the basic arc of the theological narratives remained the same though the children tended to add additional details. For example, Samantha (5) explained that "God made Israel, but the Jewish people made it their home." Lailah (4) narrated, "God made Israel because He's the only person that really created this world. Our God, the Jewish God, created Israel for the Jews, and continued to have hope in them." The theological narratives of older children, like those of younger children, situated God as the creator of Israel, but extended beyond a single moment of creation.

Children told biblical narratives beginning in second grade and continued to tell stories from the Bible throughout their elementary school years. For some children, these narratives replaced the theological narratives that their younger selves had told. These children appeared to substitute one conceptual category for another, telling stories that drew from a broader narrative from the books of Genesis and Exodus instead of stories that focused only on the moment of the creation of the world. Yet for other children, biblical narratives began to stand alongside theological narratives as an alternative way of telling the same story. At some moments, these children continued to tell theological narratives that situated God as the sole creator of Israel and the rest of the world, while at other moments they told biblical narratives that framed Israel as the result of an ongoing divine–human partnership.

Both Jewish heritage narratives and Zionist narratives were most commonly told by fourth and fifth graders. Between third and fourth grade, children tend to make an "enormous leap" in their historical understanding and begin to think about key historical concepts including chronology, change over time, and cause and effect (Levstik & Barton, 1996, p. 12). By late elementary school, children can often do what they could not in the earlier grades: understand the perspectives of multiple historical actors and grapple with the "interpretive nature of historical explanation" (Levstik, 1989, p. 117).

As these children transitioned to the upper elementary grades, they began to tell stories that focused on one example of change over time: a transition from statelessness to homeland. Some children framed this transition as a generic and timeless shift in which the Jewish people went from having no place to having a home in Israel, telling Jewish heritage narratives. Other children framed this transition as a distinctly modern phenomenon, telling Zionist narratives that attributed the transition to statehood to famous Zionist figures. Although less common, there were a few younger children who told basic Jewish heritage narratives as early as grade 1, and Zionist narratives without dates as early as grade 3.

Individual children often told multiple kinds of historical narratives throughout their elementary school years. There were two typical pathways that the children took as they developed over time: an alternative pathway and an additive pathway. In the former, children supplanted initial theological or biblical narratives that they told in early elementary school with alternative Jewish heritage or Zionist narratives in the later elementary grades. In the latter, their older selves added further narrative layers that existed alongside the stories they told when they were younger. See Figure 2.1 for the two common pathways that children took.

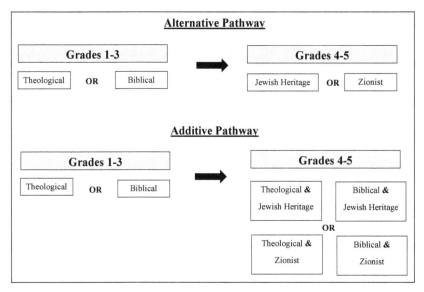

Figure 2.1. The Pathways of Children's Historical Narratives

Alternative Pathway: Developing New Stories over Time

While all children's stories changed over time, some children went through two entirely distinct phases in their storytelling. These children told one kind of story—typically a theological or biblical narrative—in early elementary school, and by fourth or fifth grade they had replaced these stories with an alternate kind—typically a Jewish heritage or Zionist narrative. No trace of the theological or biblical remained in their storytelling in the upper elementary grades, and there was no overlap in their early-elementary and late-elementary answers to who created Israel, when, and why.

This was certainly the case for Naomi, who replaced her initial theological narratives with Zionist ones. While some children hesitated momentarily before attempting to tell a story about Israel's creation, even as a first grader Naomi launched into storytelling with enthusiasm. Her first-grade story was a clear and straightforward theological narrative: "The whole world started as a big blob. Then God made things, and He made the parts of land, and Israel was one of them." A year later, in second grade, she reiterated that the origin story of Israel was "part of the creation [of the world]." To her second-grade self, it was clear that "God made the land."

Yet as a fourth and fifth grader, Naomi no longer told Israeli history as a story of creation. She pivoted, instead telling a Zionist story that set Israel's foundation in modern times. "The Zionists," fourth-grader Naomi explained, "were a group of Jews who lived not in Israel, trying to go back in Israel, but it was under Palestinian rule. Eventually they had the [1948] war. Then they got Israel back." In fifth grade, she also told a story that situated Israel's origin as a modern Zionist phenomenon. She explained:

> At first, it's called Palestine. And then Jews thought that they should have their own state, and that was called Zionism. The Zionists decided to create a state, but they didn't know where to put it. But then they put it where Israel is today. And at first there's a lot of wars, but they eventually got it (and there's still a lot of wars).

In these fourth- and fifth-grade stories, God had entirely vanished. Zionists made Israel, and they did so not at the moment of the world's creation but after "a whole bunch of countries . . . voted for Israel."

Naomi took two entirely different approaches to crafting the story of Israel's origins. Her first-and-second-grade self narrated one story, attributing the creation of Israel to God and locating it at the moment of the world's creation, and her fourth-and-fifth-grade self crafted an alternative narrative, crediting modern Zionists with transforming British Mandate Palestine into Israel. The stories she told in early elementary school faded away and were replaced by new narratives.

Additive Pathway: Layering Stories over Time

If children like Naomi had found an entirely new recipe for historical storytelling by fourth grade, then children like Tzvi told stories about the past as if they were baking layer cakes. In early elementary school, these children were able to create one-layer narratives, offering a single explanation of the story of Israel's founding. By late elementary school, these children had begun to add new elements to their stories, layering multiple kinds of narratives on top of one another. They told one kind of narrative—either theological or biblical—in first and second grade, and by fourth or fifth grade they had added elements to their story, maintaining the role of God and/or biblical characters but recasting them as a small part of a much larger story that stretched from biblical times until modern times.

Tzvi's evolving storytelling illustrates how some children took an additive pathway, layering stories over time. In second and third grade, Tzvi rooted his story about Israel's founding in the narratives of the book of Genesis. As a second grader, he explained that the moment when Israel became Israel was when "Abraham went to Canaan, and Canaan changed to be called Israel because of Jacob, which is Abraham's grandson. His nickname was Israel." As a third grader, Tzvi's biblical narrative began:

> It started out as Abraham, the first Jew. He was promised a Promised Land by God. How it got the name Israel was from Jacob, the third father of the Jewish people. God changed his name. Just like Abraham was first Abram and then He changed it to Abraham, He changed Jacob's name from Yaakov to Israel.

Although Tzvi's third-grade narrative was more verbose and detailed than his second-grade narration, the core elements of his story remained the same.

By fourth grade, however, Tzvi began to add further elements to his initial biblical story, layering a modern Zionist narrative on top of it. His fourth-grade rendition of Israel's founding was:

> First, Abraham became a Jew, the first Jew. God promised them a land of Canaan and [Abraham] having lots of descendants and children. They were traveling and there's the whole Pesach [Passover] story and Jews went into Israel after Moses died. But it wasn't really their state until 1948, when Ben-Gurion, the prime minister then, declared that Israel was a Jewish state in 1948.

His locating of the origin story in biblical times did not disappear, as it had for Naomi, but instead was paired with a story about the modern declaration of statehood.

Tzvi's fifth-grade story, like his fourth-grade rendition, contained both biblical and Zionist elements. "It all started out with Abraham," he began, and then shifted from recounting the biblical text to retelling a story from Midrash Rabbah (28:13), a rabbinic interpretation of the Genesis story.

> He belonged to a religion where they prayed down to idols. So there's a very famous story where his dad owned an idol shop. His dad went and said, "Abraham, stay there and keep watch of the idols." And then Abraham cracked a bunch of them. [His dad] came back [asking], "Abraham, why'd you do that?" And he's like, "No, the idols did it." And [his dad said], "The idols can't move." And Abraham was like, "Exactly!"

Switching back to the biblical story, Tzvi continued with a slightly different version of the story than the one quoted above:

> So God said, "*Lech l'cha* [Go forth], go to the land where I will show you. Go from the land of your birthplace, the land of your father." So [Abraham] took a bunch of cattle and sheep and livestock with his wife, Sarah. And they found Canaan. . . . So Abraham and Sarah had a child. They had Isaac. And Isaac married Rivka [Rebecca].

Jumping directly from the biblical story to modern times, Tzvi's story took an abrupt turn.

> So, it started with Herzl's idea to make a Zionist state, to make a Jewish state. And he started the Zionism movement, which was a movement where they kind of provoked a Jewish state. And Herzl started the idea, which then grew into a reality of a country. Before it was controlled by the British. It used to be called Palestine. And then, as some of the wars broke out, specifically World War II, the British kind of let Israel be in control of the Jewish people. And when Ben-Gurion signed the [proclamation], Israel came to be after a whole bunch of voting on the Palestinian territory. And after all that, Israel became a state. Israel was founded in 1948 by David Ben-Gurion.

In this fifth-grade version of Israel's founding, Tzvi suggested that Israel "started" twice: first with the story of Abraham, and then again with the story of Herzl; he jumped from a biblical story to a modern Zionist one, but he framed them as a two-part answer to the same question: When was Israel founded?

Summary of the Trajectories of Children's Narratives

In the early elementary grades, the children were most likely to tell theological or biblical stories. As the children developed over time, some of them replaced their initial historical narratives with alternative ones, instead telling Jewish heritage or Zionist narratives. Yet other children did not replace, but rather added to their initial narratives, crafting layered stories that began with theological or biblical narratives and transitioned to Jewish heritage or Zionist ones. These children were able to offer multiple explanations of the same historical event, framing and then reframing Israel's founding so that it was, in Micah's (5) words, "so many stories."

Children's Reflections on History

When children narrate stories about the past, they draw from a variety of sources in which they have encountered history: school classes and family tales, media and popular culture, visits to museums and historical sites, and more (Levstik & Barton, 2008). And, as the children in this study demonstrate, they fashion their own versions of narratives to frame past events, recrafting and reframing stories they have encountered. Yet children are capable of much more than telling stories *about* history; they are also able to reflect on the nature and meaning of history itself (Barton, 2001b).

The section below highlights the children's ideas about how history functions. First, it presents the children's reflections on the nature of historical "truth," showing that many children are able to question the very historical narratives that they tell. Next, it demonstrates that children can pay careful attention not only to the structure of stories that they tell about the past, but also to the ways that stories shift depending on who is hearing them. Thus, by late elementary school, children are able to craft different versions of history when they address different audiences.

Children's Reflections on Historical "Truth"

The historical storytelling task that we set out for kids to do focused on narratives. We asked the children to "tell me a story" about the history of Israel, but we did not ask them to reflect on any historical evidence upon which their stories might draw, nor did we ask them questions of epistemology like "How do you know what you know?" This is because while fourth and fifth graders can begin to understand that some historical accounts are more reliable than others (Barton, 1997b; VanSledright & Kelly, 1998), children in the early elementary grades do not typically think about questions of historical evidence or what makes a historical narrative reliable or verifiable (Levstik & Barton, 1996).

Nonetheless, beginning in third grade, some of the children in this study began—unprompted—to reflect aloud about questions related to historical "truth." Several children in third grade began to couch their stories with phrases like "I'm not sure that this is true, but I heard that . . ." (Gia, 3) or "I don't know but . . ." (Isabelle, 3). Lailah (3) framed her narrative with statements of doubt, beginning "I don't know but maybe . . ." and concluding, "That's all I know. That is maybe not true." Carly (4) began by stating, "I don't really know exactly" before launching into her story. None of these children were saying that they did not know of, or could not craft, a story about Israel's origins; they were instead saying that they were uncertain about the veracity of the stories they were about to tell.

By fifth grade, which for many children constitutes a shift into understanding that history constitutes its own genre (Levstik & Barton, 1996), some of the children began to voice skepticism specifically about the trustworthiness of the Bible as a historical source. These children were thinking in nascent ways about theology, history, and heritage, and as burgeoning historical thinkers they questioned whether the Bible could be considered verifiable *historical* evidence even as they continued to believe that the Bible was a source of meaning for Jewish living.

For example, Tzvi (5) reflected on God's promise to Abraham. He explained, "God said, 'I will make your children as numerous as the stars and as great as the grains of sand.' And that hasn't been true yet that much, because of the Holocaust. We've never gotten to the amount of Jews there was before the Holocaust." In Tzvi's mind, the biblical promise to Abraham "hasn't been true yet" and therefore it casts doubt on the veracity of the Bible itself.

Rina (5) also questioned whether the Bible was "true" even as she continued to tell biblical stories. She explained: "That's complicated. Really complicated. Because there's the Torah, and the stuff about Moses, and [it suggests that] the Promised Land was always their land. But how are we supposed to know if it was *actually* the Jews' land all the time?" In Rina's estimation, the fact that we don't "actually know" whether or not Jews owned or inhabited the land of Israel "all the time" means that it is impossible to determine whether the story she told about Israel's origins was true or not. "[Israel] might have been created in the time of the Torah," she explained, "but it might not have." According to Rina, "modern history" must include what "we know, based on facts, [to be] real," but the stories of the Bible could not be known in the same way because "nobody was ever there that we really know today." This spontaneous questioning about the Bible's trustworthiness as a historical source is particularly noteworthy because even older children often need prompting or directing by a teacher in order to reflect on the veracity or accuracy of a narrative about the past (Levstik, 2008b). Yet it simultaneously mirrors the historical thinking of other children who assume that the past cannot be known because people who are alive today were not there to see it (P. Lee, 1998b).

Like other children who have expressed a deep interest in learning "the truth" or "what really happened" in the past (P. Lee & Shemilt, 2004; Levstik, 1989), these children expressed discomfort with the fact that they could not easily determine whether or not the biblical story was the "real story" (Pearl, 3) of Israel's origins. Embedded in their wondering was an assumption both that there is "a real story" and that there was good reason to believe that the stories they were about to tell were not, in fact, that "real story." Their language—which distinguished "the real story" or "the truth" from their own historical narratives—demonstrated a nascent awareness of questions about evidence, argumentation, and the trustworthiness of different kinds of historical accounts.

Children's Ideas about History for Children

Even as some of the children expressed discomfort that the "real story" of what happened in the past is unknown, other children exhibited an understanding that stories about the past are created by human beings for particular audiences and particular purposes. History, in this view, is an interpretive process. Rather than being simply "real" or "fake," stories about the past may have varying degrees of trustworthiness or fidelity to the lives and experiences of those who lived in the past.

When the children were in fifth grade, we asked them about Israeli history using two different prompts. In the first, we asked children to "tell me a story" about when Israel became Israel, a question we had been asking them for five consecutive years. In the second, we used an alternate framing, explaining, "I want to write a book for fifth graders about the history of Israel. What should I tell them about how Israel started? Who made Israel, when, and why?" For some children, these questions appeared identical, and they responded to the second that the question had already been asked and answered. Some children interpreted the second prompt as a chance to circle back to their earlier stories and add details that they "forgot" (Brent, 5) to say initially. But other children interpreted these prompts as a chance to tell the story of Israel's founding moment to two distinct audiences: first to adults and then, differently, to other children their age. The alternative stories told by these children offer a glimpse into how children think about telling history specifically *to children*.[2]

The stories of Keren (5), Lailah (5), and Lior (5) demonstrate how some children framed the history of Israel in very different ways for adults and for other children. When speaking directly to an adult interviewer, Keren told a modern Zionist story, saying that "Israel was established in 1948 [but] Theodor Herzl started the idea to have a Jewish place." When imagining a book for other fifth graders, however, Keren said that the book should focus on how "God promised Abraham that his descendants would live in the land of Israel," and how "King Solomon built the Temple, the first one." To an adult audience she told a modern Zionist story, and to children she told a biblical narrative.

Lailah's (5) answers to the two prompts, like Keren's, told entirely different stories to adults and to other children. Addressing adults, Lailah began her story when "the Holocaust happened" and continued to ex-plain that "Israel became an independent country in 1948." When ad-dressing other children, however, Lailah explained that God created Israel "because He's the only person that really created this world. And our God, the Jewish God, created Israel for the Jews." She told a modern Zionist story to adults and a theological narrative to other children.

Lior's (5) stories also framed different narratives for adults and for children. To adults, Lior told a story about Herzl. Referring to Herzl's "famous quote," "If you will it, it is no dream," Lior explained that "Herzl imagined there will be a country just for Jews." When speaking to other children, however, Lior told an entirely different story. His children's book combined elements of the biblical account of Abraham with the narrative structure of a story from the Midrash, a rabbinic interpretation of the Bible. According to the Midrash (Sifre Devarim, Zot HaBeracha, 343), God approached various nations and asked, "Will you accept the Torah?" Each nation in turn asked, "What is in it?" and, upon hearing the laws of the Torah, each rejected it in turn. Finally God approached the Israelites, asking if they would accept the Torah, and the Israelites replied, "We will do and we will listen." In Lior's story for children, this rabbinic tale about the giving of the Torah was reset in the time of Abra-ham. It followed the general story arc of the Midrashic tale but recast it, framing it not as a story about the Torah but instead as an explanation of the founding of Israel. Lior explained:

God asked many people to go help Him found Israel. But they were like, "What do I get in return?" And He said, "You get as much children as you can count stars, okay?" But [one person] said, "No, I want more. I want treasure." He went to another [person] and said the same exact thing. Then God said, "Will you help me found Israel?" And the [second per-son] said, "Can I be king?" and then He's like, "Pass." And then He goes to a couple more, same thing. And then He goes to Abraham. And his wife Sarah is too old to have children, so God tells him, "You'll have as much children as you can count stars." So [Abraham] was like, "Yeah, I'm in!'" And then he went on and had a child.

Two aspects of Lior's storytelling are noteworthy. First, Lior did not just retell a story he had previously heard. He actively constructed—whether intentionally or not—a new tale that used the narrative structure from the Midrash as a way of explaining how Israel was established. His narrative was part fable, part Midrash, and part biblical allusion. Second, and perhaps more important, this story was how Lior framed Israel's origins only to other children; to adults, he told a story about Herzl, not Abraham.

Lior, Lailah, and Keren, along with the other fifth graders who explicitly addressed adults and children in different ways, initially framed Israel's origin as a Zionist story in response to a prompt asking them to "tell a story" about the creation of Israel. Yet even though they themselves clearly understood a basic version of modern Zionist history, they did not tell a modern Zionist story when suggesting a book that should be crafted for other children their age. To other children, they told only stories that contained biblical, rabbinic, or theological elements.

What accounts for fifth graders crafting different historical accounts when addressing adults and when telling stories for other children? There are multiple possible explanations. One possibility is that children misjudge the intellectual capacities of their peers. Just as adults tend to underestimate the sophistication of children's thinking and decision making (Roffey, 2012; Wilson-Keenan, 2015), it is possible that when children think about history, they, too, underestimate other children's cognitive abilities. As Rina (5) explained before telling her story for an adult audience, "It's not really stuff to share with fifth graders, but I think it's really awesome and I'm a fifth grader." While children like Rina clearly understood that the story of Israel's origin could be told in multiple ways—after all, they themselves told multiple versions of it— they seem to have assumed that their peers could handle only the elements of the story that they themselves understood in early elementary school: biblical and theological narratives.

Another possibility is that the children were responding to prompts that they interpreted as cues to tell stories of different genres. By the time children enter elementary school, they typically have a firmly established sense of storytelling conventions (Applebee, 1980). Elementary school students are capable of understanding and producing stories of different genres (Donovan, 2001; Donovan & Smolkin, 2002; Kamberelis, 1999; Pappas, 1993). Therefore it is possible that the children interpreted the prompt to tell "a story" about Israel's creation as an invitation to tell Zionist narratives, the type of children's narratives that most closely resembled a history genre, while a prompt to suggest ideas for "a book" for children elicited biblical narratives, which were more fable-like and similar in structure to children's books.

Regardless of the reason for the differences in the stories that the children told in response to these different prompts, two important facets of children's storytelling are evident: By the upper elementary grades, children are capable of telling different versions of the same story, and they can consciously choose which story to tell depending on the context. This seemingly simple act of children offering different narrations of past events challenges the prevailing wisdom in history education. It has long been understood that young people can grasp that accounts of the past can be told in different ways in different settings (Stearns, 2000). In fact, older students may deliberately choose to tell versions of history that explicitly contest school (Barton & McCully, 2005; Stearns, 2000) or official state (Wertsch, 2000, 2002) narratives. Yet prior research on younger children's historical understanding has shown that children often view different stories about the past as "copies of the same thing" (P. Lee, 1998b), suggesting that children are not yet capable of understanding different ways of framing historical events. If children can recognize differences in accounts, they are more likely to attribute those differences to intentional distortion by some authors than to differences in interpretation (P. Lee, 1998a). Yet the children in this study did not only recognize that it was possible for authors to offer multiple interpretations of the same event with different framing; they themselves did so when they narrated history.

The fact that multiple children in this study told differing stories to distinct audiences and did so according to the same pattern—telling Zionist narratives to adults and biblical or theological narratives to other children—suggests that children do more than "guess work" (P. Lee, 1998a) when it comes to thinking about the role of narrative in framing the past. They can, in fact, be deliberate and thoughtful narrators, framing and reframing stories about the past to address different audiences even if they cannot (yet) articulate how authors evaluate available evidence and make analytical decisions about how to craft their historical accounts (P. Lee & Shemilt, 2004).

Summary of Children's Reflections on History

While the children were able to tell stories about the past from the early days of elementary school, their understanding of the veracity of different origin stories and their reflections on audience transformed over time. By third grade, some children began to reflect on questions of historical truth, wondering about the credibility of the very stories that they narrated. By fifth grade, many children began to explicitly question whether the Bible could be considered a historical source. At that point, the children also developed an ability to narrate the story of Israel's origins differently to different audiences, framing stories about the past in different ways depending on whether they were crafting stories for adults or for other children. Each of these instances demonstrates that by middle childhood, children are capable of thoughtful and deliberate narration as they tell origin stories about the past.

Conclusion

From a very young age, children can and do tell stories about the past. When children tell historical origin stories, their storytelling functions as part of a larger process of making sense of how countries come into being, revealing insights into children's conceptions of how societies emerge and evolve. Using their own words and drawing upon their developing conceptions of history and myth, children are capable of reflecting both on times long gone and on the nature of historical storytelling itself.

Children's words reveal that even if elementary school students may not be learning about historical interpretation, analysis, and argumentation, they are certainly learning, in the famous words of anthropologist Clifford Geertz (1973), "the stories we tell ourselves about ourselves." Long before they are "historical thinkers" who can develop evidence-based interpretations of available historical sources and artifacts, children are "historical beings" (Wineburg, 2000) attempting to make sense of what it means to be part of a larger collective heritage that carries ties to other people, including those in the past.

For Jewish children in particular, hearing and telling stories about the Jewish past can be an important part of how they experience and make sense of Judaism. As Bella (4) explains, "Being Jewish *is* telling the stories." For her, like for so many other children in this study, stories about the past are part of the very fabric of Judaism; they permeate holiday celebrations and ritual, communal prayer and private conversations with parents and grandparents. Children, no less than adults, can understand that recalling and recounting the Jewish past is a central part of the experience of being Jewish (Heller, 1988). For, as French historian Pierre Nora explains, "To be Jewish is to remember that one is such" (1989, p. 116). Despite the fact that throughout much of the Jewish past, Jewish thinkers were decidedly uninvolved in the study of history (Schacter, 1999), many contemporary Jews "take for granted that 'Judaism' is a 'historical religion' and rests on an interpretation of historical fact" (J. Neusner, 1995, p. 56). In the eyes of these contemporary Jewish children, that Judaism is a "historical religion" often means that "Judaism is all about understanding what Jews have been through" (Hannah, 4).

As adults who care about the emotional well-being and intellectual growth of children talk to them about the past, it is important to recognize that even when children do not think about historical sources or historical evidence like adults (Gottlieb & Wineburg, 2012), they *do* think deeply about historical narratives. Children are capable of understanding and crafting multiple distinct narratives about times long gone, and as they grow they can begin to reflect on how evidence and audience might shape different historical accounts. Many curricula geared toward elementary school students underestimate the complexity of children's historical understanding, incorrectly assuming that children can think only about concrete and surface-level ideas when in fact they can understand so much more (Brophy, 1990; Levstik, 2008a).

To take seriously the developmental capacities of children would entail allowing children opportunities not only to encounter and recount multiple different stories about the past, but also to think about how and why historical stories differ. Even more important, it would require adults to explicitly model for children—not by happenstance, but as part of a deliberate process in which adults thoughtfully reflect aloud about their own thinking about the past—the multiple different strategies that adults use when hearing and telling history, ranging from "the careful sifting of the documentary record for the academic historian [to] the primacy of sacred texts and traditions for the religious believer" (Gottlieb & Wineburg, 2012, p. 26).

Adults who educate children—and especially those who hope to induct children into the stories and customs of a collective heritage—must also recognize that learning about the past can never be solely about the stories of "who we are and where we come from" (Hertzel, 2017), no matter how beautiful and varied those stories may be. For children find meaning in history both when it is "ours," revealing understanding about the communities and cultures in which we live (Levstik, 2000), *and* when it is "other," providing insight into societies in other times and places (Barton, 2001b). History education, in this view, is essential not only because it can build an understanding of the past but also because it can help young learners develop the skills needed for civic participation in democratic societies in the present, which requires the ability to understand and dialogue with people quite different from ourselves. As scholar of history education Sam Wineburg explains, "Coming to know others, whether they live on the other side of the tracks, or the other side of the millennium, requires the education of our sensibilities. This is what history, when taught well, gives us practice in doing" (2001, pp. 23–24).

As children learn about the world, past and present, they work to make sense of how their own lives and communities fit into the larger scope of human affairs, *and* they strive to make sense of how others have framed their experiences and societies. The former is often central to Jewish educational initiatives, while the latter is typically ignored or overlooked in curricula and resources for Jewish children. Yet as the American Jewish children in this study looked to Israel from afar, they directed their gaze not only to Jewish Israelis but also to Arabs, and especially Palestinians. And when they did so, they tended to see not years of coexistence work between Arabs and Jews (Abu-Nimer, 2001; Bekerman & Horenczyk) nor numerous, though often fraught, approaches to peace education initiatives (Bar-Tal, 2011; Bekerman & Zembylas, 2011; Maoz, 2010), but rather a long history of violent conflict. It is the children's narrations of that conflict, which they constructed alongside their stories of Jewish and Israeli history, that are the focus of the next chapter. For children's attempts to understand the Israeli–Arab/Palestinian conflict were inexorably tied to their ongoing quest to "learn about our history" (Gia, 4).

3

"Israel vs. the Other Team"

Children's Understanding of the Israeli–Arab/Palestinian Conflict

Samantha cannot remember a time before she knew about the Israeli–Arab/Palestinian conflict. As a 6-year-old, she insists that the conflict—which she calls "the war in Israel"—is something that she learned about in utero. Samantha's long, chestnut hair frames large brown eyes, which widen as she explains, "My mom talked about it when I was in my mom's tummy, so I learned." The conflict is so embedded in the way that Samantha thinks about the world that she cannot even imagine not knowing about it. "When I was born," she says, "I straight away knew about it."

Samantha's narration about her view of the Israeli–Arab/Palestinian conflict flies in the face of conventional wisdom. Many parents and educators, out of a well-meaning desire to protect young children from the harsh realities of the world, assume that geopolitical conflict is a developmentally inappropriate topic for young children. In public schools (Avni & Karpman, 2019) and Jewish day schools (Pomson et al., 2014), and in textbooks and resource guides for elementary-school-age children (e.g., Blumenthal, 2003; D. Neusner, 2009), young children's attention is directed toward discussions of Israeli culture and geography rather than geopolitical conflict. The goal is to turn the gaze of children away from violence and toward what is "safe," deferring more difficult conversations to the later grades (Pomson et al., 2014).

Yet Samantha spent considerable time mulling over, and worrying about, the conflict even at age 5. In fact, all of the children in this study were aware that Israel is involved in an ongoing, often violent conflict from the time they started elementary school. As they grew, their understanding of what constitutes the conflict—who it involves, why and how those people(s) clash, and how the children themselves felt about it—shifted over time. Their evolving conceptions of the Israeli–Arab/

Palestinian conflict highlight both the critical importance and the pro-found challenges of discussing violent world events with young children.

Generally, scholars who use the language of "Israeli–Arab/Palestin-ian" to name the conflict do so as a way of indicating that Arab and Palestinian are distinct yet overlapping conceptual categories with his-torical and political narratives that at times converge and at times di-varicate (Nets-Zehngut, 2011; Nets-Zehngut & Bar-Tal, 2016; Podeh, 2010). Defining the nature of the Israeli–Arab/Palestinian conflict (or conflicts) is often a central question for educators who teach about it (Avidar, 2016). Yet in the case of the children in this study, the term indicates not analytical refinement but rather the children's tendency to blur the categories as they attempt to make sense of the violence in the Middle East.

The children's evolving thoughts and feelings about the conflict are embedded both in particular phases of childhood and in particular mo-ments in time. The developmental and the sociohistorical intermingle, as children develop ideas about geography, nationality, war, and violence at the same time that current events are unfolding. Children's under-standing of the world can best be understood as a constant interaction between their own process of cognitive development and world events that they seek to understand.

This chapter focuses on the evolution of the children's thoughts and feelings about the Israeli–Arab/Palestinian conflict, highlighting both the changes and the constants in the children's understanding as they traversed elementary school. The children in this study underwent three distinct phases in their conceptions of the conflict. In early elementary school, on the heels of the 2012 Israeli Operation Pillar of Defense, the children were aware of the existence of an ongoing conflict between Israel and its neighbors, yet they tended to conflate the contemporary conflict with other historical conflicts involving the Jewish people. By the middle of elementary school, which occurred in the aftermath of the 2014 Israeli Operation Protective Edge, the children could distin-guish the contemporary conflict from other historical conflicts, and they could provide detailed, gruesome accounts of the way that the conflict was playing out. Yet they could not yet name the particular people or peoples involved in the conflict, instead conceiving of it as an ongoing war between Israel and "the other team." By late elementary school, in the wake of the election of Donald Trump, the children developed a newfound awareness of the global context in which the conflict is embedded. For the first time, they also began to imagine Arab, and not only Israeli-Jewish, perspectives of the conflict.

In each of these stages, the children spent considerable time and energy thinking about the Israeli–Arab/Palestinian conflict. Throughout childhood they remained convinced that, despite everything that has occurred, peace is still possible. They also believed that they had personally "seen" the violence of the Israeli–Arab/Palestinian conflict. Through their eyes, the conflict was not faraway or irrelevant; it was, instead, deeply intertwined with their own way of understanding both global events and their own Jewishness.

Early Elementary School (K–1): September 2012–June 2014

In November 2012 the children have been in kindergarten for a little over a month. By now they have adjusted to their new lives as elementary school students. They know the names of their classmates and teachers, and they understand the rhythm of a school day.

This early in the school year, there is a large variance in the children's reading levels. Some are working on letter–sound correspondence, while others can already sound out words. A few early readers can work through simple books. None of the children can yet read even the most basic headlines on news sources developed for children (e.g., *TIME for Kids, Newsela, Scholastic News*). When major world events occur, the children must rely entirely on auditory cues to learn about them; they may process the world around them through a variety of sensory inputs, but they learn about the world beyond their own experience by listening to others.

That November, after 20 months of intermittent, escalating rocket fire from Gaza into Israel (Siboni, 2014), Israel launched an operation aimed at killing Hamas military chief Ahmed Jabari and weakening Hamas infrastructure (R. S. Cohen et al., 2017). Israelis called the operation Amud Anan in Hebrew, or Operation Pillar of Defense in English. Palestinians in Gaza called their own offensive attacks by the Arabic Hajarah Sajeel, or Operation Stones of Baked Clay. During the eight days of fighting, Hamas and the Palestinian Islamic Jihad fired over 1,400 rockets into

Israel, while the Israeli air force hit over 1,500 targets in Gaza (Cohen et al., 2017). In that short span of time, 174 Palestinians and six Israelis were killed, and hundreds were injured on each side (UN Human Rights Council, 2013).

Operation Pillar of Defense was part of a larger Israeli strategy aimed at containing Hamas and other Palestinian militant groups in Gaza. Israel periodically launches large-scale operations that bring temporary quiet along the Israel–Gaza border, opting for intermittent calm even if the periods of escalation complicate attempts to find a long-term, sustainable solution to the ongoing conflict (Inbar & Shamir, 2014; Nguyen, 2017). Thus the 2012 Operation Pillar of Defense was sandwiched between periods of relative calm following Operation Cast Lead in 2008–09 and preceding the 2014 Operation Protective Edge.

During Operation Pillar of Defense and its aftermath, adult members of the global Jewish community grappled with both the ethics and the strategic soundness of Israel's position (Brom, 2012). Yet for the 35 children in kindergarten, the heightened tension on the Gaza border barely registered. Unlike the subsequent Operation Protective Edge, which would loom large in the children's imaginations two years later, the heightened violence that occurred during their kindergarten year had little impact on them. Not a single child mentioned any specific information tied to Israeli or Palestinian actions surrounding Pillar of Defense/Stones of Baked Clay.

Yet this doesn't mean that the children were unaware of the ongoing Israeli–Palestinian/Arab conflict. In fact, quite the opposite was true: Without exception, the children spent a good deal of time reflecting on the violent conflict. They framed that conflict not in relationship to the specific, recent violence on the Israel–Gaza border but rather in terms of an ongoing arc of Jewish history in which Jews in the land of Israel had to reluctantly fight against great enemies.

At this point in their childhood, the children's conceptions of the Israeli–Arab/Palestinian conflict can be characterized by three trends. First, the children consistently expressed an awareness of an ongoing, violent conflict between Israel and its enemies. Second, the children tended to conflate contemporary and historical or biblical enemies of Israel, framing the current conflict as part of an ongoing struggle that

Jews have faced in the land of Israel. Third, the children regularly spoke of Israel as a place that was simultaneously dangerous and one that offered a safe haven to Jews.

Awareness of an Ongoing, Violent Conflict

From the beginning of elementary school, the children understood that Israel is engaged in an ongoing, violent conflict. This conflict wove itself into the children's very definitions of Israel. For example, as the children attempted to answer the question *What is Israel?*, Hayim (K) said, "It's a Jewish state, and that's where the war happened." Carly (K) explained, "It's this place and they fight against other countries." Owen (K) defined Israel as "a place for the Jews. The Jews needed a place, needed their own country, but they didn't have one, so they had to fight for their own country." For these children, the very mention of Israel brought forth images of war and fighting.

In kindergarten, the children consistently framed Israel as a place that they associated with soldiers, wars, and Jews who had died. Rina (K) explained, "[When I think about Israel,] I think about all the people that died in Israel and the wars with other people that died." Israel made Noah (K) think about "the soldiers. . . . They died. . . . They were in a war." For Maya (K), Israel brought up "sad feelings . . . because the Jewish people, the soldiers, died." Pearl (K) "remembered the sad people who were in Israel and they were killed."

In their discussions of the conflict in which Israel was engaged, many children mentioned that Israel was fighting "enemies," "bad guys," or "bad people." Who, in their minds, were the "bad guys" that Israel faced? In kindergarten and first grade, only a few children had a specific idea about who constituted Israel's enemies. Hayim (K) spoke about how Israel "had to attack Iran." Keren (K) defined the "bad guys" as "the Arabs and the Muslims." Other children, as will be discussed below, believed that Israel's enemies were the villains from the stories they learned about Jewish holidays.

Yet most of the children had only a vague sense of some amorphous external threat facing Israel. Esther (K) defined the "bad guys" as "strangers." More typical were explanations like that of Owen (K), who said,

"There's other states, but I don't remember all of them . . . but they're not nice to Israel. They are trying to bomb Israel . . . and are trying to make Israel and Yerushalayim [Jerusalem] not beautiful at all." Maya (K) said, "I don't know [who] the bad guys [are, but they're trying to] kill the Jewish people." A year later, Maya (1) reiterated that she knows Israel fights bad guys but "I don't remember their names." Similarly, Lior (1) spoke of the "bad people," but when asked to identify them he explained, "I forgot their names." It was clear in the children's minds that Israel was under threat, but it was unclear what or who constituted that threat. Unlike their later selves, who would lament their own inability to more accurately describe the "bad guys," the children in kindergarten and first grade were perfectly content to describe an ambiguous foe.

Given their often vague sense of "the enemy," how did these young children conceive of the conflict itself? Despite the fact that the children repeatedly mentioned "the war in Israel," in the first two years of elementary school they rarely offered details about that war. Esther (K) believed the war was because the enemies of Israel were "stealing stuff." Gia (K) said it was because the enemies were "taking guns [and] stealing money, stealing kids, stealing babies." Avigail (K) talked about "the dark side [that] has swords and guns, and they were shooting people and swording people, cutting them to half." In a troubling twist on the notion that American Jews often create an image of Israel that reflects their own sentiments more than the realities in Israel itself (Sarna 1994, 1996), these children appeared to be grafting their own worst fears onto Israel's enemies, imagining them as thieves, kidnappers, and murderers. Though this would change as they grew, for the children in early elementary school the conflict was much more a reflection of their childhood conceptions of what "bad people" do than of any specific events on the ground in the Middle East.

Conflating Past and Contemporary Conflicts

At the same time that the children were imagining the conflict as a contest between Israel and the thieves and murderers who were bent on hurting Israel, they were also framing it as part of an ongoing war stretching from biblical times until today. This war, involving the ancient Israelites, the Maccabees from the second century BCE, and the contemporary Israel Defense Forces (IDF), was—in the minds of the young children—one extended conflict. Throughout their discussions of the conflict, the kindergarteners and first graders tended to conflate time, often blurring the distant past, the recent past, and the present.

The most prevalent example was the children's (K–1) tendency to conflate contemporary Israeli soldiers with the Jewish fighters of the Hasmonean Rebellion of 167-160 BCE, which the children know as "the Hanukkah story" (Olivia, K). As kindergarteners, nearly a third of the children looked at a photograph of IDF soldiers standing on rocky terrain in front of an Israeli flag and believed that those soldiers were Maccabees in "the Hanukkah war" (Hayim, K). As Dina (K) explained, she knew they were Maccabees "because I see the Israeli flag behind them . . . so I think that's the state of Israel, and I think the Maccabees live in Israel." The photograph made her think about "Judah, because Judah fighted the army and he lives in Israel. . . . They fighted King Antiochus." For Hayim, Dina, and their peers, even the tenses they used to discuss the "the armies for Israel [fighting] the Hanukkah war" (Lior, K) continuously shifted from past to present.

In first grade, the children repeated similar patterns as they thought about the relationship between the "Maccabees and the army people" (Olivia 1) and those whom they fought. Samantha (1) believed that Israeli soldiers were defending Israel from "people that weren't very nice. . . . The Greeks." Micah (1) talked about a war that's "still going. The Israeli war against the Greeks." For Ari (1), the conflict was one long fight extending from "Judah the Maccabee and then the people who lived in [Israel later]." At this age, the kids understood, in Hannah's (1) words, that "the Hanukkah story happens in Israel." They knew of the Maccabees fighting King Anticochus and the Assyrian Greeks, and they understood that the story occurred in the land of Israel. They misjudged only the timing of the story, collapsing the temporal distance between the time of the Maccabees and the modern nation-state.

While conflating the Maccabees and the modern Israel Defense Forces was the most common iteration of this trend, the children also confused the current conflict with other conflicts from the Jewish past. Pearl (K) talked about how Israelis mourn the loss of their "firstborn babies," conflating contemporary Israeli parents who have lost a child in the conflict with the parents of the book of Exodus. Hayim (1) associated the IDF with the army of King David, and Lailah (1) believed that the Israeli army's job was to defend the biblical Garden of Eden. Naomi (1) named the Roman Empire as the "bad guys" with whom Israel fought.

Research on children's understanding of time has shown that children as young as 5 can conceive of time as a quantitative entity (Levin & Wilkening, 1989), yet young children do not typically understand chronology. It is not until third grade that children generally begin to understand dates, and only by fifth grade can they usually connect particular dates with specific historical background knowledge (Barton & Levstik, 1996). Thus it is not surprising that in kindergarten and first grade, the children were unable to distinguish between different groups of soldiers fighting in or for the land of Israel at different points in history. What is noteworthy, however, is that even as they conflated different time periods, they were able to keep in mind a larger metanarrative about Israel. It was abundantly clear to the children that the stories they knew (or could imagine) about when "Jews fought" (Kevin, K) occurred in the land of Israel. Jewish battles, in the children's minds, extended across an amorphous timeline but were always clearly rooted in the same geographic place.

Israel as a Danger and a Safe Haven

As the children reflected on Israel in kindergarten and first grade, they continually pivoted between two different conceptions: Israel as a dangerous place and Israel as a safe haven for Jews. The children's reflections were marked by repeated discussions of guns, wars, and death; yet these were mixed together with their feelings of being protected and secure.

As discussed above, violence, war, and death were interwoven into the young children's discussions about Israel. Most of the children spoke about Israel as a place where "Jews died" or "Jews were killed." They populated their stories about Israel with swords, guns, bullets, and bombs, and they believed that Jews were constantly under threat.

Yet despite the children's descriptions of Israel as a place of violence, they also spoke of Israel as a place that offered safety and protection for Jews. Caleb (K) called Israel a "safe place for Jewish people" and Carly (1) described it as "Jewish and it's very safe." For Brent (K), Israel was a place where "there's a lot of Jewish people, and it's a very safe home." For Elliott (1), Israel was a place where Jews are "gonna feel much safer." He explained, "Maybe the place that they were living before wasn't a safe place for them anymore, [so they needed] to move to Israel."

Even in kindergarten, most of the children were able to *simultaneously* hold in their heads images of Israel as a safe *and* a dangerous place. Caleb (K) explained, "God made Israel, and, and then He made it safe" only moments before discussing the "bad guys [who] come to Israel." A few sentences later, he reiterated, "Israel is a safe place for everybody to go to." For Micah (1), Israel is—at once—the place of the "Israeli war" and a place where people "pray to God to be safe." As the children framed Israel as a violent place, they also spoke of ways that Israel offered protections, especially (but not exclusively) for Jews.

For many of the children, the very concepts of safety, danger, and soldiers could not be disentangled. For Bella (1), the whole reason that the Israeli soldiers "fight [is] to keep other people safe. To keep Jewish people safe." Similarly, Hayim (1) believed that the very purpose of having soldiers is to "keep Israel safe." As Owen (K) explained, "The Israeli soldiers died, but they gave their lives to us. . . . They fight and they die for us to have a safe land in Israel." These children viewed soldiers as those in Israel who fight and die to keep it safe for others, particularly Jewish children. In the children's minds, the existence of soldiers demonstrates that the world in which Israel exists is a dangerous one, yet, as Brent (K) explained, the soldiers "protect Israel, and if bad guys come to Israel they save Israel." In Maya's (K) words, "The soldiers died instead of the people that lived in Israel."

At times the children distinguished between *thoughts* of danger and *feelings* of safety. For example, Bella (K) said that Israeli soldiers made her *think about* the fighting, and that made her *feel* "that I'm going to be safe." Similarly, Ari (K) *thought about* the soldiers who were fighting difficult battles, and it made him *feel* "good . . . because they're protecting Israel." Carly (K) *thought about* "the fighting" and *felt* "happy . . . because the army stopped the fighting and [the bad guys] stopped doing bad stuff." For these children, the dangers that Israeli soldiers faced, and the protections that the children believed the soldiers offered, were inextricably linked.

Summary of Early Elementary School (Grades K–1, September 2012–June 2014)

Even in kindergarten, the children were acutely aware of an ongoing, often violent conflict between Israel and the "bad people" with whom Israel fought. Yet the children conceived of this conflict very differently than adults do, and even in distinct ways from how they themselves would see it by second grade. Escalating violence on the Israel–Gaza border barely registered for the children. For them, the conflict was not about the immediate present but rather about an ongoing battle, stretching across time, between Jews and others in the land of Israel. The children conflated the contemporary soldiers of the Israel Defense Forces with other Jewish fighters throughout time. In their minds, these brave Jews battled both the villains of Jewish holiday stories and the murderous kidnappers who inhabited the children's own worst nightmares. Yet despite the children's constant discussions of the dangers that Israel and its soldiers faced, they also believed that Israel offered safety and special protections to Jews.

For the first two years of elementary school, the Israel of the children's imaginations was one marked by conflict in the abstract. Yet the summer between the children's first- and second-grade years saw another, even more violent outbreak on the Israel–Gaza border. The children shifted their gaze from stories of the Jewish past to headlines from the Jewish present, and they saw a conflict that looked very different.

Middle Elementary School (2–3): July 2014–August 2016

In the summer of 2014, after the children completed first grade, long-simmering tensions between Israel and Hamas erupted into a 50-day escalation in hostilities. Israelis called this war Mivtzah Tzuk Eitan, literally meaning Operation Strong Cliff and nicknamed Operation Protective Edge in English. Palestinians referred to it as al Harb 'ala Gaza, the War on Gaza.

Like the name of the war itself, discussions about its casualties were highly contested. At the end of the seven-week conflagration, the United Nations reported 2,131 Palestinian and 71 Israeli deaths (OCHA, 2014). Palestinian sources point to the "lopsided" nature of these casualty numbers (Buttu, 2014), calling the Israeli use of force disproportionate (Khalidi, 2014). Israeli sources insist that Israeli fatalities would have been significantly higher were it not for the Iron Dome missile defense shield that intercepted 90% of incoming rockets and missiles (Goodman & Gold, 2015; Shamir, 2015). Furthermore, Israeli government officials argue that because Hamas deliberately uses Palestinian civilians as human shields (Baker, 2015), Hamas—not Israel—is responsible for many of the Palestinian deaths (Goodman & Gold, 2015). Despite their different ways of naming and framing the war, Israelis and Palestinians agree that these 50 days were among the most intense and deadly periods of the ongoing, intractable conflict (Chorev & Shumacher, 2015; Khalidi, 2014).

Whereas the Israel–Gaza fighting barely registered for the children two years earlier, the 2014 war loomed large in their minds. By September 2014, when the children returned to their schools as newly minted second graders, a tenuous cease-fire was in effect. Yet although the war occurred at a time when school was not in session, and none of the children reported explicitly learning about it in their classrooms, they repeatedly told stories about the death and destruction that had occurred in the Middle East.

Two shifts had occurred in the children's own lives that made the 2014 Operation Protective Edge so different for them from the previous 2012 Operation Pillar of Defense. First, in the intervening years the children had learned how to read. By second grade they were beginning the process of transitioning from what literacy experts call learning-to-read into reading-to-learn (Carroll, 1997; Duke et al., 2003; Harlaar et al., 2007). They readily understood that information could be gleaned from a wide variety of sources—many of them in written form—and that they no longer needed to rely only on what they heard from adults in order to make sense of the world.

Second, this emergent literacy was tied to the "technologization of childhood" (Plowman et al., 2010). The children had both access to and facility with a wide variety of digital platforms from a very early age. Some platforms—like FaceTime and Skype—were available to children even in early childhood, but others—like the ability to read a Facebook post or independently browse YouTube videos—were accessible only once children had learned to read. Thus, at the same time that Israelis experienced the first "WhatsApp war" in which information was transmitted through connective technologies (Malka et al., 2015), these American Jewish children were beginning to understand that they, too, could access the war, digitally tuning in from afar.

The children reported four distinct digital sources of information from which they learned about the war: television newscasts, online newscasts and videos, smartphone apps, and videoconferencing technology. Some children viewed television news programs about the war. For example, Lior (2) watched Fox News for information about it, and Hayim (2) watched CNN. Other children, like Ari (2) and Tzvi (2), watched online videos about the war, including livestreamed English language newscasts from Israel. Several children, including Gabe (2) and Elliott (2), spoke of gleaning information about the war by glancing over their parents' shoulders as the adults in their lives scrolled through Facebook feeds on their phones. One child, Carly (2), reported regularly checking Red Alert, an app on her mother's phone that tracked missile hits in Israel. Another subset of the children, including Dina (2) and Avigail (2), used Skype, FaceTime, or WhatsApp to videoconference relatives in Israel during the war. Through screens large and small, information about Israel and its involvement in a war streamed regularly into their homes.

These technologies collapsed the distance between Israel and the children's own lives, so that Israel was, at once, remote and easily accessible. For the children who had relatives in Israel, digital technologies made it possible to communicate directly with loved ones throughout the war. For example, Avigail (2) recounted Skyping her Israeli father as he was sitting in a bomb shelter during a rocket attack. In her perception, Israel is "[thousands of] miles from where I live, [but] I always feel Israel is right near me." Yet even the children without family in Israel believed that technology helped shrink the geographic space between the Middle East and the United States. As Gabe (2) explained, when he watched the news he felt "like it's near. Israel is close."

As the children used digital technologies to access a faraway place, they began to gather discrete bits of information about specific violent incidents that occurred in the Middle East. Their discussions of the conflict morphed from descriptions of a generic war to detailed accounts of particular current events.

Specific Accounts of Violent Events

Whereas their kindergarten and first-grade selves viewed the conflict as a nonspecific, ongoing fight between Jewish people and their enemies, by second grade the children understood that the conflict involved a real, contemporary war that injured and killed actual people. In Lailah's (2) words, "It's scary [because] people can die." At this age, the children populated their stories about the conflict with specific details that revealed a familiarity with the particular ways that violence manifested in the summer of 2014.

Two thirds of the children discussed specific instances of rocket attacks on Israeli civilians and/or the Iron Dome missile defense system that Israel used to intercept rockets. In Ari's (2) words, "Israel had to make the missiles explode in the air. They have the Iron Dome, which goes straight up to the missile, and it explodes in the air." As Avigail (2) explained, "One of the bad rockets got into my cousin's house, and that scared me, but Israel has good rockets, so when the bad rocket came, the good rocket smashed the bad rocket." No longer conflating the present conflict with past conflicts involving the Jewish people, these children clearly understood that the conflict was playing out in the present day, and they were able to discuss specific aspects of the Israeli Protective Edge operation.

A smaller subset of the children also spoke of the tactics that Hamas used during the war. For example, Lior (2) explained that "Hamas was digging tunnels to Israel so they could beat them." Hayim (2) expressed concern about the use of human shields, saying, "Hamas used the Gazans for shields." As will be discussed below, these children were unusual in their ability to name and explain the actions of Hamas. Yet they, like the other children in the study, clearly understood that there was contemporary violence that caused death and destruction in the Middle East conflict.

One child, Carly (2), offered a detailed account of "the three boys [who] were kidnapped." The kidnapping and subsequent search for the "three boys," Israeli teenagers Eyal Yifrach, Naftali Fraenkel, and Gilad Shaar, temporarily united a politically and religiously divided Israeli polity and served as a catalyst for intensive Israeli airstrikes into the Gaza Strip (Rudoren & Kershner, 2014). When their bodies were discovered after an 18-day search, Israelis and Jews around the world mourned. Carly, whose mother had told her about the kidnappings, knew a lot of details about their tragic story,[1] including the fact that after their deaths other Jews "named [their newborn] boys after the three boys that got kidnapped." She made the boys' kidnapping central to her own discussions of the war—though with one crucial twist. Even though she clearly knew the Israeli teenagers had died, her rendition ended with their escape. In her account, "They were trapped in a place, but they tried to get out, and they got out!" Her process of storytelling, mirroring a psychological strategy that children often use to reframe difficult moments from their own lives (Miller, 1994), indicated that she was—at once—familiar with the tragic reality and searching for a more palatable alternative.

For Carly and the other second graders, the conflict was no longer a generic fight between Jews and bad guys that stretched across time. It was, instead, a present-day war between Israel and its enemies, a war that often ended in death.

Multilayered Explanations of the Causes of the Conflict

At the same time that the children were beginning to be aware of the contemporary context of the conflict, they were also beginning to sort through its causes. Whereas their younger selves believed that the conflict was a fight between Jews (often Maccabees) and enemies of the Jews, by second grade most of the children had developed a much more textured conception of the root causes of the conflict.

What, then, did the second graders think the conflict was about? In their *A History of the Arab-Israeli Conflict*, Bickerton and Klausner (2007) ask:

> How can the Arab-Israeli conflict be explained? Is it a religious war between the followers of Islam and Judaism in which the protagonists are driven by deep-seated suspicions and hostilities concerning the Divine instructions to each other? Is it an ethnic war between traditionally rival groups, reflecting changing demographic patterns? Is it a war of nationalist aspirations in which rival militant nationalisms are seeking to establish a state and thereby find their "place in the sun"? Is it a war of self-defense

in which a newly established state is defending itself against the determination of its neighbors to destroy it? Is it a war of territorial expansion in which one state is attempting to expand its borders at the expense of its neighbors? (p. 3)

Given that the conflict can be viewed as a religious, ethnic, national, or territorial one, what—in the minds of these children—were the most salient ways of framing it?

As the children attempted to explain the root causes of the conflict, their reasons generally fell into one of three categories. Many of the children framed the conflict as a territorial dispute over land. The children also frequently believed the discord was rooted in religious differences. A subset of the children also framed the conflict as one about differing conceptions of what constitutes good and free societies.

The children who framed the conflict as a territorial dispute highlighted a fight over the land of Israel. For example, Isabelle (2) explained, "Who[ever] wins, it gets to be their land, and whoever loses, Israel is not going to be their land." According to Tzvi (2), "Israel people were fighting with mean people because mean people wanted Israel to be their land." Similarly, Gia (2) explained, "The other country wanted Israel's land, [but] the Jewish people used all their strength, and they used all their might, and they beat the other people so that they could have their land." These children viewed Israelis as the rightful inhabitants of the land, and they envisioned other peoples and places as making threats against Israeli sovereignty. Like other children this age, they privileged the claims of their own ethnic community (Aboud, 2003). Although this tendency would fade as the children grew older, at this point in time they clearly believed that the land belonged to Israelis, who were fighting off others who hoped to have it for themselves.

Many of the children also offered explanations of the conflict that focused on religious disputes. Jacob (2), for example, claimed that the conflict arose because Israel's enemies "don't want us to be chosen. They want to be chosen too. By God." Framing Jews as the "chosen people," he imagined other (unnamed) religions to be jealous of Jews' special status. For other children, the religious war could be attributed to non-Jewish groups harboring antisemitic beliefs. Hayim (2) believed that Israel's enemies wanted to "take over . . . so they wouldn't have to see synagogues any more, only churches." For Carly (2), it was because "a lot of people that are not Jewish don't like Jewish people." Later she specified, "A lot of people that are Muslim people don't like Jewish people." Like their younger selves who framed the conflict as one between Jews and their enemies, these children believed that the conflict involved Jews, not only Israelis. Yet unlike a year or two earlier, these children did not frame their discussions using the language of Jewish holiday stories; instead, they highlighted tensions among adherents to different religious traditions.

While the children's most common explanations of the conflict were about land and religion, some of them also framed it as a fight over differing ideas of what constitutes a good society. For example, Pearl (2) explained that Israel and its enemies each "don't think [the other] is a good state." Ari (2) highlighted the fact that different communities have different beliefs about appropriate dress or behavior, and Tzvi framed it as a larger fight "about freedom." Drawing upon abstract ideas, these children explained that the conflict was a battle about "the world [and] how it's supposed to be" (Isabelle, 2).

Approximately two thirds of the children offered more than one of these explanations by the time they were in second grade. Not only were these children capable of identifying some of the root causes that adult scholars attribute to the Israeli–Arab/Palestinian conflict, but they also were able to understand that intractable conflict often cannot be attributed to a single cause. By age 7 or 8, many children understood that the conflict has, in the words of Naomi (2), "so many reasons."

And yet, like a layer cake missing the final coat of frosting that binds the entirety together, their discussions lacked one essential ingredient: not a single child in second or third grade attributed the conflict to ideas linked to competing nationalisms (Peters & Newman, 2013), or the yearnings of either Palestinians or Israelis for self-determination in their own nation-state. As will be discussed below, this was in large part because they had little or no awareness of the existence of a Palestinian people. Like other young children, they understood that war is a conflict between groups (Walker et al., 2003), but they were missing the key facts that would allow them to attribute to those groups national characteristics—even though 7- and 8-year-olds generally have at least some conceptual awareness of nationality and national identity (Brown,

1980; H. Wilson, 1998). Thus, their attempts to understand the conflict were, at once, multilayered and missing key ingredients.

Missing Key Details: A Generic Other Team

The children's easy access to information about the faraway war allowed them to construct an understanding of the war's tactics and some of its root causes, but it was insufficient for helping them understand a much more fundamental idea. For, despite their knowledge of the violent means by which the war was conducted, and their clear awareness of Israeli involvement in the war, the children had very little conception of Palestinian roles in it.

After the war ended, we asked the children to tell us stories about recent events. Approximately half of the children explicitly named the "heroes" of their stories as Israelis. Another third crafted stories with Jews as the heroes, and a sixth of them narrated stories in which the protagonist was a God who protects Israelis and Jews. As is common for young children, the second graders in this study experienced strong in-group favoritism (Aboud, 2003; Bennett et al., 1998), casting their own community as the heroic actors in a grand battle.

Given the children's clear identification of Israelis and Jews as the heroes of their stories, and given the ongoing conflict between Israeli Jews and Palestinian Arabs, one might surmise that Palestinians, Arabs, and/or the Muslim and Christian communities of the Middle East would populate the children's stories as villains. Yet for most of the children, this was not the case. Even as they told stories about Jewish and Israeli protagonists engaged in violent conflict with an enemy, it was often unclear to the children who constituted the adversary with which Israel was fighting.

The majority of the children spoke of Israel's enemies in generic terms, defining them as general "bad guys" rather than any specific type of person or group. For example, Micah (2) defined his story's antagonists as "the people who are the enemies against the Israelis," but was unable to specify who those people were. Similarly, Keren (2) said the villains of her story were "the people who are fighting against Israel," Gia (2) identified them as "the other country," and Ari (2) labeled them "the other team that was fighting Israel." These children framed the antagonists of their stories as people who fought against Israel, but had no sense of the identities of such people. As Lailah (2) insisted, "I don't know [who they are] but there are bad guys in the story."

That most of the children narrated stories with generic villains says more about their positionality than about their age-specific capacities for understanding violent conflict. For children with direct experiences of conflict, conceptual awareness of the enemy is one of the most salient features of their understanding of war (Punamaki, 1999). Israeli and Palestinian children in the region certainly have a clear, often stereotypically negative awareness of one another (Bar-Tal, 1996; Brenick et al., 2010). Yet despite their classification of Israelis as heroes, most of these American Jewish children did not identify Palestinians or Arabs as villains. Even as they were acutely aware of the violent current events in the Middle East, and clearly identified with one side of the Israeli–Arab/Palestinian conflict, they lacked both the knowledge and the enmity that children with firsthand experiences of war have of the Other.

Even the small number of children (7 of 35) who offered a specific name for Israel's enemies—talking about Palestinians, Arabs, Gaza, or Hamas—readily admitted that they didn't actually know what those terms meant. They made comments, in halting tones, like "there was a war going on with Israel. With the, I think it was the Ga-, wait, Gaza. Palestine, I don't know. . . . Either the Gaza people or the Palestine people?" (Samantha, 2). Avigail (2), when asked to define the terms she had just used, said, "Well, I just know the name, nothing else," and when asked the same question, Hayim (2) said, "Uh, I do not know."

For all of the children—those who could haltingly name a specific enemy of Israel and the much larger group who spoke only of a generic Other—the inability to clearly name "the other team" (Ari, 2) was a source of great frustration. As the children reached for the language and the conceptual clarity that would have allowed them to discuss Palestinian/Arab roles in the conflict, many of them literally screamed in frustration. Maya (2) repeatedly muttered to herself, "I don't know, I don't know" as she attempted to talk about the "other side." Jacob (2) pulled his own hair as he said, exasperatedly, "Why won't anyone tell me what they're called?" As the children struggled to piece together an understanding of the Israeli–Arab/Palestinian conflict, they were missing—and *knew* they were missing—an essential piece of the puzzle.

They consistently voiced frustration that the adults in their lives had not given them adequate language that would have allowed them to fill in the missing pieces. As will be discussed in the conclusion, this is one of the most pressing correction points for Jewish education in the United States.

For the second graders struggling to make sense of the aftermath of the 2014 Israel–Gaza war, and for their third-grade selves a year later, the Israeli–Arab/Palestinian conflict was missing the second half of the dyad, transforming instead into a conflict between Israel and "the other team." For while digital proximity may have offered the children access to sounds and images that allowed them to see *how* violent conflict played out, such information was insufficient for helping the children account for *who* is involved in the conflict. In fact, in the list of questions that educators often ask students about current and historical events, there was a highly uneven understanding; at this phase in their development, the children could rapidly fire off information pertaining to the what, where, and when of the conflict, but struggled to make sense of the who. As a result, the children had a simultaneously multilayered and incomplete sense of the why.

Summary of Middle Elementary School (Grades 2–3, July 2014– August 2016)

By the middle of elementary school, which occurred in the aftermath of the 2014 Israeli Operation Protective Edge, the children could distinguish the contemporary conflict from other historical battles involving Jews, and they could provide detailed, often gruesome accounts of the way that the conflict was playing out. They also understood that the conflict has multiple causes and generally framed it as a dispute over land, religion, and/or competing visions for a good society. Despite their ability to offer multiple explanations of the root causes of the conflict, they could not yet name the particular people or peoples involved in it, instead conceiving of it as a war between Israel and "the other team." As a result, they had little sense that the conflict is also about competing nationalisms and the desires of both Israelis and Palestinians for self-determination in their own nation-states. Only in the coming years would they begin to understand the conflict not only as one between Israelis and Palestinians but also one that involved a much larger global context.

Late Elementary School (4–5): September 2016–June 2018

By the start of the 2016–17 school year, when the children were beginning fourth grade, the U.S presidential election was less than three months away. While political tensions were ratcheting up at home, relative calm reigned on the Israel–Gaza border. At least in the children's minds, the Trump–Clinton election was much more tense than the Israeli–Arab/Palestinian conflict. For the first time in their lives, the children viewed life in the U.S. as more contentious than life in the Middle East.

Then in December 2017, midway through the children's fifth-grade year and less than a year into the new U.S. presidency, Donald Trump formally recognized Jerusalem as the capital of Israel, pivoting from a decades-long U.S. policy and pledging to move the U.S. embassy from Tel Aviv to Jerusalem. As the U.S. and Israeli governments coordinated the new embassy opening for May 14, 2018, which corresponded to the 70th anniversary of the declaration of the modern Israeli state, long-simmering tensions erupted once again into violence on the Israel–Gaza border.

Between March 30, which Palestinians mark as Yom Al Ard or Land Day, and May 15, which commemorated the 70th anniversary of the Palestinian Nakba or catastrophe, tens of thousands of Gazans participated in a series of protests called the Great March of Return (Tartir & Seidel, 2019). Palestinian activists framed these protests as a way of calling attention to the plight of Palestinian refugees and the harsh conditions resulting from a decade-long Israeli blockade of Gaza (Abusalim, 2018). By contrast, many Israelis viewed the protests not as a popular uprising but as a Hamas-led military operation involving pipe bombs, guns, and grenades (J. A. Gross, 2018). Framing the events as an attack on Israeli sovereignty itself, Israeli journalist Yossi Klein Halevi (2018) argued, "The March of Return is an explicit negation of a two-state solution, with a Palestinian state in the West Bank and Gaza coexisting beside Israel. . . . The real message of the protests is . . . the creation of a Palestinian state between the Jordan River and the Mediterranean Sea, erasing Israel." When the Israel Defense Forces responded to the protesters with live fire, many Israelis viewed this military action as a justified and necessary response to violent rioting and as the best way to protect citizens from a border breach (IDF statement on Gaza border events, 2019), and many Palestinians framed it as an unjustified attack on peaceful protesters (Abu Artema, 2019). For the children, this period marked the first moment when they began to imagine the arguments of both sides.

At the same time, their understanding of the conflict expanded to include not only Israeli–Palestinian clashes but also a larger regional and global context. For the first time, the children began to speak not only about Gaza but also about other key players in the region, especially Iran. Israelis often argue that the greatest threat facing Israel is not the repeated Israel–Gaza skirmishes but rather the specter of a nuclear-armed Iran (Kaye et al., 2011). To the children, the conflict had been synonymous with the Israel-Gaza border flare-ups in the early years of elementary school, but by fifth grade they had begun to express concern about a nuclear Iran and the U.S. role in preventing this possibility.

Thus, in their final years of elementary school, the children's views of the conflict shifted dramatically. Their new understanding of it was marked by three trends: beginning to frame the conflict as a regional one involving more than Israelis and Palestinians, situating the U.S. as a key player in the Middle East, and imagining the perspective of "the other team" even while siding with "Israel's team."

A Regional Conflict

Although the children couldn't name specific national groups involved in the conflict in second and third grade, from their stories it was entirely clear about whom they were speaking when they talked about the "bad guys" or the "enemies of Israel": Palestinians. Yet as they grew, they developed a much broader understanding of who was involved in the Middle East conflict. Not only did the children begin to name and locate Palestinians, but they also developed a much more extensive vocabulary to discuss other regional players in the conflict. They started to reflect on the roles of Syria, Egypt, Jordan, Lebanon, and Iran, not only those of Israelis and Palestinians.

As the children's scope of understanding expanded, they began to consider two concepts that had previously been obscured from their vision. First, the children constructed a conceptual category of transnational-Arab, and they began to view violence in the Middle East not only as an Israeli-Palestinian conflict but also as an Israeli-Arab one. As Carly (4) explained, "Israel's sovereignty has constantly been threatened by the Arab states that surround it." In Tzvi's (4) words, the conflict was because "Arabs and Jews do not get along very well," and for Avigail (4) it was because "the Arabs were attacking Israel." In Dina's (5) description, "The Arab states that surround Israel are very frictiony with Israel, and they fight and they have wars." At this age the children were able to identify a number of Arab states, including Jordan, Saudi Arabia, Syria, Iraq, Egypt, and Lebanon.

Second, the children began to classify the Middle East into two distinct categories—"enemies of Israel and friends of Israel" (Lior, 5)—and they listed two places at the "top" of the enemies list: Palestine and Iran. The children's conceptual understanding of Palestine and Palestinians shifted dramatically between third and fourth grade. While the children had struggled to identify "the other team" in second and third grade, often expressing great frustration that they didn't have the language to name the people they were attempting to talk about, by fourth grade most of them were able to succinctly name and define this subgroup of Arabs. For example, Elliott (4) explained that the fighting in the Middle East was between "the Palestinians and the Israelis," and Hayim (4) believed it was because "Palestine wants Israel's land." Who are Palestinians, and where do they live? By fourth grade, most of the children could offer a relatively clear answer to these questions. Consider, for example, Samantha's (4) definition that "Palestinians are a certain people that live in Palestine." As Gia (4) explained, "Gaza is a little strip of land near the coast and the coastal plains that there's still Palestinian people, a lot of them living there and . . . there are so, so many of them crowded in that little place." The same children who, only a year earlier, had cried out in frustration at their own inability to name and describe Palestinians had found the language they had been seeking.

A year later, by fifth grade, the children could offer not only definitions but also emerging explanations about how Israelis and Palestinians interact in the region. Seth (5), framing Israelis and Palestinians as "rivals," explained that while Palestinians inhabit both the Gaza Strip and the West Bank, there is an international "argument about if Palestine should get their own state." Naomi (5) understood that Israel has peace with some Arab states, but that much of the current conflict focuses on Israel's relationship with the Palestinians, both in "the West Bank controlled by the Israeli army" and in the "Gaza Strip which has Palestinian" control. While the children could still not name any specific Palestinian leaders, and while only a small minority discussed particular militant Palestinian groups such as Hamas, by this age they had a clear sense of the idea that most eluded them as second graders: that Israelis and Palestinians are vying for sovereignty and national self-determination, with particular tension focused on the present and future of the West Bank and Gaza Strip.

At the same time that this idea crystallized for the children, so did another: the fact that the conflict involves Israel and Iran, not only Israel and Palestine. Whereas in fourth grade not a single child reflected on Iran's role in the conflict, by fifth grade a majority of the children understood that Iran is, in Caleb's (5) words, "the enemy of Israel." As Brent explained, the conflict between Iran and Israel centers around "Iran's nuclear weapons." While the children were fuzzy on the details of the ongoing fight over Iranian nuclear weapons, they had a general sense that "Israel doesn't like what Iran is doing" (Elliott, 5) and that, in response to some Iranian threat, "Israel [attacked] Iran's nuclear weapons" (Caleb, 5).

As a window into the children's shifting thinking about the conflict, their reflections upon viewing a Palestinian flag function as a sort of Rorschach test. Whereas in the early grades most of the children couldn't identify the flag, knowing only that it belonged to the "other team," by fifth grade most of the children *mis*identified it, believing it to be the flag of Iran. For the first time, they had begun to view Iran as Israel's biggest threat. In Hayim's (5) words, "Iran is trying to destroy Israel, and they don't like Jewish people, and they don't like people like me."

By fifth grade, the children's understanding of the conflict had expanded to include not only Palestinians but a much larger group of regional actors, with Iran as the most important among them. As the scope of their understanding broadened, a global superpower they had previously seen as distinct from the conflict began to factor into their understanding of violence in the Middle East: the United States.

The U.S. Role in the Conflict

In the early years of elementary school, the children were entirely unaware of the role that the United States plays as a power broker in the Middle East. They certainly thought about the U.S. and its political leaders, but in the children's minds the U.S was entirely distinct from anything happening in or around Israel. The election and inauguration of President Trump, who took office midway through the children's fourth-grade year, ushered in a new era in their thinking. Without exception, the children spoke about the contentious politics of the Trump election, and they began to consider ways that his administration was implicated in events in the Middle East.

The children's understanding of the communities in which they lived broadened as they studied California history (fourth grade) and U.S. history (fifth grade), and so did their conceptions of the U.S. beyond its borders. During the Obama presidency, the children had given very little thought to the U.S. role in Middle East politics or policy— including during Obama's negotiations of a nuclear-disarmament deal with Iran, which was a subject of fierce debate in the adult American Jewish community (Weisman, 2018). As Trump took office, however, the children began to pay attention to the developing relationship between the new U.S. president and the Israeli prime minister. In Gia's (5) words, "They're allies, they're friends, the prime minister and president." As Tzvi (5) explained, "Trump is helping Israel and is getting along with Bibi Netanyahu."

For the first time, the U.S. president featured as a major character in the stories that the children told about the conflict. The children, like the adults in their communities, voiced opposing beliefs about Trump and his policies. Some claimed, "I would have voted for Donald Trump" (Hayim, 4), while others explained, "I really didn't want Trump" (Lailah, 4). Yet even the children who criticized Trump and argued that "he doesn't make the right decisions" (Lailah, 5) about policies regarding the environment, immigration, or women's rights tended to believe that he was a friend of Israel. They described Trump as "standing with Israel" (Avigail, 4), "friends with Israel" (Keren, 4), and someone who "likes Israel" (Dina, 5). Although many liberal American Jewish adults were highly skeptical of the claim that Trump was good for Israel (J.

Eisner, 2019), even the children whose own politics leaned left didn't question this idea.

For the children, the Trump–Netanyahu alliance was a clear reminder of a larger friendship between their respective countries. As Tzvi (4) explained, "The United States and Israel have become practically allies." For the children, this meant that "Israel and America fight together" on the same team (Brent, 5) and "help each other out" (Seth, 5). In Naomi's (5) words, "America's never attacking Israel or visa versa."

For many of the children, this alliance was particularly important because, as Tzvi (5) explained, it "makes me feel connected to know that the two places that I see as homes connect and are friends." For Rina (5), a U.S.–Israel alliance makes it possible for her to have "a connection to Israel in some way but still live in the United States, because I know that Israel's always going to be there welcoming the United States and having friends in the United States."

Many of the children paid particularly close attention to the U.S.–Israel alliance as the Trump administration reversed a longstanding U.S. policy and relocated the U.S. embassy from Tel Aviv to Jerusalem. The children knew that this shift had symbolic import and that "the U.S. embassy went to Jerusalem to announce that it was the capital of Israel" (Keren, 5). They also knew that the move was highly controversial, catalyzing widespread protests. As Hayim (5) explained, "The U.S. opened an embassy in Jerusalem and there are a lot of protests. [The embassy] used to be in Tel Aviv, and then when our new president came he wanted it to be in Jerusalem 'cause many Jews think the actual capital of Israel is Jerusalem, so he moved it there. And a lot of people weren't happy with that."

The children were divided in their own political analysis of these current events. Some, like Keren (5), believed that moving "the U.S. embassy is doing a good job for the Jews." Others, like Samantha (5), believed that "moving the embassy wasn't a good idea [because] then the Palestinians fight the Jews and then the Jews fight back." Yet regardless of whether the children believed that "the U.S. embassy was fine where it was and it could've just stayed there and there wouldn't have been any issues" (Rina, 5), or whether they felt that the move was good for "Donald Trump and the Jews and Israelis" (Ari, 5), they all concurred about one thing: that the U.S., and not only Israel, was embroiled in the Middle

East conflict, a conflict that linked together the two countries they cared about most.

Even as the children clearly expressed affiliations with the U.S. and Israel, for the first time they also began to imagine Palestinian and Arab views of the conflict. They continued to speak in terms of "us" (Americans, Israelis, and/or Jews) and "them" (Palestinians, Arabs, and/or Muslims), but the children also attempted to give voice to the positions of those whom they viewed as on the "other team."

Imagining the Perspective of the Other

Considering the same event from the perspectives of different cultural groups is generally considered within reach of upper-elementary-school students and is often a staple of the social studies curriculum (W. C. Parker, 2012). Even though none of the children had learned about the Israeli–Arab/Palestinian conflict as part of their social studies classes, by late elementary school they had—whether knowingly or not—embraced the widely accepted idea that considering multiple viewpoints is essential for understanding any historical or current event (National Council for the Social Studies, 2016). For the children, this shift generally occurred in two steps: first understanding that Israel fights with some, not all, Arabs, and then beginning to articulate how they imagined Arabs viewed the conflict.

For most of the children, this first step occurred in fourth grade. As the children began to develop conceptual awareness of a transnational group of Arabs, they also began to understand that Israel does not fight with *all* Arabs but only with "some Arabs" (Tzvi, 4). As they spoke about Arabs, the fourth graders began to distinguish between "Arab countries against Israel" and the fact that "not all Arab people are against us" (Carly, 4). In Gia's (4) words, "Some Arabs are nice and some are mean." Like their younger selves, the children expressed strong in-group favoritism (Aboud, 2003; Bennett et al., 1998), continuing to view Israelis as the "good guys" in an extended fight. But unlike even a year earlier, the category of "bad guys" was much more complicated, with the children explaining that "there are Arabs that are bad making a war with Israel, [but] I know that not all Arabs are bad" (Avigail, 4). This ability to distinguish between "mean" Arabs who were fighting Israel and "nice"

Arabs who were not was the first step toward a much larger shift in the children's thinking the subsequent year.

By fifth grade, most of these children were able not only to distinguish between the Arabs who fought Israel and those who didn't, but also to imagine the perspectives of the Arabs with whom Israel was fighting. The same children who had previously distinguished between "good guys" and "bad guys" had begun to speak instead of the conflict with shifting perspectives, using language like "we think" and "they think." Consider, for example, Samantha's (5) explanation that Palestinians "think the Jewish people are taking Israel from them, 'cause they believe, 'Israel's ours,' even though we believe it's ours." Similarly, Ari understood that it was simultaneously possible for "us" (Jews and Israelis) to be "happy" that the U.S. embassy had moved to Jerusalem *and* for "them" (Arabs) to be unhappy because "they don't want it to be there." In Maya's (5) words, "Arabs saw that they should have Israel, and Jews thought they should have it."

The children's "we think" and "they think" language clearly reflects a larger sense of affiliation that they continued to have for Israel's side in the conflict. Yet even as they still viewed themselves on "Israel's team," they also spent substantive time considering—for the first time—the beliefs and desires of the "other team." For example, even though Hayim (5) said that he personally believed that Jerusalem belongs to "the Jews," he recognized that "other religions think Jerusalem isn't just the Jews'. They think it's theirs." Similarly, Keren (5) explained that Palestinians "think that Israel should be theirs because they think that Palestine should be a country" even though she herself thinks "they never earned it or [have] done anything to make it a country." In Avigail's words, Hamas "thinks that Israel should not be a country" even though she believes that "Israel should be there." For the first time, the children could begin to consider how Arabs—not only Israelis and Jews—might view the conflict.

Several of the fifth-grade girls were able to describe the emotions, and not only the intellectual arguments, that they imagined to be Arab views of the conflict. In Maya's (5) words, "Even though Arabs don't like Israel, they're still human beings and I kind of feel bad for them, that they didn't get Israel." Gia (5) imagined that Arabs involved in the conflict must "have felt threatened" by the Jewish people and probably responded "out of fear and out of anger." The girls who expressed such affective empathy also expressed a clear belief that "it's okay to believe in different stuff" (Olivia, 5), and they attempted to humanize the people whom their younger selves had seen only as "bad guys." For these children, the *conflict itself*, rather than the enemies of Israel, had become the problem. As Samantha (5) explained, "Everyone's kind of at fault here."

The children's newfound focus on imagining Arab views of the conflict was not, for them, a political statement. It did not reflect an expression of solidarity with Palestinian or Arab experiences (cf. Omer, 2019), nor did it portend a shift in their own primary allegiances to the United States and Israel. In fact, most of the children had never knowingly met a Muslim or Christian Arab, though many could point to Jews in their communities who hailed from Arab countries. Their attempts to imagine Arab perspectives of the conflict stemmed not from a commitment to or personal experience with intercommunal dialogue but rather from a developmental readiness for developing cognitive empathy. This kind of cognitive empathy, in which children are able to think through a conflict from the perspective of another, develops over time as children begin to understand a world beyond themselves (Feshbach & Feshbach, 2011). As these children began to develop cognitive empathy, they started to imagine global events as having both Israeli-Jewish and Arab/Palestinian narratives. They did not yet think about the gradations of beliefs and commitments *within* Israeli-Jewish and Arab/Palestinian communities, which they would begin to do only in middle school.

Summary of Late Elementary School (Grades 4–5, September 2016–June 2018)

As the children neared the end of elementary school, and in the wake of the Trump election, they developed a much more global understanding of the Israeli–Arab/Palestinian conflict. No longer viewing it as simply a fight between Israel and the "other team," the children began to understand both that Israel has global allies—including the United States—and that the "other team" consists of a transnational group of Arabs, not all of whom are engaged in fighting against Israel. At this stage, the children were also able to understand that the Israeli–Palestinian conflict is part of a larger regional conflict, and for the first time they seemed just as concerned with Iranian actions as with Palestinian ones. Although the children continued to identify with Israel, they also began to imagine Arab perspectives of the conflict, and some of the girls expressed empathy for what they imagined to be Arab views.

Constant over Time (K–5): September 2012–June 2018

Even as the children's views of the conflict clearly developed over time, two constants existed in the ways that they framed it throughout their elementary school years. First, at every age the children believed whole-heartedly that peace is possible, and that ultimately there will be a peaceful resolution to the fighting between Israel and its enemies. Second, once the children could independently access online information about the conflict, they viewed themselves as having personally witnessed events that occurred thousands of miles from their own homes and lives. The former offers a tale of hope, and the latter a tale of great caution, to adults who care about helping children make sense of a violent, intractable conflict that is geographically remote.

Peace Is Possible

At every grade level, the children talked about their hopes and prayers for peace. Even as they discussed their understanding of ongoing, violent conflict in the Middle East in one breath, they talked about the possibility of peace in the next. The children explained that when they pray, they ask that people in Israel "will have a good and peaceful life" (Micah, 3) and they "thank God there's peace" between Israel and some of its neighbors like Egypt (Avigail, 4). Several children, including Rina (K) and Gabe (4), imagined traveling to Israel in order to place notes in the Western Wall asking for peace. Some, like Carly (5), believed that praying for "peace and happiness" is part of "what it means to be Jewish." Without exception, all of the children imagined an alternative reality in which Israel "is a place full of peace, full of *shalom*" (Ryan, 5).

The children also had a belief, which remained stable over time, that Israelis—like the children themselves—want peace. The following explanations offered by six different children, one at each grade level, demonstrate the similarities in thinking across time and child. In Naomi's (K) words, "Israelis are peace" and in Ari's (1), Israelis "fight for peace."

According to Seth (2), "Israel wants peace," and Gia (3) believed that Israelis "want to be" peaceful even though they are sometimes engaged in wars. Isabelle (4) explained that "in Israel, there's a lot of people who like peace," and Rina (5) believed that "peace and harmony" were "the goal of Israel." Only in the upper elementary grades did the children begin to discuss specific actions that they believed Israel had taken in order to secure peace, such as signing peace treaties with Jordan and Egypt. Yet even before they could name specific efforts to build peace, the children viewed Israel as a place that "tries to make peace" (Samantha, 5).

For the most part, the children gave little thought to the question of whether or not Israel's enemies also want peace. Some of the children clearly believed that "Israel wants peace and Gaza wants fighting" (Seth, 2) or "the Jewish state wants to be peaceful . . . and the Arabs have said no" (Tzvi, 4). Others seemed to believe that all people must want peace because "peace is very special" (Bella, 1) and people generally want to "live together in peace" (Dina, 3). Yet most of the children didn't discuss whether or not they believed that Israel's foes wanted peace.

The children did, however, repeatedly insist that there is cause for optimism. Micah (4) explained that people are "meant to be as hopeful as you can," and Dina (1) explained that despite current wars, "I have hope." Samantha (5) insisted, "If you do end up putting [kids' ideas] in a book, you should always have an optimistic spin, saying, 'This [conflict] might happen now, but we know the Jews will [eventually] make peace because that's what they've done in the past.'"

These American Jewish children's unwavering belief in the possibility of "having peace in the world" (Carly, 3) sets them apart from American Jewish teenagers and adults, who tend to see little cause for optimism about the Israeli–Palestinian conflict (J. Hassenfeld, 2015). It also distinguishes them from Israeli and Palestinian children in the region, who often hope for peace in the abstract (Bar-Tal, 1998; Nasie & Bar-Tal, 2012) but have great difficulty envisioning a reality in which the conflict will actually be resolved peacefully (Masalha, 1993). These Jewish children in the U.S., by contrast, regularly engage in "possibility thinking," imagining the transformation between what is and what might be (Craft, 2015). As Brent (5) explained, "There might not be a lot of peace in Israel sometimes, but there can always be some harmony and peace." In Seth's (5) words, "They should just make peace already!"

"Witnessing" the Conflict

As the children learned and thought about the conflict from the safety of their home communities thousands of miles away, they repeatedly expressed a belief that they had personally "seen" the conflict. Once the children were able to independently access digital sources of information—often without the knowledge or guidance of the adults in their lives—they began to view themselves not only as knowing *about* the conflict but as actually *witnessing* it. For most of the children, this shift occurred as early as second grade and continued throughout the elementary school years.

The second, third, fourth, and fifth graders repeatedly spoke about the screens through which they gathered information about the conflict. For example, Carly (2) reported learning about the conflict from "an alert on my mom's phone," and Avigail (4) discussed how "war has been happening, and I saw news on the TV." Samantha (5) explained most clearly the children's typical process of gathering bits of information from different digital sources: "I was watching YouTube and I scrolled down and it said, 'Recent News.' There was a strip of stuff saying, 'Horror in the Gaza Strip: Jews fighting Palestinians and Palestinians fighting Jews.' And then I opened my phone the next day and there was a news story, so then I was really curious." Through a combination of accidental exposure and purposeful searching, Samantha and her peers collected information about the conflict online.

For these children, digital technologies functioned as much more than a conduit of information. In the children's accounts, as they gathered updates of the war through a screen, they perceived themselves as personally viewing it. Consider, for example, the words of second graders who viewed themselves as witnesses to the conflict. Dina (2) explained, "I just felt like I was in Israel" every time she saw information about the conflict. Tzvi (2) explained, "I heard [the conflict] myself," and Gabe (2) insisted, "I heard that the news man said that there was a war in Israel, and it was like I was there." These children described themselves as having personally viewed events in the Middle East.

At no point did the children confuse "connected presence" (Licoppe & Smoreda, 2005) with actual physical presence. As Dina's and Gabe's words exemplify, the children were able to distinguish between feeling "like I was there" and actually being there. Even so, the children repeatedly mentioned feeling "near" the conflict. Although their immediate families and their own bodies were protected, they had the ability to view—often in real time—the devastating effects of violence, and this meant that they considered themselves as having seen it.

Much of the existing research on children's conceptions of violent conflict divides the world into two kinds of children: those who have personally experienced violence, and those who have learned about it only in the abstract. Children who have personally lived through war often experience levels of both physical (Pearn, 2003) and psychological trauma (Murthy & Lakshminarayana, 2006) that are higher than adults in their communities. By contrast, children whose own homes are safe from war tend to view war and peace as abstract concepts (e.g., P. Cooper, 1965; de Souza et al., 2006). Much of this literature assumes that children were either directly exposed to the toll of war—on battlegrounds or on the home front—or did not personally experience it, left to consider war in theory only.

Yet it is clear from these children that the digital era has birthed a new kind of child—one physically removed from warfare yet virtually proximal to it via technologies that offer instantaneous connections to distant people and places. It is now possible for children to be physically removed yet digitally connected, experiencing a hybrid of "presence-absence" (Fortunati et al., 2013). In light of this digital connectivity, the dichotomy between learning about war in the abstract and encountering war as a lived experience has begun to break down. Children can now tune into conflicts from afar, witnessing the sights and sounds of violent clashes from across the globe without any physical danger.

Yet just because their bodies are protected does not mean that their psyches are. In kindergarten and first grade, before they were digitally literate enough to tune into the conflict from afar, the children expressed primarily feelings of pride when thinking about the conflict and Israel's role in it. They would say, "I'm proud of Israel" (Naomi, K) or "I'm proud to be Jewish" (Brent, 1). Yet by second grade, in the same conversations in which the children began discussing the digital sources from which they gleaned information about the conflict, they also began to use words like "worry" and "anxious" to describe their feelings about it. For example, Rina (2) felt "anxious because people might die and it's really sad when people die when they're Jewish," and Seth (3) explained, "We really worry about people dying." Several of the children explicitly linked their own emotional states to the news that they viewed about Israel. In Dina's (2) words, "Well, if there's bad news, I feel really sad. And if it's happy news, I'm happy."

As the children expressed worry, they often bounced back and forth between concern for others and anxiety about themselves. For example, Carly (2) "worried because they might be going to fight, and some soldiers, sometimes, can die. And I want to be safe," following her concern for soldiers with a desire for personal safety. Similarly, Lailah (2) said that she was "sad because people get killed sometimes and I don't like getting killed." Avigail (5) explained that her own anxiety about the conflict was linked to a widespread concern about the safety of Jews around the world, and not only Jews in Israel. "What if things like the Nazis or something like that, God forbid, happens again?" she explained. "It always makes me feel anxious, nervous."

To an outside observer it might appear that these children, whose own homes and bodies had never experienced any of the violence of intractable conflict, were far removed from it. But to the children themselves, the conflict felt "near" and anxiety producing, in large part because they believed that they had seen it. It is as if the children experienced a shared form of trauma, which I call remote trauma.

The children's trauma was remote in two senses of the word: the source of the trauma was physically far away, and it was mediated by remote controls and mouses. Like other forms of collective trauma that place traumatic events at the center of collective identity (Svašek, 2005) and therefore can be transmitted from generation to generation (Volkan, 2002), the children's trauma was directly tied to their sense of collective responsibility. Such trauma can be shared by members of a community, including those with no personal memory of traumatic events (Volkan, 2001), because it is part of a long-term socialization process in which individuals come to view themselves as part of collective history (Kreuzer, 2002).

Yet unlike other forms of collective trauma, remote trauma is tied much more closely to the *representations* of traumatic events that children can access through television and Internet sources than it is to the actual traumatic events themselves. As graphic representations of violent current events streamed into their lives, the children experienced a barrage of information about which they were both genuinely curious and deeply troubled. As a result, these children viewed themselves as witnesses to an ongoing, violent conflict in which they felt personally implicated and emotionally invested.

Conclusion

Many adults—parents, educators, clergy, and communal leaders—operate under the assumption that the Israeli–Arab/Palestinian conflict is not an appropriate topic for children. Out of an understandable desire to protect children from violence and warfare, they confine discussions and debates about the conflict to adult company, and most curricula and resources designed for children omit the conflict as a topic of study until middle or high school at the earliest. Yet the magic of childhood comes not from an innocent lack of awareness about the ills of the world; it comes, instead, from children's unfettered belief that the world can be remade.

If the children in this study are any indication, children can and do think about geopolitical conflict from the time they enter elementary school.[2] And in the absence of adults who are willing to help them process or make sense of the conflict, they turn to web searches and apps for their information. When provided with little adult guidance, they actively construct an understanding of the conflict much like building the pieces of a holographic plate; at first they have only a blurry image but by adding layers over time, the picture becomes increasingly clear (Egan, 1997, p. 86).

As the children in this study grew, some of their initial ideas fell away over time while others became increasingly refined. A conflict that they originally viewed as an ongoing war between the Jewish people and its enemies slowly transformed into a regional Middle Eastern conflict with global consequences. Table 3.1 shows the children's typical trajectory as they developed evolving ideas and beliefs about the conflict throughout elementary school.

TABLE 3.1. Typical Trajectory of Children's Ideas about the Conflict

	K-1	2-3	4-5
Conflate contemporary and historical "enemies" of Israel	✓		
Aware of Israel's involvement in an ongoing, violent conflict	✓	✓	✓
Believe that future peace is possible	✓	✓	✓
Can recount specific details of violent current events		✓	✓
Can offer multiple explanations of the root causes of the conflict		✓	✓
View themselves as "witnesses" to the conflict		✓	✓
Can name specific actors (other than Israel) involved in the conflict			✓
Can imagine non-Jewish and non-Israeli views of the conflict			✓

Over time, the children came to view violence in the Middle East not only as a faraway war but also as an essential part of their own Jewishness. They described themselves as having personally witnessed a conflict in which they have a stake, and about which they feel anxiety. And yet, for all their worry, the children continued to believe that peace is not only possible but also an inevitable conclusion to the conflict. For them, peace was woven into the very fabric of their hopes and prayers, and they could imagine no future in which the status quo persists over time.

Adults who care about the well-being of children ought to be asking not *whether* children can handle thinking about the Israeli–Arab/Palestinian conflict, but rather *what* they can grasp about it and *how* to best support them in their efforts to understand it. As educational psychologist Jerome Bruner explains, "Any subject can be taught effectively in some intellectually honest form to a child at any stage of development" (1960, p. 33). The Israeli–Arab/Palestinian conflict is no exception; at every stage of elementary school, American Jewish children can and do think about the conflict, and they deserve adult guides who are willing to help them learn about and process it.

The question of *what* kids are capable of thinking about shifts over time, and—like with all subject areas—formal curricula and informal conversations with children ought to spiral in increasing sophistication over time to reflect children's growing capacities for understanding the world. In early elementary school, the children in this study viewed the conflict as part of an ongoing war, stretching across time, between the

Jewish people and others who don't like Jews. By middle elementary school, the children understood not only conflict in the abstract but as it manifested in particular current events, and they could offer multiple explanations for why the conflict persists. At this age, they struggled to identify the "other team" and desperately wanted adult guidance in helping them name and understand Palestinians and their claims. By late elementary school, the children began to understand that the conflict is not only a fight between Israelis and Palestinians but a regional one with multiple players and numerous issues at stake. At this stage, they started to imagine non-Israeli and non-Jewish views of the conflict even as they clearly continued to affiliate with Jewish Israelis.

The question of *how* to support the intellectual and emotional journeys of children learning about the conflict is a delicate one, as it requires undertaking two distinct yet interrelated balancing acts. First, adults must allow children to learn about the problems of the world even as they help guard children's emotional well-being. Scholars of education have long recognized that children are interested in (Carter, 2004) and able to handle learning about complex political and international conflicts (Bickmore, 1999). As counterintuitive as it might seem, learning about disturbing events may actually enhance children's ability to cope with the world (Passe, 2008). The idea is to protect children by helping them build resilience for facing a complex and uncertain world, not by sheltering them from conversations about it. Yet resilience is a social-relational process, developed through interactions with family and community (Daiute, 2013), and children can develop resilience only with the guidance of adults who are willing to help them discuss and work through their fears about the world (Galante & Foa, 1986). Thus adults must walk a fine line in discussing conflict with children, neither introducing into children's minds fears they had not yet considered nor glossing over children's own concerns, questions, and anxieties about a world that they, too, inhabit.

Second, adults must allow children to learn about the world as it is and, also, hold space for children to reimagine the world as it can be. Children's hopes, prayers, and stories about peace are not merely naive articulations; they are instead inchoate versions of global problem-solving. Children have long been agents of change in global peace movements (Del Felice & Wisler, 2007; Stomfay-Stitz & Wheeler, 2003), and adults must respect children's peacemaking efforts even while helping them process a world that is not yet at peace. The goal is to answer, honestly and clearly, children's questions about the world's current ills and also invite them to be partners in the search for solutions. The stakes of this balancing act are high: If adults neglect the former, children will still seek to understand violent conflict but will be left with large questions that they are unable to answer on their own. If adults fail in the latter, children may come to understand the world but will lose the impetus to reconstruct it for the better. Thus, any attempts at this balance—helping children expand their understanding of violent conflict *and* holding space for their optimism for a better future—must simultaneously embrace reality and opportunity, inviting children to understand conflict and participate in efforts to counter or mitigate it.

As children encounter information about geopolitical conflict, they can either make sense of these events without the guidance of adults or they can do so with careful and deliberate facilitation, but they will do so one way or the other. Adults who want to be part of supporting children's emotional and intellectual journeys can do so in two ways: by understanding the trajectory of children's conceptions of geopolitical conflict, and by helping children learn about the world's current problems while simultaneously helping them process their fears and allowing them to become partners in constructing a better, more peaceful world.

Although children are capable of building foundational ideas about violent conflict that occurs between warring countries or societies, geopolitical conflict is not the only kind of serious disagreement that occurs in the world. In fact, though only some countries are embroiled in violent conflict with those outside their borders, all democratic countries give rise to internal disagreements about how society ought to function within its borders. At the heart of these disagreements lie civic and political questions. Children's understanding of these questions are the focus of the next chapter, which highlights both children's deep interest in civic and political matters and their profound frustration at what they perceive to be a lack of adult guidance as they attempt to make sense of contested civic and political issues.

4

"Why Didn't You Tell Me?"

Civics, Politics, and Children's Righteous Anger

Six-year-old Avigail is shorter than most of the children in her school, but that doesn't mean she sees herself as small. In fact, in Avigail's mind, she is already big enough to be responsible for all of the other people living in both the United States and Israel. She views both countries as "caring about" her and her family, and she sees herself as obligated to "help them."

At ages 7 and 8, Avigail envisions herself doing many different things to help the communities and countries she cares about: planting trees, picking up trash from the streets, praying for the safety of other Jews, caring for animals and friends, visiting sick relatives, and raising money to help cure diseases. She believes in taking action "because you know it's the right thing to do."

As a 10-year-old, Avigail insists that "it's an honor to be Jewish, and it's a big responsibility as well. It's also a big responsibility to be American." She describes both the United States and Israel as countries "still being built," and she believes that helping both countries is something "I have to do in life." In her mind, children "have power" to make a difference, and she intends to exercise that power by showing "respect toward other people," being "very generous," praying faithfully, and voting in U.S. elections when she is old enough to do so.

Avigail, like the other children in this study, had a belief that remained relatively consistent over childhood: a sense of personal obligation toward other Americans and Jews, and toward those living in Israel. She and her peers viewed themselves as current and future actors responsible for, and capable of, influencing the communities they cared about.

While some scholars have lamented low levels of youth political and civic engagement (e.g., Macedo, 2005; Putnam, 2000), others have pointed to the important roles that children and teens have played in the public square: as peacemakers (Del Felice & Wisler, 2007; Stomfay-Stitz & Wheeler, 2003) and political activists (Gordon, 2009; Taft, 2011), and as volunteers (Nenga, 2012; Sarre & Tarling, 2010) and participants in community organizations (Hart, 2008; Solís et al., 2013). In fact, helping young people not only understand, but also participate in, the society around them has long been seen as an important role of education (Dewey, 1916). Children and youth, in this view, are both able and entitled to learn about the problems of the community and take action in order to transform both society and the students themselves (e.g., Engle & Ochoa, 1988; Evans et al., 1996).

This chapter explores how children think and feel about civic and political engagement. In the pages that follow, the term "civic engagement" refers to children's interest in, and actions on behalf of, the common good of the communities with which they affiliate (Barrett & Pachi, 2019; Lichterman, 1996). Political engagement is a particular form of civic engagement referring to children's interest in, and participatory behavior with, political institutions, processes, and ideas (Barrett & Pachi, 2019).

From the earliest days of elementary school, the children in this study were civically engaged. They situated themselves as members of both the American and global Jewish communities, and as such they viewed themselves as responsible for helping other members of those communities in both the United States and Israel. By the middle of elementary school, as the children began to develop an understanding of political issues, institutions, and leaders, their experiences of and feelings toward U.S. and Israeli societies diverged. They came to understand that the United States grapples with important and contested political questions, but they developed little sense of Israeli civic and political matters. As a result, when children *did* encounter the civic and political issues that permeate contemporary Israeli life, they were caught off guard, and they expressed profound anger toward the adults in their life who they believed inadequately prepared them. Taking children's anger seriously will require shifting educational practices in order to help children learn about the civic and political issues that they so desperately want to understand.

Children's Civic Engagement

Children's civic engagement—their interest in, and actions on behalf of, the common good of their communities (Barrett & Pachi, 2019; Lichterman, 1996)—is one way that children are able to shape their own lives and the societies in which they live (K. A. Payne et al., 2020; Percy-Smith, 2010). Children are invested in a range of civic issues not because they parrot adults, but because they understand these issues to be relevant to their own lives (e.g., Drakeford et al., 2009; O'Toole et al., 2003). And while childhood has long been associated with egocentric thought (Piaget, 1923/1926, 1927/1930), children are often interested in, and able to deliberate about, what constitutes the common good (Hauver, 2019). Although some attempts to involve children in civic causes and institutions result in mere tokenism, consulting children without actually taking their ideas seriously (O'Connor, 2013; Wyness et al., 2004), in other instances children are actively involved as agents of change in their own communities (Pontón & Andrade, 2007; Silva & Langhout, 2011).

Children's Beliefs about Civic Obligation

As the children in this study reflected on the communities that mattered to them—local, national, and global—they situated themselves as capable of advocating and working on behalf of the common good. Without exception, the children viewed childhood not only as a time when "our parents take care of us" (Brent, 1) but also as a time when "you can help people" (Ryan, K).

All of the children spoke of ways in which they, or other children they personally knew, worked to contribute to their own communities. They discussed how children could "take care of nature" (Naomi, 3), visit sick relatives (Lailah, 3), "help the elderly" (Dina, 2), donate or serve food to people who are hungry (Bella, 2), raise money for medical research (Avigail, 4), recycle (Olivia, 4), and more. The most common way that the children envisioned contributing to the community was by caring for animals. Hannah (1) explained, "I love animals, and I like to take care of them so they can live." In Naomi's words (3), "There's so many reasons to take care of animals." Whether they spoke of caring for animals, people, or the environment, it was clear that the children viewed themselves as responsible for those beyond their own families and schools.

Not surprisingly, the children viewed themselves as particularly obligated to care for the United States and those who live there. As Isabelle (3) explained, "It's our home, and we take care of it so it's healthy." Well before the political rise and rhetoric of Donald Trump, the children viewed themselves as responsible for helping making America a "good" (Caleb, K) and a "great" (Carly, 1) country.

All of the children envisioned contributing to "America, our home" (Tzvi, 4), and most of the children offered the same explanation about how they could do so: by exhibiting "care and love" (Ryan, K; Lior, 1; Pearl, 5). The children spoke of their "care of animals" (Hannah, K), "care of things" (Naomi, 3), "care about the environment" (Olivia, 4), and "care about people" (Maya, K). Many children explicitly specified that their care of other people included both "care about non-Jewish people and Jewish people" (Avigail, K). The children framed both private acts of kindness like sharing with others (Hayim, 2) and public acts of service like launching a fundraising campaign to search for a cure for a friend's genetic disorder (Avigail, 4) as part of a larger ethic of care (Noddings, 2002, 2013). For many children, it felt important to state that "I care about, and I worry about, and I love" (Elliott, 5) those in their local communities even when no interviewer asked them to do so.

Most of the children framed their obligations toward the United States and their own local communities not as a result of the responsibilities of American citizenship but rather as an outgrowth of their Judaism. For example, Keren (2) believed that helping others is part of what Jews do. In her words, "Jews help. They help and they don't keep things [for] themselves, so they give things to other people." Similarly, Gia (5) explained, "Being Jewish means being aware that other people are there [and] they may need your help. To be Jewish, you need to understand that if other people need help, you'll help them." A few of the children framed their own responsibilities as those of citizens, like Ryan (3) who said that "everyone's a citizen who [must] help around the state." But it was much more common for the children to describe themselves as responsible for others not because they were citizens, but because they were Jews. In Dina's (2) words, Jews "always do *mitzvot* [obligatory deeds] to help other people."

As Jews, the children believed that their obligations to help others extended well beyond the boundaries of the United States. As they looked to address global problems, they were particularly focused on the impact they might have in Israel. From the age of 5 or 6, and continuing through adolescence, the children expressed a belief that "Israel is counting on all the Jewish people" to make it better (Avigail, K), and that, as Jews living in the United States, "I can help in that" (Gia, 3). Woven into their very definitions of being Jewish was an idea "that Jews help" (Keren, 3), and while they clearly believed that Jews needed to "help save the [entire] world" (Pearl, 3), they were especially concerned with helping "Jews who live in Israel" (Dina, 2).

In the early grades of elementary school (K–3), the children had a relatively unified conception of what it meant to "feel like I just have to help Israel" (Avigail, K); they viewed Israel as an impoverished place and themselves as obligated to "help poor people in Israel" (Dina, 2). Israel has relatively high poverty rates, especially among its elderly, Charedi (Ultra-Orthodox), and Arab populations (Giorno, 2016), and approximately one in every five Israelis lives below the poverty line (Weiss, 2016). In the children's minds, this poverty was one of the most striking things about Israel, even though their own city of Los Angeles has among the highest poverty rates of any large city in the United States (Bishaw & Fontenot, 2014). They frequently talked about how Israelis are "a little poor" (Bella, 3) and discussed "the parts [of Israel] where Jews are poor" (Hayim, K). They were especially concerned about "my people, [the Jewish people], that didn't have food" (Maya, K) or "don't have a lot of food" (Ari, 1). For example, Samantha (2) recounted a story told to her by her Israeli-born teacher, who "said when she was in Israel when she was a little girl, they had not a lot of food." She told a second anecdote about a classmate's Israeli grandfather, who faced such poverty in his youth that "all he wanted for his birthday was a box of cereal." For the children, this food insecurity was profoundly troubling.

The children did not view poverty in Israel as a phenomenon either irrelevant to their own lives or outside their own control; they believed that they were both personally obligated and capable of helping to solve this problem. For example, Pearl (K) spoke in one breath about "when the poor people were sad in Israel" and how happy she felt "because we help them." Bella (1) believed that part of the beauty of Israel is that you get "to make food to help other people." Dina (2) insisted that Jews like her "always help other people less fortunate [than] them, and they always help poor people in Israel, because they give them *tzedakah* [charitable donations]."

The most striking example of the children's sense of obligation toward Israel comes from Avigail, who in kindergarten explained, "I just have to help Israel . . . I'm going to make money, and then I'm going to give it to . . . [Israeli] people that don't have any money." In Avigail's mind, "Israel is not a great place. It's dirty, and ucky, and yicky, but you have to make it a better place. You have to clean and work hard." Avigail viewed herself as personally obligated as a Jew to assist in efforts to improve the imperfect Jewish state.

While American Jews have long invested financially in Israel's social infrastructure (C. I. Waxman, 2010), the primary way that these children imagined working to improve Israeli society was through physical labor, not financial contributions. Avigail (K) imagined traveling to Israel to pick up trash from the streets. She explained, "Every time people drop trash in Israel, I'm just going to take a bag every single day, and help [clean]." Bella (1) envisioned herself cooking meals for Israeli "people that are hungry." Samantha (2) and Gia (3) wanted to work the land on a kibbutz so that the fruit of their labor could feed hungry people living in Israel. This emphasis on physical, rather than financial, contributions may stem from the fact that children take years to develop an understanding of money and its worth (Berti & Bombi, 1981), but it may also be because contemporary Jewish children—like the American Jewish community writ large—are seeking interactions with Israel that are more personal and experiential (Sasson, 2014).

As the children grew, they developed a much more expansive sense of civic engagement. While in early elementary school (K–3) the children equated contributing to Israeli society with feeding hungry Israelis, by late elementary school (4–5) they began to develop other ideas about how they might act as "people who want to help Israel" (Keren, 4). For the most part, the children continued to believe that "being Jewish means if other people need help, you'll help them" (Gia, 5) and they continued to "feel like I should be there [in Israel] helping" (Lior, 5). But the ways that they envisioned themselves helping expanded to include "donating to Jewish funds in Israel" (Keren, 5), "standing up for Israel" when people criticize it (Olivia, 4), protecting the environment as a way of protecting Israel (Lailah, 5), and expressing gratitude for the "brave men or women who are fighting for us [as part of the Israeli army], thanking them very much for being courageous and brave" (Brent, 5). Although in the older grades the children continued to stress the importance of "helping each other out [so every Israeli can] have a roof over their head and some food" (Hayim, 5), fighting poverty became one of many ways that the children imagined their own contributions to Israeli society.

Summary of Children's Civic Engagement

From the earliest days of elementary school, the children were civically minded. They viewed themselves as part of a larger community, and they believed they were responsible for helping others in their community, which included people in both the United States and Israel. The children framed their commitment to civic engagement as stemming directly from their obligations as Jews. They described themselves as helping by caring for people, animals, and the environment, and they spoke of specific ways that they and other children whom they personally knew were working toward the common good. As the children reflected on their own local communities in the United States, they pointed to a range of public and private actions that they viewed as expressions of care. As they thought about helping Jewish communities in Israel in particular, they were especially concerned with alleviating poverty and hunger.

Children's Political Engagement

If children's civic engagement consists of a wide variety of beliefs and actions regarding their contributions to the common good, then children's political engagement is a particular subset of civic engagement in which they seek to understand and contribute to their communities through political actions and beliefs. The first step in understanding children's political engagement is recognizing, in the words of renowned child psychiatrist Robert Coles, that "there most assuredly [is] a political life among children, and that its significance [is] well worth attending" (Coles, 1986b, p. 8). Once politics are understood as a common feature of children's lives, it is necessary to consider three interrelated factors that comprise their political engagement: children's political participation, their political interest, and their political understanding.

Political *participation* encompasses a range of activities that have "the intent or effect of influencing government action—either directly by affecting the making or implementation of public policy or indirectly by influencing the selection of people who make those policies" (Verba et al., 1995, p. 38). Understanding children's political participation is especially complex because children are barred from many forms of conventional political participation like voting or running for political office even as they are capable of engaging in other actions that can be viewed as political such as letter writing or participating in political protests (Barrett & Pachi, 2019). A long scholarly debate has highlighted children's often ambiguous role as political actors who are—at once—autonomous individuals and under the guidance and protection of adults (Jans, 2004). Should children be shielded from political life and spared the burden of responsibility for participating in the public sphere (Arendt, 1959; Kallio & Häkli, 2013)? Are young people "citizens-in-the-making," neither ready for full political participation nor detached from political life (Gordon, 2009; Gordon & Taft, 2011)? Are children both capable of and interested in political participation even as adults marginalize youth (Drakeford et al., 2009; Roche, 1999)? Each approach reveals different beliefs that adults have about what kinds of political actions are ideal and which should be promoted specifically for young citizens (Nenga & Taft, 2013) even as children themselves often embrace all of these different beliefs about their own political participation (Drakeford et al., 2009; Stordal & Hellem, 2005).

Yet political participation is only one form of children's engagement with political matters. Children may have interest in, or knowledge, feelings, or opinions about, political matters even if they do not take any specific political action, and thus both political interest and political understanding are seen as essential elements of children's political engagement (Barrett & Pachi, 2019). Political *interest* is often viewed as a proxy for political engagement in children because people who express interest in political issues are typically more likely to become those who participate in political activities (e.g., Brady et al., 1995, Emler, 2011; Schulz et al., 2016). *Understanding* of political issues, processes, and policies is necessary for the formation of well-informed beliefs and attitudes, and young people's political understanding often correlates with future political participation, especially voting patterns (e.g., Torney-Purta et al., 2001; Zukin et al., 2006). For very young children, political understanding often begins with knowledge about the head of state (R. D. Hess & Torney, 1967), and thus young children's views of their political leaders offer an important glimpse into their emerging political knowledge and beliefs.

As the children in this study reflected on their "favorite" countries, the United States and Israel, they spoke about political issues, political institutions, and especially political figures. Yet if the children tended to frame their civic responsibility toward U.S. and Israeli societies in largely similar ways, consistently viewing themselves as obligated to and capable of contributing to the common good of both countries, the same was not true of their political engagement. In the early elementary grades, the children developed initial and parallel understanding of political figures and institutions in both places. Yet by fourth grade, as the children's political awareness and political interest developed, they began to view the two countries in markedly different ways, articulating emerging positions about U.S. political issues and leaders but not Israeli political issues or leaders. These differences were reflected in both the children's views on political participation and their political understanding.

Children's Reflections on Political Participation

Although children may be barred from many forms of political participation, including voting and running for office, other forms of participation are both permissible and accessible to them. These include attending protests or political demonstrations, writing letters to public officials, fundraising for political causes, expressing political positions in public or online forums, and other political actions that children can engage in alongside, or under the supervision of, adults (Barrett & Pachi, 2019; Barrett & Zani, 2015). None of the children in this study discussed, at any point in time, their own current or past participation in any of these types of activities. Even though several children spoke of their own fundraising efforts through events like bake sales, book sales, and lemonade stands, the causes for which the children reported raising money were all civic rather than political (e.g., curing a friend's disease or supporting a local animal shelter).

Nonetheless, many of the children did discuss their plans for *future* political participation, especially voting. In kindergarten through third grade, the children rarely mentioned voting processes (a political institution) or voting preferences (a political belief), even as the 2012 presidential election and the 2014 congressional midterm and California gubernatorial elections occurred during these years. In fourth grade, by contrast, leading up to the 2016 presidential election, many of the children spoke of both voting processes and voting preferences, framing the right to vote as a fundamental right of all U.S. citizens. As Rina (5) explained, "Being American means that you help the government, and you pay your taxes, and when you're age 18 you can go vote." Similarly, even though Caleb (5) knew that he was too young to vote, he believed that "we, all the U.S. citizens, have rights and we get to vote for our new leader of country." By fourth grade, many of the children also expressed clear voting preferences, articulating whom "I would have voted for" (Hayim, 4) in U.S. national and statewide elections. Some of the children also offered analyses about whom "most of the Jews voted for" (Avigail, 4) in these elections. Not only did the children view themselves as future participants in U.S. elections, but by the time they were in fourth grade they also viewed themselves as having clear political preferences in the present.

The children's plans for future political participation applied only to the U.S. context, not to Israel. None of the children—including those who were dual citizens of the U.S. and Israel—ever described themselves as future voters in Israeli elections, and none ever mentioned whom they "would have voted for" in any Israeli election that occurred during their childhood. By fourth grade, the children clearly knew that Israel is a democratic country in which "people run for [office] because they want to make good decisions for Israel" (Olivia, 4). Many of the children also knew that Israeli policies allowed "Jews like me to make *aliyah* [immigrate and obtain citizenship] to Israel" (Samantha, 5). Nonetheless, they never described themselves as having a voice—or a stake—in Israeli elections.

At first glance, this disparity makes sense. After all, there are many barriers between the children and the Israeli electoral process. The children are not yet of voting age. Even when they will be, these children—all of whom live in the United States—would have to go through great effort to first obtain Israeli citizenship (if they are not already citizens) and then to travel to Israel in order to vote, as Israeli law does not permit absentee ballots except for those serving abroad on official state business. Yet upon further consideration, it is actually quite puzzling that not a single child at any point during elementary school ever expressed any beliefs about whom they "would have voted for" if they could vote in Israel. After all, they frequently used this language about the United States, and they repeatedly insisted that "I really care about Israel" (Isabelle, 2) in ways that often mirrored their descriptions of the United States. In fact, the children cared so much that they freely described themselves as planning to travel to Israel in order to pick up trash from the streets and cook meals for people who are hungry. Why didn't the children extend this same sense of obligation to political participation in Israel?

There are two reasonable explanations for the fact that the children viewed themselves as obligated to travel to Israel to fulfill their civic duty but described no such political obligations. First, it is possible—though no child ever stated so explicitly—that the children were developing a nascent belief that American Jews ought to engage with Israeli civic causes but let Israeli citizens decide on political matters. This position, both common and contested among American Jewish adults, suggests that American Jews ought not to get involved in Israeli political matters "because they don't live there" (Beinart, 2012, p. 50). Stated most concisely by Anti-Defamation League director emeritus Abraham Foxman, this belief suggests that "Israeli democracy should decide; American Jews should support" (Frankel, 1996, p. 222). The children may have been grappling with a nascent form of this position even if they were not yet able to verbalize this idea. Based on the data in this study, there is no evidence to either support or refute this possibility.

A second explanation is that the children did not view themselves as beholden to any political process in Israel even as they did in the United States because they did not really understand Israeli political issues and the Israeli political system. In fact, there were profound differences in the children's conceptual understanding of U.S. and Israeli politics, and the children themselves were aware of their own limited knowledge about Israeli political matters. Thus while the first explanation—that the children may have believed that as U.S. citizens they ought not to get involved in Israeli politics—is possible, the second—that the children understood less about Israeli politics than U.S. politics—is most certainly true, and the pages that follow explore this phenomenon and its consequences.

Children's Political Understanding

That the children described themselves as civically engaged with both U.S. and Israeli societies, but politically engaged only with the United States, stemmed from their very different conceptions of the role of government and politics in U.S. and Israeli societies. While adults typically have a broad conception of government and politics, children tend to equate government with the personal figure of the head of state (R. D. Hess & Torney, 1967). Thus an examination of the children's conceptions of the U.S. president and the Israeli prime minister sheds light on how they thought about government and politics, and how their ideas and beliefs developed over the course of childhood.

The children in this study went through two distinct phases in their conceptions of the U.S. and Israeli political leaders. In kindergarten through third grade (fall 2012 to spring 2016), when Barack Obama and Binyamin Netanyahu served as heads of state, the children tended to view both leaders as benevolent figureheads protecting their countries and the world. Beginning in fourth grade (2016–17 school year), during and after the election of Donald Trump and at a major point of growth in the children's conceptual understanding of politics, the children began to diverge in their conceptions of the political leaders of the two countries. While they continued to view the Israeli prime minister as a benevolent leader of his country and the Jewish people, they began to view the U.S. president as a highly political and polarizing figure.

In the first four years of elementary school (K–3), the children viewed the U.S. president and the Israeli prime minister in similar ways. Regardless of the political leanings of their parents, and with only one exception, the children assumed that U.S. president Barack Obama was working in the best interest of the United States and the world, and that Israeli prime minister Binyamin Netanyahu was protecting and caring for Israelis and Jews around the globe. It is typical for elementary-school-age children to express personal attachment to, and trust in, the government and the head of state (Barrett, 2007; Easton & Dennis, 1965, 1969; R. D. Hess & Easton, 1960; R. D. Hess & Torney, 1967) and to view the head of state as a benevolent leader (Barrett, 2007; Greenstein, 1960, 1961, 1965, 1975).[1] For these American Jewish children, expressions of trust in a caring and competent leader initially applied to both their conceptions of U.S. and Israeli heads of state. The children believed that each "makes good choices for his people" (Dina, 2).

As the children reflected on U.S. president Barack Obama, they wholeheartedly believed that "the president is trying his hardest to make this a very nice country" (Avigail, 2). They understood that Obama was the "first African American United States of America president" (Lior, K) and that "our president lives in the White House" (Carly, 2). The children described Obama as "so smart" (Gabe, 2), "strong," (Gia, 2), "nice" (David, 2), and "a good president" (Hayim, 2). They viewed him as "a person that could stand up for us" (Elliott, 3), "take care of America" (Gia, 3), and "always help us" (Carly, 1). Under his leadership, the children felt "safe" (Carly, 2), "lucky to have him as president" (Rina, 3), and "in good hands" (David, 3). In their descriptions of the U.S. president, the children whose parents had voted for Obama sounded indistinguishable from those whose parents had not. With the notable exception of Lior (3), who said that "I don't like Obama a lot," all of the children believed, in Olivia's (3) words, that "he's a really good president and he would never do anything mean."

In these early-elementary-school years, the children's descriptions of Israeli prime minister Binyamin Netanyahu were just as glowing as their praise of U.S. president Barack Obama. Despite the fact that Netanyahu is a polarizing figure among American Jewish adults (Pew Research Center, 2021), and even though the children's own parents express a wide range of beliefs about Israeli politics, Netanyahu evinced a uniformly positive reaction from the children in early elementary school. They consistently articulated that he is "a really good person . . . [and] really nice" (Bella, 1). The children viewed Netanyahu as a leader who not only "cares for his country" (Lior, 2) but who also "takes care of the world" (Bella, 1). Without fail, the children expressed confidence that "he will always help people in Israel" (Carly, 1), "make Israel a better place" (Isabelle, 3), "tell Israelis the right thing to do" (Carly, K), and "make the choices of Israel that are good for Israel" (Avigail, K). They viewed Netanyahu as "a really good [leader] for Israel" (Olivia, 3) who can "run Israel and make sure everything runs smoothly" (Samantha, 3).

The children viewed the heads of state of both the U.S. and Israel as "really good" (Olivia, 3) in part because children in early elementary school tend to have limited understanding of the roles that government and political leaders play in society (Easton & Dennis, 1969; S. W. Moore et al., 1985). When describing the work of the U.S. president and Israeli prime minister, the children believed that these heads of state "wave flags" (Bella, 1), "wear ties" (Olivia, 1), "make speeches" (Dina, 2), "make laws" (Carly, 2), and "help all around the world" (Maya, 2). Before age 9, children do not generally have a clear conceptual understanding of the political structure (Berti, 1994) and often confuse the titles and roles of various leaders (Connell, 1971). Like other early-elementary-school students, these children often misnamed and misidentified the roles of political leaders. For example, they often described the Israeli prime minister as the "president of Israel" (Caleb, K), the "Jewish president" (Brent, 1), or the "ruler of Israel" (Micah, 1). Some of the children imagined the Israeli leader lived in a blue house that corresponds with the U.S. president's white house (e.g., Avigail, K; David, 2), and others imagined that new leaders were elected in both countries "every few months" (Pearl, 2). In the first several years of elementary school, the children had no sense of the different political structures in the U.S. and Israel, believing that both heads of state function in the same way because "they're both presidents" (Hayim, K).

As they grew, the children developed a much different understanding of political leadership. As early as second grade, some children were able to correctly identify that the U.S. head is called the president while the Israeli head is called the prime minister (e.g., Hayim, 2), and others began to distinguish between U.S. governmental leaders at the state and federal level (e.g., Carly, 2). Yet the biggest shift in the children's understanding occurred in fourth grade as they began to view the U.S. head of state—though not the Israeli one—as a political and polarizing figure.

Two shifts occurred in fourth grade to usher in a change in the children's conceptions of political leadership, one developmental and one political. Developmentally, children at age 9 and 10—the typical age for a fourth grader—undergo a transition in their understanding of governmental structure and function. While many fourth graders continue to view the head of state as a benevolent leader (Greenstein, 1960, 1975), this is also the age at which children begin to understand the difference between the state and private sectors (S. W. Moore et al., 1985), the power hierarchy within the state (Berti, 1994; Connell, 1971), and the fact that government functions through institutions and not only individuals (Dennis et al., 1968, 1972).

Yet for the children in this study, this key developmental shift also happened at a time of great political change. The children were in fourth grade during the Trump–Clinton election, a time that brought not only new political leadership but also a new era of divisive politics. For the children, this election ushered in a new phase in their own political consciousness, as for the first time they viewed the U.S. president as political and polarizing, not merely benevolent. Children often develop nascent political ideas even before they can describe what "politics" means (Coles, 1986b), but for the children in this study an acute awareness of both the meaning and societal implications of politics began to emerge in fourth grade. No child, in any research interview or task, used the word "politics" before then, but at that point many of the children began to explicitly think "about politics, and how much politics there is in America" (Tzvi, 4). If in early elementary school the children uniformly believed that the president was "a good president" (David, 3), by fourth grade some believed that the new president was "going to do good things for America" (Isabelle, 4) while others thought that he had "bad ideas" (Maya, 4) and expressed concern that he "might do bad things" (Pearl, 4). The children were united in their belief that, with the election of a new president, "America is changing" (Naomi, 4) and "the world is gonna change" (Hannah, 4). They were divided in their beliefs about whether it was, in Naomi's (4) words, "changing for the better or worse."

Whereas in kindergarten through third grade, the children's conceptions of the U.S. president were uniform, by fourth grade the children began to split along political lines, for the first time resembling their parents more than one another. It is common that children's political preferences are often closely aligned with those of their parents (R. D. Hess & Torney, 1967; Jennings & Niemi, 1968; Niemi & Jennings, 1991), and by fourth grade the children began to articulate nascent forms of political partisanship that often mirrored those espoused by the adults in their immediate families. Some children explained that "if I could have voted, I think I would have voted for Donald Trump" (Hayim, 4), while others said "I don't really like Donald Trump that much" (Ryan, 5) or "I really wanted Hillary to win" (Maya, 4).

What is noteworthy about this shift is not only that the children began to differentiate from one another, but also that they began to articulate specific policies or issues with which they agreed or disagreed with the president. Whereas their younger selves liked the president out of a generic sense that "the president is trying his hardest to make this a very nice country" (Avigail, 2), in fourth and fifth grade the children spoke about their support or distrust for the president based on his approaches to the U.S. relationship with other countries, immigration policy, the environment, and other substantive issues. For example, Trump's rhetoric about building a wall on the Mexican border mattered both to the children who supported him (e.g., fifth-grader Brent's assertion that Trump's plan to "build a wall [is because] he really just wants to protect and fight for America") and those who opposed him (e.g., fourth-grader Gabe's belief that "they shouldn't be building a wall because migrant workers should be able to come and work, because that's where they get their money and [how] people have fruits and vegetables"). For the first time, the children focused their attention on the president's policies rather than the figure of the president.

For all of the children, Trump supporters and detractors alike, late elementary school was a time in which they developed a marked increase in awareness of political issues and understanding of the U.S. political context. They spoke unprompted about issues ranging from the environment (Olivia, 4) and unemployment (Gabe, 4) to Iran's nuclear capacity (Brent, 5) and U.S. negotiations with North Korea (Micah, 4). They no longer viewed the U.S. president as a symbolic figurehead automatically deserving of support from all Americans because he "can do great things for our country" (David, 3). Instead, they began to view the president as the head of his party and a person pushing for particular partisan interests. They *decided* whether or not they supported the president, and they did so based on their understanding that "he is a Republican" (Hayim, 4).

Yet the children made no equivalent shift in their understanding of the Israeli prime minister. In fourth and fifth grade, the children were just as likely as in the earlier grades to refer to the Israeli prime minister as someone who "stands up for Israel" (Elliott, 4), "cares about Israel" (Isabelle, 4), and "makes good decisions" (Olivia, 5). All of the children, regardless of their parents' views on Netanyahu's leadership and irrespective of their own beliefs about U.S. politics, continued to view Netanyahu as a benevolent head of state and figurehead of the Jewish people. They assumed that Netanyahu "knows what he's doing" (Carly, 4), can handle "all the responsibilities" (Olivia, 4), and is "looking out for the Jews" (Samantha, 5). Not a single child questioned his leadership style or any particular policies of his government, a stark contrast with their views on President Trump.

Why, then, was there such a gap between the children's views of the U.S. president and of the Israeli prime minister in late elementary school? Both Trump and Netanyahu were polarizing figures in the adult American Jewish community during and after their respective tenures as head of state, and adults in both countries clearly recognized each head of state to be partisan. Yet the children continued to view the Israeli prime minister as a symbolic figurehead for Israelis and Jews long after they understood that the U.S. president plays a political role and shapes particular policies.

The gap between the children's developmental capacities—which indicated they were capable of understanding both political issues and the political role of the head of state—and their views of the Israeli prime minister—who remained only a unifying and symbolic figurehead in their eyes—can be explained in two ways. First, while the children had viewed a change in both leader and party in the United States when they were in fourth grade, they experienced no such change in Israeli leadership. The children, all born in 2006 or 2007, had lived through Ehud Olmert's term as prime minister, but by the time they were old enough to remember, Netanyahu had already taken office. Although multiple Israeli election cycles occurred during their elementary school years, these elections only solidified Netanyahu's power, and it was only during the children's final days of middle school that he was replaced by Naftali Bennett. Hence, in the children's experience, the Israeli prime ministership—unlike the U.S. presidency—was not an office filled by different people, each functioning as the head of a particular political party; instead, the Israeli prime minister was synonymous with only one person. Thus Netanyahu remained, in the children's eyes, a leader who "commands Israel" (Tzvi, 4) and "[brings] all Jews together" (Olivia, 5), long after the U.S. president had become, for them, a contentious political figure.

Second, and even more important, the gap between the children's developmental capacity for understanding political leadership and their views on Israeli political leadership in particular stemmed from the fact that the children had little knowledge of key domestic policy issues in Israel. While the children knew quite a lot about the Israeli–Arab/Palestinian conflict and many of Israel's related foreign policy issues (see chapter 3), they knew virtually nothing about internal Israeli conversations about the economy, issues of systemic racism, or religion and state. Even Israeli policy issues that were hotly debated in the American Jewish community, such as the 2018 nation-state law and the Western Wall agreement that many American Reform and Conservative Jewish adults deeply care about (Gordis, 2019), were largely unknown to the children. Their conversations about Israel with adults, both in formal learning environments and in informal interactions with family and community members, generally focused on Israeli history or culture—not politics.

Therefore, when asked to discuss current Israeli issues, Ari (4) insisted, "I don't know any." Ryan (5) explained that he didn't know enough about policies in Israel to determine whether they are "kind or bad." In response to the question "What's been happening in Israel recently?," several children mentioned the Israeli–Arab/Palestinian conflict but not a single child spoke of any other issue in Israeli political life. These children understood, in theory, that Israel has internal issues that the political leaders seek to address. Yet they had no way of assessing whether they agreed or disagreed with the Israeli prime minister and his government in large part because they had no sense of the domestic issues with which any Israeli government grapples.

The children's limited knowledge of Israeli political issues, however, should not be mistaken for a lack of *interest* in those issues. Even though the children's commitment to participate in political life and their understanding of political issues was much higher for the United States than it was for Israel, the children themselves expressed a deep frustration that their knowledge of Israeli politics hadn't kept pace with their knowledge of U.S. politics. In fact, the children consistently spoke of being angry about the fact that they believed that the adults in their lives had concealed from them important information that would have allowed them to better understand Israeli civic and political life. The sections below examine moments when the children expressed dissatisfaction with the limits of their own understanding and begged to know more about the very civic and political issues they were aware that they did not sufficiently understand.

Summary of Children's Political Engagement

In the early grades of elementary school, the children did not spend much time thinking about the role of politics in society. They did not envision themselves as participants in a political system, nor did they view heads of state as political leaders. By fourth grade, the children began to understand that one important element of civic engagement is developing political beliefs. They viewed themselves as future voters in U.S. elections, and they could articulate clear stances about both contemporary political issues and U.S. political leaders. Yet while the children came to understand the U.S. president as a politically polarizing figure, they continued to view the Israeli prime minister as apolitical. This reflected a larger gap between children's developmental capacity to understand politics and their limited understanding of politics in Israel in particular. Even as they ended elementary school, the children could name no particular political issues in Israel beyond those related to the Israeli–Arab/Palestinian conflict. As the pages below show, the children themselves were actually quite upset as they became aware of this gap.

Why Didn't You Tell Me?

In order for young people to understand civic and political issues, they must understand that societies grapple with profound questions about how people ought to live together (D. E. Hess & McAvoy, 2014). Many of these questions spark significant disagreement (D. E. Hess, 2009) and matter deeply even as both experts and the general public lack consensus about how to proceed (J. Zimmerman & Robertson, 2017). The children in this study developed an emerging understanding of contentious and contested issues in the United States during their elementary school years. Yet the same children often had very little sense that Israel is a society that, like all societies, grapples with public conversations and public disagreements about matters of collective importance.

In early elementary school (K–1), the children were generally content without this knowledge. They never expressed awareness of, or frustration with, their own limited understanding. But beginning in second grade, the children began to realize that they were ill-equipped to make sense of key issues related to the Israeli public square. Many of the children recounted moments of epiphany in which they realized that even though they cared about both the United States and Israel, their understanding of the latter had not kept pace with their understanding of the former; they were missing key information about Israeli civic and political life. In those moments, the children expressed profound anger at the adults in their lives who, they believed, had insufficiently prepared them to engage with important matters affecting the Israeli and global Jewish communities. The stories told by Gia and Avigail illustrate this larger pattern in the children's reflections.

Gia's Visit to the Western Wall

Third-grader Gia sat cross-legged in her chair, her back straight and rigid. Her long braids dangled on either side of her face, often covering the large dark eyes that looked earnestly ahead. Gia has always been unfailingly polite, though adults sometimes have to strain to hear what she has to say. And so it came as somewhat of a shock that Gia, one of the most demure children in the study, was the first to use what the children call "the s word": stupid. She hurled the epithet not at another human being, but at a place that only a year earlier she had described as a magical wonderland: HaKotel HaMaaravi, the Western Wall.

Gia first visited Israel with her family when she was a baby, and although she had no memory of the visit, she often spoke of how special it must have been to be near the greatness of the Kotel (Wall). Like so many of the children in the study, Gia (grades K–2) viewed the Western Wall as a place where wishes and dreams come true. For these children, the Kotel had the power of a fairy godmother: A wish there need only be articulated and it would be magically granted. Gia knew of the tradition that Jews traveled from around the world to place prayers and supplications, rolled on small pieces of paper, in the cracks of the Kotel's ancient walls. Even in kindergarten Gia imagined herself standing by the time-worn stones, adding her own prayers to those of so many others. It was, in her mind, a holy religious site.

Then, in the summer before third grade, Gia and her family visited Israel for the first time that she could remember, and their trip included a visit to the place she had often dreamed of visiting. Yet as she stood at the large plaza that serves as an entryway to the Kotel, she realized that the Western Wall of her imagination was a place quite different from the actual place that loomed before her eyes. In all of the times she had learned about the Kotel in her Jewish school, and all of the times she had heard her rabbis and teachers talk of its ancient stones, until she stood before it Gia had no sense of how the physical space of the modern Western Wall is laid out. What drew her attention were neither the stones nor the pilgrims placing prayers in their cracks—the two aspects of the Wall she had been prepared to see. Instead, Gia saw only the *mechitzah* (partition) between male and female worshippers, which in her eyes was a massive barrier.

Gia's initial reaction to seeing the Kotel was one of shock. As a child raised in the Reform movement, where men and women pray together, Gia was surprised to find that not only were men and women at the Kotel divided, but the men's side is significantly larger than the women's side. When, in kindergarten, her class took a pretend trip to Israel on a mock El Al plane, and visited a reconstructed Kotel in the school's multipurpose room, that Kotel had not been gender divided. Yet as she looked at the Kotel that actually stood in Jerusalem, the first thing she noticed was the smaller women's side, and it upset her. She explained, "Separating the women from the men is wrong because they should stay together. You see how the women's side is smaller than the men's side? I don't think that's fair!" Seeing the layout of the space felt as if Jewish men were saying, in Gia's words, "Oh, we don't care about you. We'll get the bigger side; you'll get the smaller side. You have to stay home cooking and cleaning. We'll go to school, and that kind of stuff."

But Gia's initial feelings paled in comparison to what happened as it slowly dawned on her what the layout of the Kotel's physical space would mean for *her*. Gia and her brothers have two fathers, and so as she stood at the entrance to the Western Wall and took in the gender-segregated space for the first time, a terrifying thought crossed her mind: If she, as an 8-year-old girl, wanted to touch the walls of the Kotel, would she need to brave it alone? As her brothers and her dads went to one side, would she be sent to the other without any adults? She felt utterly alone in a place where she had expected to feel a sense of connection to all of the Jewish worshippers who surrounded and preceded her.

In the end, Gia explained, her tour guide "showed me a little section where families can pray together. Women and men could stay together." There, at Robinson's Arch, Gia and her family were able to remain with one another. But the moment of panic she felt was enough to transform the entire experience. As she stood before the ancient stones, Gia buried her belief in the Kotel as a magical space and resurrected it as a political place. She started asking questions about why the Kotel was laid out in this way, and as she began to understand that the space functions as an Orthodox synagogue, she came to see that a place she had been taught about as a symbol of Jewish unity was also a place of contentious intra-Jewish disputes about the power of the Orthodox rabbinate in Israeli society. She wanted to know more about "the rules" of that society, and how and why they had been made.

After returning to the United States, Gia continued to reflect on her experiences at the Kotel. Year after year she revisited the same story, each time making sure to explain her "mixed feelings" about it (Gia, 5). On one level, Gia felt "happy" that she had an opportunity to visit a place she had only imagined before. She expressed gratitude that the ancient stones are "there for me to see, and my dads to see, and when I grow up, my children to see. It makes me feel happy that Jews are still praying on that wall" (Gia, 3).

Yet the generally mild-mannered Gia also repeatedly expressed feeling "angry" about her experiences at the Kotel. Some of that anger stemmed from her belief that the Kotel had come to symbolize a place where "women can't": Women can't have a prayer space of equal size to men's, women can't wear a *kippah* (religious head covering) or a *tallit* (prayer shawl), and—worst of all—women can't stand and pray with their fathers (Gia, 3). Even more profound, however, was the anger she expressed *toward* her fathers. Why did they wait for her to see the Wall before they explained that "the [Orthodox] rabbis made up the rule[s]" about how it functions (Gia, 3)? And why hadn't her teachers explained to her any of the real issues—political or spatial—that she experienced at the Wall? Why had these adults left her to imagine a beautiful and spiritual prayer space when what she encountered was a much more complicated and unpleasant reality? In middle school, Gia explained what her younger self had only begun to articulate: When thinking about Israel and the adults who taught her about it, "I'm disappointed that they do many things right, except in my eyes, this" (Gia, 6).

Avigail's Move to Israel

The child of two Israeli parents—an Israeli father living in Israel, and an Israeli-born mother who had come to the United States as a young adult and who had raised Avigail in a bilingual (Hebrew and English) home in Los Angeles—Avigail spent the first part of her childhood immensely proud of her connections to the state of Israel and the Hebrew language. As a kindergartner, Avigail would say things like, "Israel is meant for Hebrew, and I'm meant for Hebrew" and "I really, really, really want to be in Israel. Because Israel is meant for me." As she talked about Israel she consistently tied herself to it, and envisioned both her present and her future as bound together with a place that, in her words, was "a special place for Jewish people."

Despite her family's connection to Israel, Avigail (K) hadn't actually been there since she was a baby, and she had no recollection of that trip. Nonetheless, she had created a clear mental image of what she believed Israel to be: a place of great "caring," a term that she and many of her peers framed as a key component of civic responsibility (Hauver, 2019).

Israel was not, in her young imagination, a perfect place. Avigail (K) envisioned Israel as a particularly violent place where "bad guys" attacked Jews and sometimes even killed Jewish children in horrifically violent ways "like shooting people and swording people, cutting them to half." But she also believed that Israel was where Jews worked to make their imperfect reality a better place for all—for Jews and for "people that's not even Jewish." It was a place where Jews could contribute to the collective and, in her words, "make Israel a better country."

Then, in the summer before Avigail started third grade, she and her mother moved to Israel. Overnight, Avigail went from being the strongest Hebrew speaker in her class to the weakest, and from the child who best understood Israeli culture to the one who least understood it. Part of what Avigail experienced was culture shock of the kind that any child might encounter in moving to a new country. She was taken aback by the differences in school schedules, the lack of familiar stores and brands, and she had an especially hard time adjusting to what she experienced as markedly different gender norms in how "girls play with the boys" at her school in the United States and her school in Israel.

Yet Avigail also experienced a profound sense of loss as she realized that the Israel of her early imagination did not live up to the reality she was experiencing in her day-to-day life as a new Israeli resident in one particularly important way: Avigail's imagined Israel was a place where Jews treated one another and the world around them with the utmost care and respect. She was shocked when she realized that in Israel, "when an ambulance comes and it's an emergency, the cars don't go to the side." She was upset when she discovered that in her neighborhood in Israel, cats roamed the street and no people stepped forward to care for them. "It's not really good for the cats," she lamented. Most of all, she was devastated to realize that Jews in Israel littered on the streets of their own Jewish state. She explained, "You know how some people litter in America? I thought that because this is the Jews, they won't litter, but they do." Her belief that "because they're Jews, they [shouldn't] litter because it's in the Torah" collided with her lived experience in which she watched Jewish people drop trash in public places.

Like the other children in this study, Avigail believed that all community members are responsible for caring for people, animals, and the physical world. These three categories were central to her understanding of civic responsibility, and yet she watched her neighbors blatantly ignore what she believed to be in the interest of the common good on all three fronts. As this occurred, she felt a great sense of anger bubbling up within her.

Avigail did not direct her fury at the Israelis who were, in her eyes, doing great damage to people in ambulances, stray cats, and the neighborhood itself. Instead, she lashed out at her mother. She was angry not that her mother had taken her away from her friends and the life that was familiar to her, but instead that her mother hadn't done more to prepare her to make sense of Israeli society. She turned to her mother and screamed, "I didn't really know that much about Israel when I was there [in the United States]. You only told me the things that I already knew!" (Avigail, 3). Implicit in her words was a harsh condemnation: She felt she had been insufficiently educated.

As she imagined talking to her friends back in the United States about life in Israel, Avigail wanted to adjust the images she thought they were getting about her new place of residence. The idea of Jews from different ethnic backgrounds living in harmony? "I want to tell them about Israel that it's a really nice place to be, but if you're a Persian [it's best] not to live here." There is too much racism in Israel, she explained, so "I'm recommending you don't come." The belief that all Jews, regardless of religious denomination, could coexist? She imagined telling her friends, "Some people are religious and some are not, and that's really hard." As she thought about all of the tensions that existed between different Jewish subgroups in Israeli society, she lamented, "I didn't know those kinds of things. I never learned those kinds of things."

Avigail wanted to teach her friends in Los Angeles what she felt she should have learned before she moved, but her friends were far away. So instead she turned to her mother and she screamed, "Why didn't you tell me?"

Children's Righteous Anger

Gia and Avigail are children of loving, thoughtful parents and students of talented, caring educators, and their stories of frustration with these adults whom they deeply love demand attention. Over the course of several years, Gia maintained her disappointment over the fact that her parents and teachers had, in her mind, ill prepared her to understand the Kotel as a civic-political space and not only a religious site. Avigail expressed anger at her mother and the educators who, she believed, had insufficiently helped her understand how her conceptions of civic responsibility might (not) graft onto the Israeli context. These girls, while exceptional in both the clarity with which they expressed their emotions and the frequency with which they revisited these stories, were not alone in their outrage.

They were, in fact, joined by many of their peers who increasingly voiced a shared frustration as they grew. As discussed in chapter 3, many of the children exploded in anger as they grasped for the word "Palestinian" or struggled to understand Palestinian narratives to which they had limited access. Jacob (2) literally tugged on his hair as he screamed, "Why won't anyone tell me what they're called?" Rina (3) repeatedly shouted, "I'm so angry!" when she thought about how her day school teachers had not taught her what she believed to be sufficient Hebrew, which in her mind was the key to understanding important conversations happening in Israeli society. "I need more direction!" she shouted. Maya (4) was "mad" that no adults helped her sort through what was so confusing to her: a society based on the Jewish ideal that all human beings "are created equal" in which a public space like the Kotel could "separate the women and the men." After all, she knew from reading books about U.S. history that "separate" was not "equal," and yet no adults talked to her about how to reconcile that with the fact that in parts of Israel, men and women are "supposed to be separate." Hayim (5), using more precocious words to reflect the same sentiment, yelled in frustration, "I just want to learn more about [Israel's] political climate and its relationship with other countries!"

At every grade level from second grade onward, the children expressed that they were "angry," "mad," and "frustrated." In order to understand the children's anger, it is necessary to consider both the objects of their frustration—at whom the children were "mad"—and the subjects of their anger—the topics about which the children did, and did not, feel angry.

The children expressed anger primarily at their own parents and teachers, the adults they most love and trust, and this fact challenges the prevailing discourse about young American Jews and Israel. For Jewish public intellectuals have argued about whether young Jews' anger stems from what Israel *does*—the actions that Israel takes that are antithetical to the overwhelmingly liberal population of young American Jews (Beinart, 2012)—or whether it is a pushback against what Israel *is*—signifying young American Jews' discomfort with Jewish nationalism and ethnic democracy (Gordis, 2019). Yet these American Jewish children, as clear and articulate in their expressions of anger as any teenager or young adult, were not angry at Israel at all. They were, instead, angry at the adults in their lives responsible for *teaching* them about Israel, and their frustration was more about their own education regarding Israeli civic and political life than about Israeli politics itself. Like older Jewish teens who reflect on their elementary school learning and feel disillusioned by its simplicity (Reingold, 2017), these children expressed deep frustration that they "didn't learn" (Lior, 3) what they most wanted to.

On one level, the children's expressions of anger appear to be an analogue to the outrage of Jewish young adults affiliated with the progressive Jewish organization IfNotNow. A movement of young Jews committed to "ending American Jewish support for the [Israeli] Occupation [of Palestine]" (S. Zimmerman & Lieberman, 2017), IfNotNow has both political and educational aims. The name of one of its education campaigns, #YouNeverToldMe, is nearly identical to the pressing question voiced by third-grader Avigail, "Why didn't you tell me?" Young adult participants of IfNotNow voice "explicit resentment at their elders and educators" (Omer, 2019, p. 32), upset that their Jewish educational experiences did not address Palestinian narratives (A. Cooper, 2017; Fishman, 2017) or "[teach] them to confront the injustice of the Occupation" (Heisler, 2017).

Yet in two respects the children's anger was much broader than that of the #YouNeverToldMe young adults. First, #YouNeverToldMe supporters are politically progressive, whereas the children in this study who expressed anger come from both liberal and conservative households and themselves affiliate with both Democratic and Republican positions. Avigail, for example, was "happy that Trump won the election" (4) and was "grateful for what he's doing" (5), a position that IfNotNow supporters eschew. (As discussed above, the children did not have as clear of a sense of how they might affiliate on Israeli political issues.) While progressive young adults say #YouNeverToldMe, children with both liberal and conservative political leanings ask, "Why didn't you tell me?" Second, supporters of IfNotNow's #YouNeverToldMe campaign believe they were "betrayed by the institutional Jewish world which told us stories of Israel's glories but no stories of the horror and impact of occupation on Palestinians" (Brammer-Shlay, 2017). Some children, like Jacob, were similarly upset about not being taught enough about Palestinian experiences, and they appear to be responding to a similar omission of Palestinian narratives in Jewish educational institutions as IfNotNow. Yet as a whole, the children asked "Why didn't you tell me?" about a wide range of civic and political issues that included Israel's relationship with Palestinians but also the contentious politics regarding the role of

the Orthodox rabbinate in Israel, racism in Israeli society, and other issues related to "Israel's political climate" (Hayim, 5).

That so many of the children expressed anger at their parents and
teachers could be explained in two ways: as a healthy and normal process
of child development, or as a cautionary tale for parents and educators.
The former assumes that children always build their initial conceptions
of the world on an illusory simplicity, and a process of disillusionment
is natural and expected as children come to realize the complexity of the
world and the fallibility of the adults in their lives (Winnicott, 1991/1971).
The latter presumes that expressions of anger are one important way that
children communicate a sense of injustice and a desire to bring about
change (Grindheim, 2014). In this case, the latter explanation is more
compelling because these children did not express a general sense of
disillusionment as they came to increasingly recognize the complexities
of the world; instead, they targeted their anger at specific issues. The
children never described feeling angry or even frustrated at their parents and teachers as they considered historical questions (see chapter 2)
or questions of belonging (see chapter 1). Never once did a child yell in
frustration as he tried to explain the abstraction of a symbolic homeland
or as she attempted to tell stories about a past she never lived through. In
these instances, even when the children recognized that there was much
they did not yet understand about the world, they described their emotional states primarily as "curious" (Rina, 3; Olivia, 4) or "fascinated" (Elliott, 5; Samantha, 4). Yet they frequently raised their voices or described
themselves as "angry" (Rina, 3; Avigail, 3) when striving to understand
civic and political questions—questions focused on how people ought to
live together in society (D. E. Hess & McAvoy, 2014).

The children's anger over what they perceived as a failure to teach
them the concepts necessary to grapple with these questions mirrored
their language in only one other context: when talking about racism.
Gia (3) was "angry at some white people" when she thought about the
American legacy of slavery and racism. Rina (5) was similarly angered,
saying, "It's so unfair that [in our society] we treat people by what they
believe in and what color their skin is." Avigail (3) was incensed by comments she overheard in Israel that had racist overtones against Jews of
Middle Eastern origin.

The thread that tied together the two contexts in which the children expressed anger—when reflecting on racism and when speaking about the fact that they "wish that the [adults] taught me more" (Avigail, 3)— was a sense of righteous indignation aimed at fixing a broken system (Ellenson, 2008). Though systemic racism is both more insidious and more entrenched, the children's descriptions of their emotions surrounding racism and the fact that the adults "don't tell me much" (Rina, 3) were identical. The parallelism signaled that in both cases the children believed that a great injustice had been done, and they wanted to see a change.

Summary of Children's Righteous Anger

Despite the fact that the children in this study viewed themselves as responsible for caring for both U.S. and Israeli societies, they often had very little understanding of public conversations and debates regarding important civic and political issues in Israel. In the initial years of elementary school (K–1), these children appeared perfectly content without that understanding. Yet beginning in second grade, the children started to describe themselves as "angry," "mad," and "frustrated" about the fact that they were missing—and knew they were missing— information that was essential for helping them understand some of the most critical issues in contemporary Israeli society. The children's anger was directed at the most trusted adults in their lives, their loving parents and caring teachers, whom the children asked with great frustration, "Why didn't you tell me?"

Conclusion

Civic and political questions—questions that surface discussions and disagreements about what constitutes the common good (Reich, 2019) and how people ought to live together (D. E. Hess & McAvoy, 2014)— lie at the heart of democratic societies. Understanding and deliberating about civic and political matters is a *learned* process; it requires people to develop, over time, the ability to weigh multiple and often competing values, consider evidence, listen compassionately to others, build arguments, and identify compromises.

Children and youth can both express interest in and reflect thought-fully about civic and political matters (Barrett & Pachi, 2019; Hauver, 2019), yet civic and political questions are often absent from school cur-ricula. As political polarization in the United States grows (Abramowitz, 2013), one common response is to "keep politics out" of the classroom (D. E. Hess & McAvoy, 2014, p. 20). Diana Hess, a social scientist of edu-cation and expert on classroom political discussions, explains, "Many adults either want schools to mirror their ideas or fear that adding con-troversy to the curriculum *creates* controversy, as opposed to more sim-ply teaching young people how to deal more effectively with the kinds of political controversies that exist outside of school" (2009, p. 24). The result is that at the very time that engaged members of the public have to make increasingly stark choices among polarized positions (Abramow-itz, 2010), young people have less practice learning to understand and deliberate about these matters. As historian Jonathan Zimmerman and philosopher Emily Robertson argue, "Our schools teach many things. For the most part, though, they have not taught us how to engage in reasoned, informed debates across our myriad differences" (2017, p. 4).

Jewish educational institutions in the United States reflect this larger trend, and nowhere is this more glaringly true than in Israel educa-tion. Even as questions about civic and political matters in Israel are among the most contested issues in contemporary American Jewish life (Kurtzer et al., 2019; D. Waxman, 2016), "strikingly few" Jewish educa-tors address "Israel's political situation or social challenges the country currently faces" (Pomson et al., 2014, p. 12)—the very kinds of ques-tions that the children in this study begged to know more about. As sociopsychologist Bethamie Horowitz explains, many Jewish educators "bracket the political issues because these are so divisive within the Jew-ish communal-organizational world, and because [they believe that] much work in Israel education, particularly as it relates to young chil-dren, is separate from the political" (2012, p. 15). Therefore, even when politics are taught as part of a larger educational trajectory, they are not typically addressed with elementary-age children.

The tendency to avoid political conflict is an especially striking omis-sion in Jewish education. Integral to the study of classical Jewish texts is the value of *machloket l'shem shamayim*—literally meaning "argument for the sake of heaven" and often framed for children as "constructive conflict" (Roth, 2017). Jewish schools have long encouraged differing interpretations of religious texts, resting on the assumption that "there is no one authoritative understanding of the text, but rather a range of views" (Holtz, 2013, p. 35). An engagement with morally complex issues that arise from those texts is also common in Jewish classrooms (Z. R. Hassenfeld, 2019a). Yet questions about Israeli civic and political life—also morally complex and subject to multiple different viewpoints—do not receive the same treatment. Even as Jewish political advocacy organizations have proliferated and flourished (Sasson, 2014), Jewish political education has not.

Nonetheless, understanding civic and political matters—including the most highly contested issues—is necessary for making sense of any democratic society. In fact, the topics about Israel that are typically taught to children in Jewish educational institutions—geography, history, arts, and culture—are all implicated by civic and political questions (Sinclair, 2013). There is no way to deeply understand Israel's borders, Zionist history, or Israeli music without knowing that Israelis and Jews, past and present, have articulated different visions for the common good and worked toward enacting differing approaches to living together—both within Israel's borders and as part of a larger world.

The children in this study clearly articulated the unintended consequences of educational systems—both American and Jewish—that gloss over civic and political questions or defer them to the teenage and young adult years. In the early grades of elementary school, the children expressed unmitigated excitement as they spoke of learning about Israel. They understood that children can make an impact on their communities, and they viewed themselves as responsible for contributing to both U.S. and Israeli societies. Yet as the children grew, they came to believe that their own understanding about Israel was, in Maya's words (4), "not enough" to allow them to do so. Many felt a great sense of injustice—and expressed profound anger—when they realized that they were ill-equipped to make sense of important issues in Israeli civic and political life. They believed, in Avigail's (4) words, that they should have been taught "much more."

The children's anger ought to be taken seriously. It illuminates both that civic and political matters can be meaningful to children and that current educational approaches must shift if they are to address children's concerns. Thus, as Diana Hess argues, it is a "mistake for schools to wait until students are older to introduce these discussions" (2009, p. 168). The elementary school years have great potential for helping students develop the skills and dispositions needed to understand and participate in communal conversations about civic and political life.

Taking children's thoughts and feelings seriously necessitates developing new educational frameworks that are simultaneously more developmentally sensitive and more attuned to civic and political questions, including contested ones. For American Jewish education in particular, this will require educators and parents to focus less on cultivating personal connections to Israel (Chazan, 2016; Horowitz, 2012) and more on helping young people investigate and deliberate about matters of collective discourse and disagreement. It is to such an educational framework that I turn in the book's conclusion, outlining an approach that both honors the thoughts and feelings of children and is rooted in a more explicit commitment to civic and political education.

Conclusion

*"I Want to Learn More": Next Steps for Children and the Adults
Who Support Their Learning*

It is May 2020, Keren is in seventh grade, and she is living through what
she likens to "a zombie apocalypse." Keren's home in Los Angeles is under
"safer at home" orders due to the Covid-19 crisis, and "nobody's out.
Everyone is inside. It's all gloomy [and] everything is totally upside down."

"One of the difficult things about [life during the Covid-19 pandemic]
is 'synagogue' online," she explains, drawing large quotation marks in the
air when she says the word "synagogue." "It's just not the same. When
everyone is together in person, you can actually feel like you're *with* everyone. But when you're just sitting on your couch and watching the
livestream, you're alone, not together."

Despite feeling isolated, Keren acknowledges that her life has shifted
much less than that of other children her age. "It's not as big of a difference for me because I'm homeschooled. So the school is pretty much
the same." While other children lamented that the shuttering of schools
made life "really different and really hard to cope with" (Rina, 7), much
of Keren's routine has stayed the same. For her, the biggest shift has been
the canceling of afternoon activities, which means that she has extra
time to play piano, read, and explore topics that interest her. One of
those topics is the Israeli political system.

After Keren's Hebrew tutor mentioned that "the new government [in
Israel] is going to be sworn in," she explained, "I got interested and I
read some more about the topic." Keren scoured multiple online sources,
none mediated or suggested by the adults in her life, about the newly
forming Israeli government. She explained:

> The leader of the Likud [political party] is Netanyahu, and the leader
> of Blue and White [political party] is Benny Gantz. So, I was looking at

what their agreement was for their coalition, because it took them forever to finally do something. And so I found out that . . . [if this plan works] Netanyahu will get one and a half years of being the prime minister, and then Gantz will get the rest. Together they have 69 seats out of 120, which is enough. They made a coalition with a few other smaller parties, and now they have around close to 90, which is a very big deal compared to the rest of the elections. And I read about how they're splitting all of the ministries, I guess like Ministry of Justice, Economy, all that. So yeah, [I was] just looking it up.

Despite doing so much independent research, Keren insists, "I [still] want to learn more about the politics in Israel, [and] how the government works." Keren was not alone in her desire to understand more about the Israeli political system. In fact, many of the adolescents expressed an interest in better understanding both "politics in Israel" (Ryan, 7) and "wars in the Middle East" (Jacob, 7). "I don't really know much about them," lamented Lailah (7), "but I know if I had a class about it, I would ask a lot of questions." As these middle schoolers reflected on their prior learning as elementary school students, they repeatedly insisted that they had not learned enough about either the political tensions within Israeli society or the conflict between Israel and its neighbors. As seventh-grader Rina put it, "We should see the bigger picture and not just a tree. We should see the whole forest." But, she continued, in her experience adults talk with children about some "trees" like biblical stories and not other "trees" like war and political conflict. In Keren's (7) words, that means young people like her know only "half of the story."

Lest the words of Keren and her peers be mistaken for the newly burgeoning political interests of young teens, these middle schoolers were reflecting—albeit in more precise language—the very points that they had been making since the middle of elementary school. By second or third grade, most of the children in this study began insisting that they needed more help making sense of conflicts *between* Israel and the Arab world, and by fourth grade most children also expressed frustration and anger that they didn't have sufficient context for making sense of civic and political conflicts *within* Israeli society and the global Jewish community.

Three aspects of these children's reflections are noteworthy and form the bedrock for the conclusions offered in this chapter. First, Keren and her peers insisted, year after year, that they "care about" and "want to learn more about" Israel and Israelis (Keren, 6). Keren's own interest stemmed from her belief that "we're supposed to care about all other Jews" (6); she viewed learning about Israel as one aspect of her own Jewish life. Second, many of the children expressed a particular interest in learning more about inter- and intrasocietal conflict in particular, and they voiced frustration or anger because they felt that they had insufficient support from adults when attempting to understand that "half of the story" (7). Third, in the absence of adult guidance, Keren and her peers did not tune out of conversations about Israel; instead, they "logged on" and "looked up" (7) the information they felt they had been missing. When taken as a whole, these three trends in the children's reflections offer a profound challenge to adults who care about children's intellectual and emotional well-being.

Throughout this book, I have argued that children invest a great deal of intellectual and emotional effort in making sense of how countries and societies do, and ought to, function. Yet even as Jewish children build foundational conceptions of civics, history, and politics in both the United States and Israel, they often feel ill-equipped to make sense of contested issues in contemporary Jewish and Israeli life. Taking children's ideas seriously requires a shift in educational practices in order to help children better navigate a world in which people disagree, both within and between countries and communities. This conclusion reviews this argument and how it situates children's thoughts and feelings at its center. It then turns to concrete suggestions about what might be done to shift educational practices in order to help children better understand and navigate a world in which contested issues and polarized positions are, increasingly, the norm.

Taking Children' Ideas Seriously: A Review

In the previous chapters, we have seen that children think carefully and care deeply about many of the complex questions that sit at the heart of civics, history, and politics: What values do and should animate country and nation, and what constitutes home and homeland? What are the stories that matter to who we are, and how might we narrate these stories for different audiences? Why does intractable conflict persist, and what might be done to alleviate it? What does it mean to be a responsible member of society, and how ought communities care for people, animals, and the environment?

To argue that children think carefully and care deeply about these questions is not to say that children think like adults. It is only over time, as we saw early in chapter 1, that children are able to sort through some of the ways that countries function as both real and symbolic spaces bounded both by geography and by national culture and values. Children's stories of the past, as chapter 2 demonstrates, are not chronological or evidentiary in the ways that historians frame history. And there is much that children do not yet understand—and know that they do not yet understand—about political and geopolitical conflict, as chapters 3 and 4 have illuminated.

To argue that children spend a great deal of intellectual and emotional energy on these questions is not a claim that children think about adult questions. It is, rather, to say the opposite: that many of the questions that adults, at times, assume are not appropriate for children are, in fact, the very questions that matter deeply to them, that capture their interest, and that animate their imaginations and their Internet searches.

The care with which children think about how countries and societies function is evident as they reflect on a range of issues and questions related to civics, history, and politics. In chapter 1, we saw that elementary-age children begin to understand not only that countries exist as distinct geographic and cultural entities but also that different countries and societies prize different values. As they grow, children develop increasingly multilayered theories both about the values that animate different societies and about what it means to be part of, or connected to, such societies. In chapter 2, we explored how children begin to think deeply about countries' origin stories well before children's own stories adhere to the conventions of history. Throughout elementary school, children are capable of both retelling and reflecting on historical stories, and by late elementary school they can deliberately craft different versions of historical narratives for different audiences. Children also think about, and attempt to understand, conflicts both between and within countries, as we saw in chapters 3 and 4 respectively. Yet, if the children in this study are any indication, children often receive little adult guidance to help them make sense of political and geopolitical conflict. They are missing—and are frustrated that they are missing—key information and contextual understanding that would help them make sense of current and past events. The children report that their formal schooling; their informal conversations with parents, grandparents, teachers, and clergy; and their independent Internet searches all leave them simultaneously interested in learning more and flailing as they seek to comprehend a world in which people disagree about important issues.

After paying careful attention to the experiences and reflections of the children in this study for more than nine consecutive years, it seems clear that their learning about Israel is marked, in equal measures, by curious interest and by frustration and anger. They are intrinsically curious about the world around them even at moments when their schools are not structured around children's interests and explorations (Engel, 2011), and they wish they had more adult help thinking about a topic they find "really interesting" (Caleb, 7). In short, the children often view Israel as "one of my favorite things" (Micah, 2), but they experience their education *about* Israel as something that "makes me feel frustrated!" (Rina, 3).

Pillars of Education for Children

This disconnect between children's interest in learning and their experiences of learning need not be the case. It is certainly possible to create the kinds of educational experiences that children deserve (Kohn, 1999). Such education must be structured around children's interests, questions, and concerns, and thus it must be undergirded by three pillars: (1) It must be developmentally sensitive, responsive to the particular ways that children think and feel. Given that how children think is often discipline-specific, developmentally sensitive education must build upon an understanding of how children grapple with ideas and questions related to a specific subject matter. (2) It must allow children to ask and investigate the kinds of questions that capture and hold their attention. Questions that sustain children's interests over time are not the kinds of common questions asked in elementary classrooms, to which the teacher has predetermined an acceptable answer or set of answers (Edwards & Westgate, 2005). Rather, children express sustained interest in questions that I call prism questions because they necessarily reflect a spectrum of human beliefs, opinions, and experiences. (3) It must explicitly help children make sense of civic and political matters about which people disagree. In other words, contested questions and issues—not settled ones—ought to be centered in the conversations that adults have with children.

In the pages that follow, we will explore each of these pillars that ought to uphold educational experiences for elementary-age children. As has been true throughout this book, we will use the particular case of Israel education to highlight issues that have broader implications for children's education writ large, drawing upon the words of sociologist Sara Lawrence-Lightfoot, who explains that "in the particular resides the universal" (1997, p. 14).

1. Developmentally Sensitive

The importance of developmentally appropriate practice is certainly not a new idea in education (Bredekamp, 1987). It is a vision of best practice in which learning activities for young children are designed to be age appropriate, socioculturally appropriate, and appropriate to the particular needs of the individual learner (Goldstein, 2015). It relies on a deep understanding of the stages that children undergo at different ages (Wood, 2007), as well as a respect for the values, beliefs, and social and cultural practices of the learners' communities (Bredekamp & Copple, 1997).

Developmentally appropriate practice is a particular educational approach rooted in early childhood, a period of life that bridges early childhood education and early elementary education (Copple et al., 2013, 2014a, 2014b). Yet many of the principles of developmentally appropriate practice, including a commitment to children's agency and a belief that children have both common progressions of development and individual differences (National Association for the Education of Young Children, 2020), can apply to middle childhood and adolescence as well. Therefore, I use the term "developmentally appropriate practice" to refer to the important ideas and literature that have emerged from a deep commitment to understanding and honoring the developmental needs of young children in particular, and the term "developmentally sensitive education" to refer to a broader approach that embraces age-appropriate and socioculturally appropriate practices for learners of any age.

Scholars and practitioners of education have developed discipline-specific visions for what constitutes developmentally appropriate practice. Drawing upon a deep commitment to meeting the developmental needs of young learners in particular (Copple & Bredekamp, 2009), there is a growing understanding of developmentally appropriate education in mathematics (e.g., Seo & Ginsburg, 2004; Stipek & Johnson, 2020), science (Chaille & Britain, 1997; Yoon & Onchwari, 2006), and language and literacy (Elliott & Olliff, 2008; Neuman et al., 2000). Situated at the heart of this work are two interrelated assumptions about education: that "any subject can be taught effectively in some intellectually honest form to a child at any stage of development" (Bruner, 1960, p. 33), and that no child is too young to begin to explore the key questions at the heart of these disciplines (Kahn, 2021).

Despite the importance of developmentally appropriate practice for making schools places that are good for children, it is certainly not the case that all elementary school classrooms are driven by children's developmental needs. In fact, elementary schools are increasingly places where children are asked to "sit still and pay attention" rather than invited to investigate the questions and problems that capture their imaginations (Paley, 2004, p. 43). Problems of developmentally inappropriate practice are especially common in the early elementary grades (Jackson, 2009; Zeng & Zeng, 2005). For even when teachers of elementary-age students *believe* in the importance of age-appropriate classrooms, their *practice* does not always follow suit (A. Parker & Neuharth-Pritchett, 2006).

In Jewish education, this challenge is compounded by the fact that scholarship has lagged behind other disciplines in articulating the "ages and stages" of Jewish learning. Despite recent inroads into understanding the experiences and ideas of young Jewish learners as they engage with biblical and rabbinic texts (e.g., Z. R. Hassenfeld, 2016, 2019b; Kent & Cook, 2019), Hebrew language (e.g., Benor et al., 2020; Walters, 2019), Jewish history (e.g., J. Hassenfeld, 2016; M. L. Katz & Kress, 2018; Reingold, 2018), and other subject areas that comprise Jewish learning, there remains little understanding of the developmental stages that young learners undergo. Thus while Jewish educational institutions often tout their own developmentally appropriate practices, there remains little shared understanding of what might constitute developmentally sensitive Jewish education.

In Israel education in particular, scholars have long raised concerns that Jewish educational settings often "communicate developmentally inappropriate messages" (Pomson et al., 2014, p. 48) and do not spiral curriculum and instruction "in a developmentally sensitive fashion" (Pomson & Deitcher, 2010, p. 60). It is clear that Israel education must reorient in order to become more developmentally sensitive (Gerber & Mazor, 2003; Horowitz, 2012; Sinclair, 2014). But what would developmentally sensitive Israel education entail?

On the most basic level, a developmentally sensitive approach to Israel education would build upon an understanding of how children think about the particular subject matter of Israel. Yet common practices in Jewish education regularly both overshoot and underestimate children's developmental readiness to engage with particular ideas and concepts.

The starkest example of overreaching children's capacities occurs in the ways that Jewish educational resources commonly use the geography and terrain of Israel as a way of focusing children's gaze. Many of the picture books designed to introduce young children to Israel take readers on a journey through Israel's landmarks: the Dead Sea, the Kotel (Western Wall) in Jerusalem, the beach in Tel Aviv, and other locations (e.g., Balsley & Fischer, 2016; Gehl, 2015; Groner, 2004; Newman, 2011; Rauchwerger, 2018). Similarly, many of the textbooks designed specifically for children—and thus the curricular choices that educators make based on these books—are structured around Israel's terrain and famous landmarks; chapters focus on the particular geographies and cultures of Jerusalem, Tel Aviv, Eilat, and the Galilee (e.g., Blumenthal, 2003; Feldman, 1995; Gervitz, 2009). Yet understanding geographic location, and even more so the interaction between a city's culture and its location and terrain, was conceptually out of reach for most of the children in this study in the early elementary grades (K–3). Even when they could name and identify landmarks like the Kotel, they had little sense of the distances—physical and cultural—between different places in Israel, and they had no sense of the kinds of people who might inhabit different kinds of spaces. In fact, it is not uncommon for children to struggle with spatial-geographical understanding and in particular with the nested nature of geography that would allow them to make sense of the fact that landmarks are places within cities, which exist within countries, which are part of larger geographic regions (Barrett, 2007). Elementary school students often find it difficult to make sense of geographical concepts related to space and often have difficulty with the nomenclature used to discuss geography (Platten, 1995a, 1995b). Thus resources for children often focus on precisely the aspect of Israel that early elementary school students have to strive most to understand.

Yet even more common than overreaching children's cognitive capacities is the tendency to underestimate the depth and sophistication of children's thinking and questioning. Nowhere is this phenomenon clearer than in the ways that Jewish educators tend to shy away from education about the Israeli–Arab/Palestinian conflict and Palestinian claims to the land. "Strikingly few" Jewish educators aim to "expose their students to challenging features of contemporary Israel" (Pomson et al., 2014, p. 12), and educators often worry that "it may not always be appropriate to discuss *ha-matzav* [the current geopolitical situation], particularly with very young children" (Litman, 2004; see also Horowitz, 2012). Yet while there is no reason to think that Jewish children wonder and worry about the conflict in preschool (Applebaum et al., 2020), there is ample evidence—as shown in chapter 3—that elementary-age Jewish children spend considerable mental and emotional effort attempting to sort through the contours of a conflict that they often investigate with minimal adult guidance. Elementary-age children ask pressing questions both about why the conflict persists and what it might take to shift the current reality. In children's own telling, these questions are not out of grasp but rather precisely "what I think about" (Rina, 3).

Developmentally sensitive Israel education—like developmentally appropriate practice in other subject areas—involves honoring both the depths and the limits of children's thinking while making complex subject matter accessible. In the words of one Jewish educator interviewed by historian Jack Wertheimer (2009):

> In order to accommodate the developmental level of your students, it doesn't mean making a complex thing simple. It [means making] a complex thing apprehensible. But if you do that by stripping out all of the

sophistication, all of the complexity, the kids will be left feeling that this is a simple thing that they have mastered and there's nothing else there. . . . That's one of the most difficult tightropes that we walk. (p. 20)

Those who care deeply about children's developmental needs— educators, but also parents, grandparents, clergy, and others—must allow children to encounter and investigate intellectually and morally complex questions without assuming that all conceptually complicated ideas are within children's grasp. The ability to walk this tightrope—neither over-shooting nor underestimating children's capacity for thinking about complex ideas and relationships—relies on a solid understanding of the subject-specific ways that children think about the world.

2. *Exploring Prism Questions*

While understanding children's subject-specific developmental capaci-ties is a necessary pillar of elementary education, by itself it is insufficient for cultivating educational environments sensitive to children's needs. This is because developmentally appropriate practice is not only about what children of any age are *capable* of knowing, but also about what they are *interested* in knowing (Goldstein, 2015). To understand chil-dren's interests, children themselves must be invited to weigh in on the question of what counts as appropriate content (e.g., H. P. Ginsburg et al., 2001).

The idea that children's questions and interests ought to be a rich source for curriculum and instruction has deep roots in educational discourse (e.g., Dale, 1937). Scholars have long argued that children's "real questions"—questions generated by children's engagement with problems and topics that are of genuine interest to them—ought to sit at the heart of education (Wells, 1999, p. 91). Children are often driven by variations of the question *How can I lead an interesting and meaning-ful life as a participant in my family, community, and culture?* (Hedges & Cooper, 2016).[1] Yet despite the fact that children's questions "are al-ways much larger [and] much more serious than we imagine" (Olsson, 2013, p. 230), classrooms regularly require children's self-generated ques-tions to give way to questions imposed upon them by their teachers (M. Gross, 2006).

As Jewish children learn about Israel in particular, it is often the case that children's deep questions about the relationships among self, family, community, and nation are set aside in the interest of focusing on much simpler factual information. In these moments, the issue is not a mismatch with children's developmental understanding—there is neither overshooting nor undershooting of their conceptual capacities—but rather a mismatch with children's genuine interests and questions.

A prime example of this phenomenon occurs in lessons about the colors and symbols of the Israeli flag, a common topic in elementary Israel education (e.g., Gervitz, 2009). There is nothing developmentally inappropriate about teaching children about the Israeli flag. Unlike attempts to teach them about the geography and terrain of Israel, which most young children in this study found conceptually too difficult to grasp in the early grades of elementary school, even children in kindergarten and first grade were easily able to explain the symbols and the "blue and whiteness" (Olivia, K) of the flag in their own words. Many of the children were able to articulate that "Israel's flag's colors are blue and white" (Isaac, 1) and that "the blue and the white remind us about the *tallit* [prayer shawl] that we wear at the temple, and the Magen David [Star of David] is to remember David, who was the king of Israel once" (Owen, K).

Yet the children in this study found little joy in learning facts about the flag, at least not the kind of sustained joy that elementary school students can find in active, engaged efforts to attain new knowledge or understanding (Opitz & Ford, 2014; Rantala & Määttä, 2012). The children were certainly able to restate and retell information they had learned about the Israeli flag, but they did not speak about the flag unless they were specifically prompted to do so, did not ask their own unsolicited questions about it, and did not seek out any additional information beyond what had been provided by adults.

There were many other kinds of questions—ones much more complex than "What are the colors and symbols of the Israeli flag?"—that *did* elicit these types of responses from the children. For example, the questions "What makes a place Jewish?," "What might it take to bring lasting peace to the Middle East?," and "How can I best contribute to the communities I care about?" were all questions that the children themselves wondered about year after year, offering new and often increasingly sophisticated and varied language about them. Even when the children were not specifically prompted to address these questions, and even when they had already formed initial answers in previous years, they remained engaged in building emerging theories about these questions. The children sustained interest in these questions over time, and in their attempts to investigate, many children even sought out information beyond what they ever learned as part of a formal classroom environment.

The questions that *did* sustain children's wondering and theory building over time had many possible answers that highlighted differences among people. It is these prism questions—questions that, in the process of answering them, necessitate grappling with a spectrum of answers—that children revisited year after year, rethinking and refining their emerging ideas about them, and sometimes even researching them on their own time. Prism questions are distinct from the kinds of factual questions that many teachers ask, questions that have an answer known by the teacher and elicited from the students (Good & Lavigne, 2018). "What are the colors of the Israeli flag?" is a factual question that invites a single correct answer: blue and white. Children can and do engage with these kinds of questions, but they are not the questions that animate their sustained interest and curiosity over time. "What makes a place Jewish?," by contrast, is a prism that separates into a spectrum of answers, highlighting the myriad ways that Jews across time and space have structured and sustained Jewish homes, communities, and institutions both within and outside of a Jewish state.

Prism questions share much in common with the kinds of essential questions that many educators use to frame children's learning (McTighe & Wiggins, 2013; Wiggins & McTighe, 2005). Both kinds of questions are open-ended and do not have a single, final, and correct answer, and both kinds of questions lead to asking other rich questions. Yet prism questions meet one additional litmus test that essential questions need not: The process of attempting to answer these questions reveals a spectrum of human beliefs, opinions, and stances.

Some essential questions—How can I sound more like a native (Hebrew) speaker? How can we know what *really* happened in the (Jewish) past?—direct students to discipline-specific strategies for thinking about knowledge (McTighe & Wiggins, 2013). These questions are important for helping children understand key ideas and processes, but they do not necessarily point to a range of human beliefs and experiences.

Prism questions, by contrast, function like triangular prisms that separate white light into a spectrum of colors, revealing a vibrant array of responses:

- What makes a place a home?
- How should governments balance the rights of the minority with the will of the majority?
- When should we draw upon tradition and when should we innovate?
- When is military action warranted?
- What are the hallmarks of a free and just society?
- Is _____ good for the Jews? For the world?
- What would an ideal society look like?

None of these questions can be settled with facts alone, though certainly learning key facts can help illuminate an array of answers. All of these questions rely on human judgment and discernment. More so, different human beings—those living in different times, in different societies, and even within the same communities today—have addressed and will continue to answer these questions in different ways. It is not possible to seriously consider any of these questions without taking into account a spectrum of human beliefs, ideas, and experiences.

Children's learning ought to be centered on these kinds of prism questions. This is because, first and foremost, inviting children to engage with these genuine questions situates children not as passive recipients of adult knowledge but as co-constructors of ideas and beliefs about the human experience. Children are, as this book has shown, both interested in and capable of participating in conversations about these questions; more so, they ask versions of these questions year after year as they grow (even if their exact formulations of the questions change over time). In fact, these are the very types of questions about which elementary-age children's sense of wonder and wondering is sustained over time.

Second, and perhaps even more important, when children have no adult guides to help them deliberate about these questions, and the range of answers to them, they turn to the one source that *is* accessible to them: the Internet. Thus, like sex education, adults have two choices: they may speak with children in thoughtful ways, or they may exclude children from conversations about these topics. Either way, children will ask and investigate, and they are much more likely to understand what they want and need to know with the guidance of adults.

3. Investigating Contested Civic and Political Matters

There is one particular subset of prism questions that the children in this study were especially keen to investigate on their own because they wanted to make sense of ideas that they believed adults didn't sufficiently help them understand. These questions revolved around civic and political matters, and they often pointed to children's attempts to understand contentious issues. Helping children make sense of contested civic and political matters is a third pillar that must undergird elementary education if it is to respond to children's own interests and queries.

Contested civic and political matters are those about which there is a live controversy about what a community, or its members, ought to do. Drawing upon the work of Diana Hess (2009), I define these issues as ones that spark significant disagreement among members of a community and that require "deliberation among a 'we' to determine which policy is the best response to a particular problem" (p. 37). This is not to say that all questions about which people disagree ought to be deliberated in schools. Questions about which experts agree even if some members of the public dissent (for example, the existence of global warming or the historical veracity of the Holocaust) are neither appropriate nor educative for classroom debates (J. Zimmerman & Robertson, 2017). Yet open policy questions—matters of public concern about which there is no widespread consensus—are certainly worth deliberating, and schools can provide an important forum for doing so (D. E. Hess & McAvoy, 2014). For young children in particular, having an opportunity to locate, name, inquire about, and reflect on open policy questions about which people disagree is crucial for helping them understand the issues and values that animate their communities.

The claim that children must have dedicated time and space to investigate contested civic and political matters runs counter to recent trends in education. Despite a long and rich tradition of understanding teachers and schools as essential for helping children learn democratic norms and responsible citizenship (e.g., Dewey, 1916), rising political polariza tion has ushered in an era of "keep[ing] politics out" of education (D. E. Hess & McAvoy, 2014, p. 20). In fact, as issues become more contentious outside of school, they also often become more taboo inside schools (J. Zimmerman & Robertson, 2017).

At the heart of the matter lie two interrelated questions: whether *any* schools ought to be places for political deliberation and debate, and whether *elementary* schools in particular are appropriate places for highlighting contested civic and political issues. Both questions I answer in the affirmative.

It is clear that schools can and do play a crucial role in helping young people understand democratic norms and participate in democratic processes. When schools explicitly teach civic skills (e.g., debating or letter writing), and when they deliberately create an open classroom climate for discussing political issues, they are able to cultivate a student body committed to civic and political participation (Torney-Purta, 2002; Zukin et al., 2006). When students themselves are invited to discuss and analyze political issues, rather than simply regurgitating facts about governmental systems and processes, they develop deeper understanding of political issues and are more likely to be actively involved in political discussions outside of school (Ichilov, 1991; Niemi & Junn, 1998). When schools make space for students to engage in classroom conversations about controversial issues that are of interest to them, and when they allow students to express opinions that differ from one another, students are more knowledgeable about, more interested in, and more able to participate in the conversations that matter in their communities (Barrett & Pachi, 2019).

While it is widely understood that schools serve an important role in helping students learn to participate in democratic society, it is a little more radical to claim that learning about contested civic and political issues ought to occur not only in high schools but also in elementary schools. Although education has long been understood as a political enterprise (Apple, 1979; Freire, 2018/1968; Nieto, 2006), teachers and parents often believe that children are too young to grapple with political issues and conversations (Husband, 2010; May et al., 2014). Many elementary educators navigate this tension by emphasizing the civic importance of community service while downplaying more partisan forms of political engagement (Martin, 2008). Yet elementary-age students are certainly able to deliberate about complex topics with political resonance (T. A. Beck, 2003; Bickmore, 1999; K. A. Payne & Journell, 2019), and they are capable of discussing and negotiating their ideas with other children (Hauver et al., 2017; James et al., 2017). The children in this study desperately wanted to know more about civic and political matters, and they were often very angry that their parents and teachers avoided these topics. Therefore, I join a growing chorus of scholars who insist that teachers and parents should not wait until middle or high school to begin conversations with young people about political issues (e.g., D. E. Hess, 2009; K. A. Payne & Journell, 2019).

The importance of starting these conversations in childhood—not adolescence—stems from two roots. First is the reality that children can and do think and ask about issues and institutions that are political in nature. The children in this study wondered and worried about issues that have civic import and political implications—gun violence, racism, food insecurity, and more—even in the early grades of elementary school, and by fourth grade most were able to take explicitly political stances about both political leadership and policy matters. Assuming that politically contentious issues are not developmentally appropriate for children misunderstands the ways that children *do* think about politics, and the fact that children often feel responsible for fixing structural issues in society when they view those matters as relevant to their own lives (Hauver, 2019).

Second is the fact that the primary skills needed for civic and political engagement take time to develop. These skills—the ability to understand and assess the credibility of information, to deliberate about what constitutes good and fair outcomes, to weigh the relative merits of multiple possible paths forward, to communicate clearly with and listen compassionately to others, to find mutually agreeable points of compromise—must be practiced and honed over time. Each has long-term implications for conventional forms of political participation like voting (Barrett & Pachi, 2019), but each can also build upon the particular ways that children reflect on and negotiate issues of fairness, power, and authority (Berti, 2005; Paley, 1992). Thus providing children time and opportunity to cultivate and reflect on these skills ought to have a place in elementary education.

To argue that elementary-age children ought to have time and space to investigate contentious civic and political matters is not to argue that adults ought to tell children *what* to think about any particular issue. The goal, rather, is to help children practice *how* to deliberate, discuss, and decide on what actions they want to take. As Diana Hess explains, discussions of contested issues ought to function "not as a soapbox for [teachers], but as a forum for their students" (2009, p. 75). Schools play a crucial role in this process both because schools themselves function as a civic space for children and because teachers can scaffold instruction to practice and develop these complex skills.

Yet even if investigating civic and political matters is appropriate for elementary education writ large, why ought it have a place in Jewish education in particular? After all, Jewish education is more typically framed as a form of identity education (Levisohn & Kelman, 2019), heritage education (Kelner, 2010), or religious education (Rosenak, 1987), not civic or political education.[2] Despite this, many of the most profound questions that the Jewish children in this study have asked about their own lives and communities are not about identity, heritage, or religion per se. They are instead about the children's desires to make sense of what it means to be part of a larger community in which people do not agree about how that community ought to function. These are questions that can be addressed only by helping children understand Jewish life as a complex civilization (Kaplan, 1934/2010) that, like all societies, must negotiate the needs, desires, and beliefs of multiple individuals who are part of (and outside and on the margins of) the collective.

This kind of educational approach requires an adjustment to what typically happens as children are inducted into Jewish communal life. It may certainly include elements of the "typical" Jewish education for young children—a focus on Jewish holidays and rituals, Bible stories, "Jewish values," Hebrew language, and prayer literacy—but it cannot include *only* these, as they alone cannot help children understand the civic and political issues and structures that have shaped and been shaped by Jewish communities across time and place. These are issues that are addressed only when the study of history, civics, and politics is part of larger conversations about Judaism and its meanings. This vision for Jewish education is inherently pluralistic in that it necessarily requires learning about the contours of difference among "many different Jews" (Keren, 2) from distinct Jewish denominations, cultural backgrounds, geographic locations, political orientations, and moments in time.

Israel education, in this view, is an important component of Jewish education because it offers a particularly rich case for exploring civic and political aspects of Judaism and Jewish life, and the ways that civics and politics interact with religion, culture, heritage, and identity. Not only does it provide opportunities for exploring the possibilities and limits of Jewish political sovereignty in Israel, but because Israel has become such a lightning rod in both American and American Jewish political discourse (Sasson, 2014; D. Waxman, 2016), Israel education is also a particularly powerful way of investigating the civic and political questions of contemporary American Jewish communities. In this view, Israel education matters not because of its role in helping young Jews forge an affective relationship to Israel (cf. Chazan, 2016; Horowitz, 2012) but because it provides a multidimensional case for exploring the prism questions that animate contemporary Jewish life. Approaching Israel education in this way requires shifting the balance of Jewish education from the individual toward the collective (Winer, 2019) and from the settled to the contested.

Next Steps for Adults

Children's educational experiences ought to be more developmentally sensitive and should explore prism questions that refract into a spectrum of human beliefs and experiences, including a subset of those questions that are explicitly political in nature. An educational approach undergirded by these pillars will require shifts in both the attitudes and the actions of the adults who love children and support their learning. These shifts can occur only with changes in three crucial areas: materials, mindsets, and mentoring.

Materials

Curricula and resources for elementary-age learners will need to highlight both the kinds of open-ended prism questions that sustain children's interest and curiosity, and an array of human responses and interpretations to those questions. Elementary school curricula, which are increasingly focused on "fixing" the gaps in children's knowledge rather than allowing time for children to explore and investigate the worlds around and within them (Paley, 2004), will need to provide children more opportunities for asking, wondering, investigating, and deliberating about these questions—all of which requires prioritizing the time for doing so.

In addition to reallocating time, there will need to be changes in the written materials that children encounter. Textbooks often have hidden authors, concealing from young readers thinking and decision-making processes (Bain, 2006). If children are to learn how to grapple with important and especially unsettled questions, they will need to encounter written materials that contain both words and graphics that require students to engage in interpretive processes (Barton & Levstik, 2015; Guo et al., 2018). Jewish curricula and textbooks in particular will need to shift from focusing on the transmission of knowledge and tradition to highlighting the ways that Jews—both today and across Jewish history—have co-constructed Jewish communities, rituals, and beliefs.

Yet even if new curricula and textbooks are developed for school use, this alone will be insufficient for shifting children's experiences. This is because when children ask questions and don't get answers they believe to be sufficient, they keep asking (Chouinard et al., 2007) and, if the children in this study are any indication, when they have particularly complex questions, they turn not to their parents or teachers but to the vast expanses of the Internet. By the time they could read well enough to do so, which for most children in this study occurred in second or third grade, they began conducting untargeted searches on Google and YouTube and attempted to make sense of whatever information they happened to stumble upon.

Part of what is needed is a new form of digital-literacy education that helps young people understand who creates digital resources and for what purposes (Breakstone et al., 2018; Wineburg, 2018). This will allow children to reframe their understanding of the Internet from a font of all knowledge to a public square for contemporary discourse.

In Israel education, digital-literacy education must also be accompanied by the development of new digital resources. This is because when the children in this study wondered about issues in their home communities in the United States—questions, for example, about the U.S. electoral process—many of them turned to online resources that their teachers had directed them to. These sources, like *Newsela* or *Time for Kids*, were specifically designed to provide accessible information to children with varying reading levels and background knowledge. Yet no such digital content exists to take Israeli news and current events and translate them—both linguistically and culturally—for Jewish youth in the English-speaking world. Given how Jewish children use the Internet— often believing online sources to be more accessible and more reliable than their teachers, parents, and rabbis—the creation of curated content geared specifically to helping young people understand the complex political and social reality of life in Israel is a necessary next step.

Mindsets

Currently, much of children's education centers on teaching children what adults already know about the world. Water moves in a cycle that includes evaporation, condensation, and precipitation. A letter *e* at the end of a word is silent. Both sides of an equation are equal in value. The U.S. president lives in the White House. Israel's head of state is called the prime minister. The questions are clearly defined and the answers are known. Yet there are many questions that are developmentally within children's reach and interest and that have no set answers—either because of an array of possible answers, because the issues are contested, or both.

Three interrelated stances are essential for (re)positioning education to help children make sense of the unsettled and/or the unknown. An inquiry stance situates both adults (Cochran-Smith & Lytle, 2015) and children (Lindfors, 1999; Metz, 2004) as capable of investigating important questions, including questions that have no settled or commonly agreed-upon answer. A participatory stance views children—no less than adults—as interested in and capable of contributing to both the production of knowledge (Pascal & Bertram, 2009) and the process of schooling (Groundwater-Smith et al., 2014). A deliberative stance positions knowledge itself as necessary but insufficient for guiding human actions, viewing dialogue and deliberation as both essential for society (Thomas, 2010) and possible to be cultivated in classrooms (McAvoy & Hess, 2013).

When taken as a trio, these stances position education not as a process of transferring knowledge from adults to children but as one of providing children opportunities to investigate, uncover, and reflect on complex ideas over time, with the guidance and support of adults. In this view, adults are not the keepers of the answers but interlocutors and guides in asking and investigating the questions. None of these stances are static traits, either present or absent. Instead, they are "malleable, capable of being cultivated" over time (Feiman-Nemser & Schussler, 2010, p. 181).

In the specific context of Jewish education, these stances offer a departure from more common approaches in which Jewish educators situate themselves as key role models and exemplars of Jewish living (Z. R. Hassenfeld & Levisohn, 2019; Pomson et al., 2014). They reposition adults and children, assuming that both have lived Jewish experiences and profound questions about Jewish life.

Only when adults and children together develop inquiry, participatory, and deliberative stances can education be sensitive to both children's developmental capacities and their interests. Helping adults in particular embrace and enact these stances will likely require explicit opportunities for learning, coaching, and support.

Mentoring

Mentoring adults who are responsible for children's learning is crucial for improving the practices of teaching and learning. Any effective approach to mentoring and adult education will rest upon three assumptions about adults as learners. First, most adults involved in children's learning care deeply about children and are committed to their physical, emotional, and intellectual well-being—even at moments when they may struggle to offer the kinds of educational experiences that children want and need. Second, as adults learn more about how children learn, it is often easier for them to embrace this new knowledge in theory than in practice (Schneider, 2014), and thus there often remains a gap between what they say and what they actually do (Feiman-Nemser & Schussler, 2010). Third, and most important, with deliberate and ongoing coaching and support, adults can reflect upon and learn from their words and actions in ways that improve children's learning and educational experiences (Darling-Hammond, 2008).

The professional-development literature in education, which focuses on both preservice support for those seeking to enter the field and in-service learning for those who are already working as professional educators, reveals that effective professional learning opportunities have many shared characteristics. They are not onetime or episodic, but rather offer opportunities for sustained learning over time (Feiman-Nemser, 2012). They situate teachers as both learners (Dorph, 2011; Feiman-Nemser, 2012, 2001) and collaborative partners who are jointly responsible for creating a culture of teaching and learning in their institutions (Darling-Hammond & McLaughlin, 1995; Little, 1982; Stodolsky et al., 2004). These professional learning opportunities help educators better understand not only their subject matter but also how students *learn* this subject matter (Darling-Hammond & Bransford, 2005; Garet et al., 2001), and thus how to transform subject-matter knowledge into "teachable subject matter with a structure and logic that students will understand" (Feiman-Nemser, 2011, p. 952). They also provide opportunities for educators to reflect on and learn from their own practice and the practices of their colleagues (Ball & Cohen, 1999; Feiman-Nemser, 2012).

Despite the critical importance of sustained, collaborative, professional learning that has a direct relationship to matters of teaching and learning, professional development in Jewish education has not always reflected these criteria (Holtz et al., 2000). Although Jewish institutions offer myriad opportunities for professional learning, most are short in duration and not part of a larger coordinated professional trajectory (Sales et al., 2008). Sustained conversations about teaching and learning rooted in practice are rare (Stodolksy et al., 2006).

In Israel education in particular, many professional-development opportunities remain episodic and top-down (Sinclair et al., 2012). Recent inroads in offering sustained professional learning in Israel education—by the iCenter for Israel Education, Makom, the Shalom Hartman Institute, and other organizations well positioned to reach Jewish professionals—have made important advances in helping educators develop both deeper content knowledge and a wider array of pedagogical strategies. Even so, ongoing professional learning in which educators investigate and tinker with their own practices based on developing understanding of how their students learn about Israel has been missing—

largely because knowledge of children's thinking has rarely been the focus of scholarship and discourse in Jewish Studies and Jewish education. When educators *do* learn more about the complex ways that young Jewish learners think and feel about Israel, they often struggle to adapt their teaching accordingly, and thus they need mentors who can support and challenge them as they adjust both their understanding and their practice (Applebaum & Zakai, 2020). The next step for professional learning in Israel education, building on the existing institutional infrastructure, is to develop professional learning and mentoring trajectories specifically focused on helping educators better understand and collaborate with their learners—especially when those learners are children.

In Jewish education, high-quality learning opportunities for professional educators must be accompanied by other kinds of adult education. Given the bidirectional nature of children's and parents' Jewish education, such that each influences the other (Pomson & Schnoor, 2008, 2018), Jewish educational institutions will need to provide ongoing support and learning opportunities for parents. Given the outsized role that grandparents can play in the Jewish education of their grandchildren (P. Beck, 2005; Sasson et al., 2015), providing grandparents education and support may be just as crucial. In addition, members of the clergy—many of whom make educational decisions for their communities even in the absence of formal educational training—need opportunities for learning about the educational practices and stances that will allow them to transform their own commitment to learning *lishma* (for its own sake) into learning in the service of children's learning (Dorph & Feiman-Nemser, 1997). Adult education for each of these groups must focus on three areas: (1) developing deeper understanding of children's developmental capacities, (2) cultivating distinct strategies for talking with children about contested and unsettled matters, and (3) navigating, and helping children navigate, new ways of finding and assessing information in the digital era.

Conclusion

Standing on the threshold between elementary and middle school, Rina fantasized about getting a chance to visit "cool places" in Israel because "I've always wanted to do that" (5). Although she had never been there,

Rina imagined that "if I were to go to Israel one day, then I would know how to get my way around that place" because "it's something that I've been learning about since kindergarten" (5).

If Rina were to look back at her younger self, she would see that even in kindergarten she had viewed Israel as "very special to me" (K). Over the years, she had come to think about Israel in ways that were increasingly multilayered, so that her kindergarten belief that Israel was "a country where some Jewish people live" had developed into a view of Israel as "a country that was the Promised Land by God in the Torah [the Five Books of Moses], but now it's the modern country. It has Jewish-y stuff like the Western Wall from the Second Temple [but] it's not just for the Jews" (5). As she reflected on her own educational journey, Rina explained, "I've been learning about [Israel] for so long, and I still feel a really big connection," but she also felt frustrated by the fact that there was so much about the politics of Israel that "I don't really know" (5).

If Rina were able to see forward from that moment in time, getting a glimpse of her older self, she would see that both her desire to visit Israel and her frustration with her education about it would only continue to grow. "Israel makes me feel kind of a sense of longing. I've been learning about this for a long time, and I really just want to go see it," Rina (7) would explain at the midpoint of her middle school years. "But I'm not going to lie. I think a lot of middle schoolers only know a little part of the story. And [when we learn more,] it's like, 'surprise!'" Rina critiqued her prior education in elementary school, saying, "Teachers will teach us about the Torah, but they'd never *really* talk about present-day Israel." She was particularly upset that she hadn't learned more about "disagreeing between countries" and "disagreeing between people," each of which she considered to be essential to her own developing understanding. "I think that it would help society and middle schoolers a lot more," she explained, if adults would begin to think more "about the stuff that they don't really teach us."

Rina's words, and the words of all of the children whose voices have contributed to this book, offer both a promise and a warning. The children ought to be taken seriously.

ACKNOWLEDGMENTS

This book is possible only because of the dedication of 35 children and the commitment of their parents. Thanks to each of you for helping me answer the questions I began with 10 years ago, and for raising so many more questions for me in the intervening years. Your wisdom continues to astound me.

Another group of children, whose words are not quoted in this book, have also helped shape it. These children let me "audition" interview questions and research prompts with them, offering important feedback and reflections about the type and wording of questions that are (and are not) accessible for their age groups. Thank you for steering me in the right direction.

In 2012 the leaders of three Jewish day schools were brave enough to open their doors to me. At a time when so many schools that I approached said that they'd be willing to show me their signature Israel education programs but not let me interview their students, the school leaders at these three institutions understood how much the children in their schools could contribute to conversations about Jewish education. Although your names and institutions will be kept anonymous, you and I know what a great service you have done in allowing the children at your schools to speak freely. Thank you.

The Children's Learning About Israel Project and the research for this book and its publication were made possible by the generous support of the Jack, Joseph, and Morton Mandel Center for Studies in Jewish Education, a partnership between Brandeis University and the Jack, Joseph, and Morton Mandel Foundation of Cleveland, Ohio. A block grant from CASJE, the Collaborative for Applied Studies in Jewish Education, helped support the Children's Learning About Israel Project and other projects at the center.

Along with the financial support of the center since 2014, its director Jon Levisohn has offered ongoing encouragement, asking just the right questions to help me see the bigger picture each time I got bogged down in the details. Sharon Feiman-Nemser, Jonathan Krasner, and Joe Riemer have all offered valuable guidance and feedback as this project has unfolded. A team of people at the center, including Susanne Shavelson, Shani Winton, Pamela Endo, and Masha Lokshin, have offered crucial behind-the-scenes assistance.

The Dorot Foundation, and especially Steve Jacobson, helped to turn a pedagogical question into a longitudinal study. Funds from the foundation made it possible to transcribe the first set of interviews with the children, and advisers to the foundation asked probing questions that helped shape the structure and scope of the project.

The amount of data from this project is immense, and it is only because of the work of Hannah Tobin Cohen that I was able to collect and make sense of it. Her approachable demeanor with the children, and her consummate professionalism with the data, have been invaluable to this project. Even when it is not visible, her work is on every page of this book. Additional research assistance from Emma Jaszczak Maszi, JR Small, Tammy Cohen, Shira Sergant, and Samuel Hainbach made it possible to catalog and categorize, organize and order the children's words and mine.

In the decade that I have been working on this project, my colleagues at the Hebrew Union College–Jewish Institute of Religion and, before then, at the American Jewish University have been my source of guidance and inspiration. Miriam Heller Stern, who supported this project from its infancy, has made it possible for me to carve out precious time for this work. Sarah Benor is my guide in navigating all tricky methodological questions. Laura Novak Winer helped me see the order of the book's chapters. Lauren Applebaum, Tamara Eskenazi, Reuven Firestone, Sharon Gillerman, z"l, Leah Hochman, Joshua Holo, Bruce Phillips, and Dvora Weisberg all offered guidance and support at precisely the moments I needed it. Rachel Lerner and Michael Berenbaum believed in this book before I did.

To my colleagues who carefully read and commented on draft work—Lauren Applebaum, Sharon Avni, Sarah Benor, Jonah Hassenfeld, Ilana Horowitz, Jane Kanarek, Jonathan Krasner, Oren Kroll-Zeldin, Lesley Litman, Matt Reingold, Jack Schneider, Ronit Stahl, Laura Novak Winer, and Laura Yares—I am so grateful for your discerning eye. To my colleagues who were able to help me answer specific questions outside of my own area of expertise—Dina Danon, Ziva Hassenfeld, Jeffrey Kress, and Michael Shire—I am grateful for your wisdom. To my teachers, Sam Wineburg above all, thank you for showing me how to ask and investigate deep questions.

At NYU Press, Jennifer Hammer has championed this work and given feedback with a perfect balance of encouragement and redirection. Martin Coleman and Veronica Knutson have patiently answered all my questions.

Ronit Stahl and Lauren Applebaum, you double-team as my compass and whetstone, setting me straight when I am lost and sharpening my ideas when I am dull. I quite literally cannot imagine my work, or my life, without your voices in my head.

My own children's many talented teachers, beloved babysitters, and adoring grandparents, aunts, uncles, and cousins have all provided the kind of necessary support that makes it possible to be a working parent. I have always appreciated you, but the pandemic has made the essential nature of your support even more visible!

I stand on the shoulders of my parents, Leah Kroll and Michael Zeldin, and their parents, Joan and Irving Kroll and Isaiah and Florence Zeldin. It is because of your great example that I believe in the transformative power of teaching and learning.

Igor Zakai, if I ever have any sense of inner calm, it is because of you. I am blessed to have a family and a life with you.

My own children, Eytan, Ilan, and Liam, were the first to teach me about how deep children's ideas and how sophisticated children's questions can be. The children of the Children's Learning About Israel Project remind me of that every day. This book is for all of them.

NOTES

1 In order to participate in this study, called the Children's Learning About Israel Project, both the children and their parents had to agree to a multiple-year commitment so that the children could share their thoughts and ideas as they developed over time.

2 Although the Covid-19 pandemic has temporarily hampered travel between the United States and Israel, there is reason to believe that it has created pent-up demand for Israel educational travel experiences, which will only increase as restrictions decrease. As Anne Lanski, founding CEO of the iCenter, explains, "Far from waning, demand for these [travel] experiences is as robust as ever" (2021, p. 93), with growing waitlists for Israel travel programs.

3 As a result of multiple allegations of sexually inappropriate contact (Dreyfus, 2018; McGinity, 2018), the work of sociologist Steven M. Cohen has come under much-warranted scrutiny. Despite widespread public condemnation of his actions, there has been a much more uneven response to his scholarship. As Karla Goldman explains, "Some admire and some look askance at the way Cohen's scholarly agenda has been driven by his devotion to sustaining Jewish peoplehood" (2020, 195). Because of concerns about recent attempts to rehabilitate Cohen's reputation (Dreyfus, 2021; Hanau, 2021), I want to make transparent my choices about referencing his work. Throughout this book, I have cited Cohen's work when and only when it is coauthored by other reputable scholars. This decision is an attempt to balance two priorities: (1) to acknowledge that his scholarly work has shaped much of the discourse on American Jews and Israel, even when scholars like myself push back against his framing, and (2) to uphold serious concerns about the ways that his contributions have been part of larger misogynistic and patriarchal systems (Berman et al., 2020; Rosenblatt et al., 2018).

4 The longitudinal study continued to track these children during the middle school years (2018–21). Although that research generally falls outside the scope of this book, at times the children's comments from middle school have shaped the present framing.

5 The work of interviewing children is delicate. Children tend to shut down in interviews if they have to listen too much, but also if they feel like they are being interrogated (McConaughy, 2013), and thus a delicate balance must be struck in the amount of talk between the interviewer and the child. The interviews we con-

ducted with the children were semistructured, based on a prewritten script but allowing for fluid conversation between interviewer and child (Gillham, 2005; Miles & Huberman, 1994). The semistructured nature of these interviews allowed both focus and flexibility, each of which is useful when interviewing children (Drever, 1995). Like all of the research methods we use with the children, these interviews assume that children, no less than adults, are capable of recounting and reflecting on their own experiences (Greene & Hogan, 2005).

6 When paired with interviews, photo and music elicitation exercises (Allett, 2010; Harper, 2002) can evoke longer and more comprehensive responses from participants than interview questions alone (Collier, 1987). Such exercises, which call forth not only what participants see and hear but also what is brought up for them internally when they interact with the prompt (Banks, 2001), also have the benefit of helping children distinguish the questions of the researcher from the kind of teacher questioning that regularly occurs in schools (Cappello, 2005). In addition, verbal interviews rely heavily on linguistic communication, which can be challenging for some young children, and thus including visual prompts can mitigate some of the challenges of extensive back-and-forth questioning between researcher and child (Epstein et al., 2008).

7 For children, telling stories can be a way of making sense of the world, serving as "a child's way of exploring, inquiring, probing, and . . . playing her way into deeper understanding" (Lindfors, 1999, p. 149). Stories allow children to process the world as they understand it to be, or to imagine the world as they would like it to be. For, whether they tell stories that are factual or fictional, children's narratives reveal how they interpret and view the world around them. Drawing upon the work of VanSledright and Brophy (1992), who found that children can construct coherent narratives of events even when they mix up or imagine some details, this methodological approach assumes children to be intelligible narrators including at moments when they provide counterfactual accounts. It examines children's stories not only to ascertain their accuracy, but more so to illuminate their ways of thinking and feeling about past and current events.

8 Any product that a child creates, like an art project or an essay, can offer a glimpse into what the child knows and how the child thinks. These artifacts of learning are external representations of a child's constructed knowledge (Sawyer, 2014). Even when they are produced as part of formal schooling, they often reflect children's understanding of issues that fall well beyond the scope of the primary school curriculum (Vasquez, 2014).

9 Given that parents function both as "gatekeepers" for children's participation in research and as potential contributors to "thick" descriptions of children's voices (Carnevale, 2020), the parents of the children in this study were offered multiple (optional) opportunities to provide information about their children. At several points we invited parents to fill out surveys in which we asked about the demographic backgrounds of their families, any recent family visits to Israel, and any additional information they would like to provide about their children

or themselves. Multiple parents sent us unsolicited emails about their children's experiences, recounting stories their children had shared with them. In particular instances, we reached out directly to parents to ask them specific questions about their children or their families. Periodically we asked the children's schools about the curricula, resources, and textbooks they were using, and at times teachers sent us samples of both their work and the work of their students.

10 The latest censuses of American Jewish educational institutions have found that approximately 230,000 children attend supplementary schools (Wertheimer, 2008), over 292,000 attend day schools (Besser, 2020), 73,000 attend Jewish day camps (Soifer & Stark, 2018a), and 81,000 attend Jewish overnight camps (Soifer & Stark, 2018b), with some overlap between camp and school attendees. Although these censuses were conducted in different years, they paint an overall picture that suggests that fewer than half of the 1.8 million children residing in American Jewish households (Pew Research Center, 2021) engage in formal Jewish learning in any school or camp context.

11 All members of the 2012–13 kindergarten classes from the three cooperating schools were invited to participate in the longitudinal study. Recruitment letters were sent home to all parents by way of the kindergarten teachers, and all children whose parents gave permission to participate in the study were enrolled in it. Several other day schools were invited to participate but declined. In addition, a group of supplementary schools were invited to participate. While the leadership of several of these supplementary schools signed on, the schools were unable to gather sufficient parental consent to continue with the study.

12 In the initial design of the study, we did not include an Orthodox day school among our partner schools because previous research about Israel education has shown that students attending Orthodox day schools understand and relate to Israel in markedly different ways than their non-Orthodox peers, and researchers have needed to disaggregate data collected on Orthodox day school students (e.g., Pomson et al., 2011). However, several of the children in this study self-identify as Orthodox and affiliate with Orthodox synagogues while attending non-Orthodox day schools, and I have found no marked differences between these children and the others in the study. It is possible that such differences will arise as the children grow older; it is also possible that these children's liberal day school education has made them more similar to their classmates than to Orthodox children attending Orthodox day schools.

13 Twelve of the thirty-five children had left their original schools by fifth grade, and we have been able to consistently follow many, though not all, of them. Over the six-plus years of the study, there has been some attrition so that 29 of the original 35 children recruited in kindergarten participated in the fifth-grade year of the study.

14 Some scholars suggest that the deficits of young American Jews reflect larger "deficiencies in knowledge" of Americans in general (e.g., Phillips et al., p. 104), whereas others situate American Jewish youth in relation to the "psychological

and emotional deficit" of other young Jews around the world (e.g., Liebman, 1999, p. 7). In both cases, American Jewish youth are portrayed as deficient.

1. "THE PLACE WHERE I BELONG": CHILDREN'S CONCEPTIONS OF HOME AND HOMELAND

1 See S. W. Moore et al. (1985) for an important exception to this rule.
2 Children are generally understood to be capable of developing complex theories about how the world functions even when those theories do not align with those of adults or expert wisdom in a particular field (e.g., Brewer & Samarapungavan, 1991).
3 There is evidence that Jewish preschoolers, like Jewish children in the early years of elementary school, relate to Israel in this concrete way, describing its physical distance from their own lives (Applebaum et al., 2020).
4 Identifying a "Goldilocks Zone" for learning is a distinct though similar concept to the more commonly used Vygotskian "zone of proximal development" (Vygotsky, 1978.) The former focuses on learning while the latter highlights development, processes that are linked but not identical (Chaiklin, 2003).

2. "ONCE UPON A TIME GOD MADE ISRAEL": CHILDREN'S NARRATIONS OF ISRAEL'S HISTORY

1 Their stories offer the first empirical evidence on how American Jewish children conceptualize Israeli history. For while scholars have examined how Israeli (e.g., Goldberg et al., 2011; Porat, 2004) and North American Jewish teenagers (e.g., J. Hassenfeld, 2016, 2018; Reingold, 2017, 2018) narrate Israeli history, there has heretofore been no investigation of American Jewish children's understanding of Israel's past.
2 Although the stories that the children told during their middle school years are generally outside the scope of this book, the trend continued into sixth and seventh grade, with a growing number of children each year telling markedly different versions of Israeli history when addressing adults and when addressing others their age.

3. "ISRAEL VS. THE OTHER TEAM": CHILDREN'S UNDERSTANDING OF THE ISRAELI–ARAB/PALESTINIAN CONFLICT

1 Despite her familiarity with the story of the "three boys," Carly indicated no awareness of the death of another boy, Mohammed Abu Khdeir, a Palestinian teenager who was kidnapped and burned alive in revenge for the deaths of the three Jewish teenagers (Rudoren, 2014). Jewish-Israeli extremist Yosef Haim Ben-David, along with two teenage accomplices whose names are sealed in the Israeli court system because they were minors at the time, were convicted for Abu Khdeir's murder in 2016, and the state of Israel officially recognized Abu Khdeir as a victim of terror (Hasson, 2016; Wootliff, 2016). Although many American Jewish adults were acutely aware of Abu Khdeir's murder, made even more prominent

after the release of the 2019 HBO drama series *Our Boys* based on these events, Carly appeared to know only of the deaths of the Jewish teens.

2 Preschool-age Jewish children, by contrast, do not yet think or wonder about the conflict (Applebaum et al., 2020).

4. "WHY DIDN'T YOU TELL ME?": CIVICS, POLITICS, AND CHILDREN'S RIGHTEOUS ANGER

1 Because children's attitudes can undergo generational shifts, some recent studies have suggested that even as contemporary American children continue to view the *office* of the president in high regard, they no longer have a uniformly favorable view of the *person* who occupies that office (Oxley et al., 2020).

CONCLUSION

1 Although many questions that children ask are variations of the larger question *How can I lead an interesting and meaningful life as a participant in my family, community, and culture?* (Hedges & Cooper, 2016), the specific iterations of their questions need to be categorized and rephrased by adults in order to create conceptual categories that can inform curricular and instructional decision making (Hedges, 2010). Therefore, I have taken the specific phrasing of children's questions and created from them a larger category, which I call prism questions, as a way of simultaneously reflecting children's words and giving them clearer pedagogical and curricular implications.

2 Pomson and Held offer a notable exception to this framing, asking "whether it might be fertile to conceive of Israel education in the diaspora as a form of Jewish civic education" (2012, p. 98, n. 2). While Pomson and Held distinguish between civic and political education, considering the former to be more relevant to the lives of American Jewish high school students, the children in this study expressed interest in *both* civic and political questions.

BIBLIOGRAPHY

Aboud, F. E. (2003). The formation of in-group favoritism and out-group prejudice in young children: Are they distinct attitudes? *Developmental Psychology, 39*(1), 48–60.

Abramowitz, A. (2010). *The disappearing center: Engaged citizens, polarization, and American democracy.* New Haven, CT: Yale University Press.

———. (2013). *The polarized public: Why American government is so dysfunctional.* Boston: Pearson.

Abu Artema, A. (2019, March 30). How the Great March of Return resurrected Palestinian resistance. *Al Jazeera.* Retrieved from www.aljazeera.com.

Abu-Nimer, M. (2001). Education for coexistence in Israel. In M. Abu-Nimer (Ed.), *Reconciliation, justice, and coexistence: Theory and practice,* 235–254. Lanham, MD: Lexington Books.

Abusalim, J. (2018). The Great March of Return: An organizer's perspective. *Journal of Palestine Studies, 47*(4), 90–100.

Acer, D., & Gözen, G. (2020). Art detectives: Young children's behaviour in finding and interpreting art elements within picture books. *Education 3–13, 48*(6), 716–732.

Aharon, N., & Pomson, A. (2018). What's happening at the flagpole? Studying camps as institutions for Israel education. *Journal of Jewish Education, 84*(4), 337–358.

Ainslie, D. (2000). Word detectives. *The Reading Teacher, 54*(4), 360–362.

AJC Survey of American Jewish Opinion. (2021, June 14). New York: American Jewish Committee. Retrieved from AJC Global Voice, www.ajc.org.

Alderson, P., & Morrow, V. (2011). *The ethics of research with children and young people.* Thousand Oaks, CA: Sage.

Alexander, H. A. (2015). Mature Zionism: Education and the scholarly study of Israel. *Journal of Jewish Education, 81*(2), 136–161.

Alldred, P. (1998). Ethnography and discourse analysis: Dilemmas in representing the voices of children. In J. Ribbens and R. Edwards (Eds.), *Feminist dilemmas in qualitative research: Public knowledge and private lives,* 147–170. London: Sage.

Allen, D. (1995). The Joint Authority for Jewish Zionist Education. *Journal of Jewish Education, 61*(3), 4–7.

Allett, N. (2010). Sounding out: Using music elicitation in qualitative research. NCRM Working Paper. Realities/Morgan Centre, University of Manchester.

Apple, M. W. (1979). *Ideology and curriculum.* Boston: Routledge & Kegan Paul.

Applebaum, L., Hartman, A., & Zakai, S. (2020). "A little bit more far than Mexico": How 3- and 4-year-old Jewish preschool students understand Israel. *Journal of Jewish Education, 87*(1), 4-34.

Applebaum, L., and Zakai, S. (2020). "I'm going to Israel and all I need to pack is my imagination": Pretend trips to Israel in Jewish early childhood education. *Journal of Jewish Education, 86*(1), 94–119.

Applebee, A. N. (1980). Children's narratives: New directions. *The Reading Teacher, 34*(2), 137–142.

Arenas, A. (2001). "If we all go global, what happens to the local?" In defense of a pedagogy of place. *Educational Practice and Theory, 23*(2), 29–47.

Arendt, H. (1959). Reflections on Little Rock. *Dissent, 6*(1), 45–56.

Ariel, J. (2020). Jewish engaged citizens as hope in Israel education: A response to Jon Levisohn. In J. Ariel (Ed.), *Israel education: The next edge,* 67–73. Jerusalem: Makom/Jewish Agency for Israel,

Attias, S. (2015). What's in a name? In pursuit of Israel education. *Journal of Jewish Education, 81*(2), 101–135.

Avidar, G. (2016). Israel education at a crossroads between transmission and transition: A comparative case study of three Jewish day high schools (Doctoral dissertation, New York University).

Avni, S., & Karpman, A. (2019, September 18). Hebrew learning in American public schools: An under-the-radar educational experience and resource. *eJewishPhilanthropy.* Retrieved from www.ejewishphilanthropy.com.

Backenroth, O., & Sinclair, A. (2014). Vision, curriculum, and pedagogical content knowledge in the preparation of Israel educators. *Journal of Jewish Education, 80*(2), 121–147.

Bain, R. B. (2006). Rounding up unusual suspects: Facing the authority hidden in the history classroom. *Teachers College Record, 108*(10), 2080–2114.

Baker, A. (2105). The legal war: Hamas' crimes against humanity and Israel's right to self-defense. In H. Goodman and D. Gold (Eds.), *The Gaza War 2014: The war Israel did not want and the disaster it averted,* 61–76. Jerusalem: Jerusalem Center for Public Affairs.

Ball, D. L. (1993). With an eye on the mathematical horizon: Dilemmas of teaching elementary school mathematics. *Elementary School Journal, 93*(4), 373–397.

Ball, D. L., & Cohen, D. K. (1999). Developing practice, developing practitioners: Toward a practice-based theory of professional education. In L. Darling-Hammond & G. Sykes (Eds.), *Teaching as the learning profession: Handbook of policy and practice,* 3–22. San Francisco: Jossey-Bass.

Balsley, T., & Fischer, E. (2016). *Shalom everybodeee!: Grover's adventures in Israel.* Minneapolis, MN: Kar-Ben.

Banks, M. (2001). *Visual method in social research.* Thousand Oaks, CA: Sage.

Barnett, M. N. (2016). *The star and the stripes: A history of the foreign policies of American Jews.* Princeton, NJ: Princeton University Press.

———. (2019, August 21). The growing gap between Israel and American Jews. *Moment.* Retrieved from www.momentmag.com.

Barrett, M. (2005). Children's understanding of, and feelings about, countries and national groups. In M. Barrett & E. Buchanan-Barrow (Eds.), *Children's understanding of society,* 251–285. Hove, UK: Psychology Press.

———. (2007). *Children's knowledge, beliefs, and feelings about nations and national groups*. Hove, UK: Psychology Press.

Barrett, M., Bennett, M., Vila, I., Valencia, J., Gimenez, A., Riazanova, T., Ravlenko, V., Kipiani, G., & Karakozov, R. (2001). *The development of national, ethnolinguistic and religious identity in children and adolescents living in the NIS*. Final Report to the International Association for the Promotion of Cooperation with Scientists from the New Independent States of the Former Soviet Union, Open Call 1997, Project No. 1363.

Barrett, M., Lyons, E., Bennett, M., Vila, I., Gimenez, A., Arcuri, L., & de Rosa, A. (1997). *Children's beliefs and feelings about their own and other national groups in Europe*. Final Report to the Commission of the European Communities, Directorate-General XII for Science, Research and Development, Human Capital and Mobility Programme, Research Network No. CHRX-CT94–0687.

Barrett, M., & Pachi, D. (2019). *Youth civic and political engagement*. New York: Routledge.

Barrett, M., & Zani, B. (2015). Political and civic engagement: Theoretical understandings, evidence, and policies. In M. Barrett & B. Zani (Eds.), *Political and civic engagement: Multidisciplinary perspectives*, 3–25. London: Routledge.

Bar-Tal, D. (1996). Development of social categories and stereotypes in early childhood: The case of "the Arab" concept formation, stereotype and attitudes by Jewish children in Israel. *International Journal of Intercultural Relations, 20*(3), 341–370.

———. (1998). Societal beliefs in times of intractable conflict: The Israeli case. *International Journal of Conflict Management, 9*(1), 22–50.

———. (2011). Challenges for constructing peace culture and peace education. In E. Matthews, D. Newman, & M. Dajani (Eds.), *The Israeli-Palestinian conflict: Parallel discourses*, pp. 209–223. London: Routledge.

Barton, K. C. (1996). Narrative simplifications in elementary students' historical thinking. In J. Brophy (Ed.), *Advances in research on teaching* (Vol. 6). *Teaching and learning in history*, 51–83. Greenwich, CT: JAI.

———. (1997a). History—it can be elementary: An overview of elementary students' understanding of history. *Social Education, 61*(1), 13–16.

———. (1997b). "I just kinda know": Elementary students' ideas about historical evidence. *Theory & Research in Social Education, 25*(4), 407–430.

———. (2001a). A sociocultural perspective on children's understanding of historical change: Comparative findings from Northern Ireland and the United States. *American Educational Research Journal, 38*(4), 881–913.

———. (2001b). "You'd be wanting to know about the past": Social contexts of children's historical understanding in Northern Ireland and the United States. *Comparative Education, 37*, 89–106.

———. (2008). "Bossed around by the queen": Elementary students' understanding of individuals and institutions in history. In L. S. Levstik and K. C. Barton (Eds.), *Researching history education: Theory, method, and context*, 159–182. New York: Routledge.

Barton, K. C., & Levstik, L. S. (1996). "Back when God was around and everything": Elementary children's understanding of historical time. *American Educational Research Journal, 32*(2), 419–454.

———. (2008). *Researching history education: Theory, method, and context.* New York: Routledge.

———. (2015). Why don't more history teachers engage students in interpretation? In W. C. Parker (Ed.), *Social studies today: Research and practice, 35–42.* New York: Routledge.

Barton, K. C., & McCully, A. W. (2005). History, identity, and the school curriculum in Northern Ireland: An empirical study of secondary students' ideas and perspectives. *Journal of Curriculum Studies, 37*(1), 85–116.

Beck, P. (2005). *A flame still burns: The dimensions and determinants of Jewish identity among young adult children of the intermarried.* New York: Jewish Outreach Institute.

Beck, T. A. (2003). "If he murdered someone, he shouldn't get a lawyer": Engaging young children in civics deliberation. *Theory & Research in Social Education, 31*(3), 326–346.

Beinart, P. (2012). *The crisis of Zionism.* New York: Macmillan.

———. (2014, September 22). American rabbis these high holidays talk about Jewish texts, not the Jewish state. *Haaretz.* Retrieved from www.haaretz.com.

———. (2017, March 8). I support boycotting settlements. Should I be banned from Israel with my children? *Forward.* Retrieved from www.forward.com.

Bekerman, Z., & Horenczyk, G. (2004). Arab-Jewish bilingual coeducation in Israel: A long-term approach to intergroup conflict resolution. *Journal of Social Issues, 60*(2), 389–404.

Bekerman, Z., & Zembylas, M. (2011). *Teaching contested narratives: Identity, memory and reconciliation in peace education and beyond.* Cambridge: Cambridge University Press.

Bennett, M., Lyons, E., Sani, F., & Barrett, M. (1998). Children's subjective identification with the group and in-group favoritism. *Developmental Psychology, 34*(5), 902–909.

Benor, S. B., Krasner, J., & Avni, S. (2020). *Hebrew infusion: Language and community at American Jewish summer camps.* New Brunswick, NJ: Rutgers University Press.

Berman, L. C., Rosenblatt, K., & Stahl, R. Y. (2020). Continuity crisis: The history and sexual politics of an American Jewish communal project. *American Jewish History, 104*(2), 167–194.

Berti, A. (1994). Children's understanding of the concept of the state. In M. Carretero & J. Voss (Eds.), *Cognitive and instructional processes in history and the social sciences, 49–75.* Hillsdale, NJ: Lawrence Erlbaum.

———. (2005). Children's understanding of politics. In M. Barrett & E. Buchanan-Barrow (Eds.), *Children's understanding of society, 69–104.* New York: Psychology Press.

Berti, A., & Bombi, A. (1981). The development of the concept of money and its value: A longitudinal study. *Child Development, 52*(4), 1179–1182.

Besser, M. (2020). *A census of Jewish day schools in the United States, 2018–2019.* New York: Avi Chai.

Biale, D. (1986). *Power and powerlessness in Jewish history*. New York: Schocken.

Bickerton, I. J., & Klausner, C. L. (2007). *A history of the Arab-Israeli conflict* (5th ed.). Upper Saddle River, NJ: Pearson Prentice Hall.

Bickmore, K. (1999). Elementary curriculum about conflict resolution: Can children handle global politics? *Theory & Research in Social Education, 27*(1), 45–69.

Bishaw, A., & Fontenot, K. (2014). *Poverty 2012 and 2013: American community survey briefs*. Washington, DC: United States Census Bureau.

Bjorklund, D. F., & Causey, K. B. (2018). *Children's thinking: Cognitive development and individual differences* (6th ed.). Thousand Oaks, CA: Sage.

Blumenthal, S. E. (2003). *The great Israel scavenger hunt*. Springfield, NJ: Behrman House.

Bosacki, S. L. (2008). *Children's emotional lives: Sensitive shadows in the classroom*. New York: Peter Lang.

Brady, H. E., Verba, S., & Schlozman, K. L. (1995). Beyond SES: A resource model of political participation. *American Political Science Review, 89*(2), 271–294.

Brammer-Shlay, S. (2017, September 20). This year, we must address the moral crisis of our Jewish generation. *Forward*. Retrieved from www.forward.com.

Breakstone, J., McGrew, S., Smith, M., Ortega, T., & Wineburg, S. (2018). Why we need a new approach to teaching digital literacy. *Phi Delta Kappan, 99*(6), 27–32.

Bredekamp, S. (Ed.). (1987). *Developmentally appropriate practice in early childhood programs serving children from birth through age 8* (expanded ed.). Washington, DC: National Association for the Education of Young Children.

Bredekamp, S., & Copple, C. (1997). *Developmentally appropriate practice: In early childhood programs*. Washington, DC: National Association for the Education of Young Children.

Brenick, A., Killen, M., Lee-Kim, J., Fox, N., Leavitt, L., Raviv, A., & Al-Smadi, Y. (2010). Social understanding in young Israeli-Jewish, Israeli-Palestinian, Palestinian, and Jordanian children: Moral judgments and stereotypes. *Early Education and Development, 21*(6), 886–911.

Brewer, W. F., & Samarapungavan, A. (1991). Children's theories vs. scientific theories: Differences in reasoning or differences in knowledge? In R. R. Hoffman & D. S. Palermo (Eds.), *Cognition and the symbolic processes: Applied and ecological perspectives*, 209–232. New York: Psychology Press..

Brinkerhoff, J. M. (2009). *Digital diasporas: Identity and transnational engagement*. New York: Cambridge University Press.

Brom, S. (Ed.). (2012). *In the aftermath of Operation Pillar of Defense: The Gaza Strip*. Tel Aviv: Institute for National Security Studies.

Bronfenbrenner, U. (1979). *The ecology of human development: Experiments by nature and design*. Cambridge, MA: Harvard University Press.

Brophy, J. (1990). Teaching social studies for understanding and higher order applications. *Elementary School Journal, 90*, 351–417.

Brophy, J., & Alleman, J. (2006). *Children's thinking about cultural universals*. New York: Routledge.

Brophy, J., VanSledright, B. A., & Bredin, N. (1992). Fifth graders' ideas about history expressed before and after their introduction to the subject. *Theory & Research in Social Education*, 20(4), 440–489.

Brown, J. A. (1980). Children's development of concepts related to country and nationality: A Canadian perspective. *Canadian Journal of Education/Revue Canadienne de L'éducation*, 5(3), 55–65.

Bruner, J. (1960). *The process of education*. Cambridge, MA: Harvard University Press.

———. (1966). *Toward a theory of instruction*. Cambridge, MA: Harvard University Press.

———. (1990). *Acts of meaning: Four lectures on mind and culture*. Cambridge, MA: Harvard University Press.

Bryfman, D., & Cohen, S. (2015a, June 30). A case for more teen Israel trips. *New York Jewish Week*. Retrieved from www.jewishweek.timesofisrael.com.

———. (2015b, July 13). To fight BDS, focus on teens. *Jewish Telegraphic Agency*. Retrieved from www.jta.org.

Buttu, D. (2014). Blaming the victims. *Journal of Palestine Studies*, 44(1), 91–96.

Cappello, M. (2005). Photo interviews: Eliciting data through conversations with children. *Field Methods*, 17(2), 170–182.

Carnevale, F. A. (2020). A "thick" conception of children's voices: A hermeneutical framework for childhood research. *International Journal of Qualitative Methods*, 19, 1–9.

Carrington, B., & Short, G. (2000). Citizenship and nationhood: The constructions of British and American children. In M. Leicester, C. Modgil, & S. Modgil (Eds.), *Politics, education and citizenship*, 183–193. London: Falmer.

Carroll, V. (1997). Learning to read, reading to learn, 1–8. Retrieved from http://lib-proxy.usc.edu.

Carter, C. (2004). Scary news: Children's responses to news of war. *Mediactive*, 3: 67–84.

Chaiklin, S. (2003). The zone of proximal development in Vygotsky's analysis of learning and instruction. In A. Kouzlin, B. Gindis, V. S. Ageyev, & S. M. Miller (Eds.), *Vygotsky's educational theory in cultural context*, 39–64. Cambridge: Cambridge University Press.

Chaille, C., & L. Britain. (1997). *The young child as scientist: A constructivist approach to early childhood science education*. New York: Longman.

Chaudron, S. (2015). Young children (0–8) and digital technology: A qualitative exploratory study across seven countries. Ispra, Italy: Joint Research Center.

Chazan, B. (1979). Israel in American Jewish schools revisited. *Journal of Jewish Education*, 47(2), 7–17.

———. (2002). The world of the Israel experience. In H. Goldberg, S. Heilman, and B. Kirshenblatt-Gimblett (Eds.), *The Israel experience: Studies in Jewish identity and youth culture*, 5–20. New York: Andrea and Charles Bronfman Philanthropies.

———. (2015). A linguistic analysis of the role of Israel in American Jewish schooling. *Journal of Jewish Education*, 81(1), 85–92.

———. (2016). *A philosophy of Israel education: A relational approach*. Lincolnshire, IL: Palgrave Macmillan.

Chorev, H., & Shumacher, Y. (2015).The road to Operation Protective Edge: Gaps in strategic perception [translated from the Hebrew]. *Israel Journal of Foreign Affairs, 8*(3), 9–24.

Chouinard, M. M., Harris, P. L., & Maratsos, M. P. (2007). Children's questions: A mechanism for cognitive development. *Monographs of the Society for Research in Child Development*, i–129.

Christensen, P., & James, A. (Eds.). (2017). *Research with children: Perspectives and practices*. New York: Routledge.

Cochran-Smith, M., & Lytle, S. L. (2015). *Inquiry as stance: Practitioner research for the next generation*. New York: Teachers College Press.

Cohen, R. S., Johnson, D. E., Thaler, D. E., Allen, B., Bartels, E. M., & Cahill, S. E. (2017). *From Cast Lead to Protective Edge: Lessons from Israel's wars in Gaza*. Santa Monica, CA: RAND Corporation.

Cohen, S. M., & Kelman, A. Y. (2007). *Beyond distancing: Young adult American Jews and their alienation from Israel*. New York: Andrea and Charles Bronfman Philanthropies.

———. (2010). Thinking about distancing from Israel. *Contemporary Jewry, 30*(2–3): 287–296.

Coles, R. (1986a). *The moral life of children*. New York: Atlantic Monthly Press.

———. (1986b). *The political life of children*. New York: Atlantic Monthly Press.

———. (1990). *The spiritual life of children*. Boston: Houghton Mifflin.

Collier, J. (1987). Visual anthropology's contributions to the field of anthropology. *Visual Anthropology, 1*, 37–46.

Connell, R. W. (1971). *The child's construction of politics*. Carlton, Australia: Melbourne University Press.

Cooper, A. (2017, September 7). What they didn't teach me at Solomon Schechter. *Jewschool*. Retrieved from www.jewschool.com.

Cooper, P. (1965). The development of the concept of war. *Journal of Peace Research, 2*(1), 1–16.

Cooper, P. M. (2009). *The classrooms all young children need: Lessons in teaching from Vivian Paley*. Chicago: University of Chicago Press.

Copple, C., & Bredekamp, S. (2009). *Developmentally appropriate practice in early childhood programs serving children from birth through age 8*. Washington, DC: National Association for the Education of Young Children.

Copple, C., Bredekamp, S., Koralek, D. G., & Charner, K. (Eds.). (2013). *Developmentally appropriate practice: Focus on preschoolers*. Washington, DC: National Association for the Education of Young Children.

———. (2014a). *Developmentally appropriate practice: Focus on children in first, second, and third grades*. Washington, DC: National Association for the Education of Young Children.

———. (2014b). *Developmentally appropriate practice: Focus on kindergarteners*. Washington, DC: National Association for the Education of Young Children.

Cordesman, A. H. (2010, June 2). Israel as a Strategic Liability? *CSIS Commentary.*

Corsaro, W. A. (2017). *The sociology of childhood* (5th ed.). Thousand Oaks, CA: Sage.

Cracraft, J. (2007). Faith in history. *Journal of the Historical Society, 7*(1), 137–149.

Craft, A. (2012). Childhood in a digital age: Creative challenges for educational futures. *London Review of Education, 10*(2), 173–190.

———. (2015). Possibility thinking: From what is to what might be. In S. Robson and S. F. Quinn (Eds.), *The Routledge international handbook of young children's thinking and understanding.* New York: Routledge.

Daiute, C. (2013). Relational resilience. In C. Fernando & M. Ferrari (Eds.), *Handbook of resilience in children of war,* 147–162. New York: Springer.

Dale, E. (1937). Children's questions as a source of curriculum material. *Educational Research Bulletin, 16*(3), 57–66.

Damon, W. (1988). *The moral child: Nurturing children's natural moral growth.* New York: Free Press.

Darling-Hammond, L. (2008). Teacher learning that supports student learning. In B. Z. Presseisen (Ed.), *Teaching for intelligence,* 91–100. Thousand Oaks, CA: Corwin.

Darling-Hammond, L., & Bransford, J. (2005). *Preparing teachers for a changing world: What teachers should learn and be able to do.* San Francisco: Jossey-Bass.

Darling-Hammond, L., & McLaughlin, M. W. (1995). Policies that support professional development in an era of reform. *Phi Delta Kappan, 76*(8), 597–604.

Davies, S. (2013). History and heritage. In P. Lambert & P. Schofield (Eds.), *Making history: An introduction to the history and practices of a discipline.* New York: Routledge.

Del Felice, C., & Wisler, A. (2007). The unexplored power and potential of youth as peace-builders. *Journal of Peace, Conflict and Development, 11.* Retrieved from http://repository.ubn.ru.nl.

Dennis, J., Lindberg, L., & McCrone, D. (1972). Support for nation and government among English children. *British Journal of Political Science, 1,* 25–48.

Dennis, J., Lindberg, L., McCrone, D., & Stiefbold, R. (1968). Political socialization to democratic orientations in four Western systems. *Comparative Political Studies, 1,* 71–101.

Dershowitz, A. (2004). *The case for Israel.* Hoboken, NJ: Wiley.

de Souza, L. K., Sperb, T. M., McCarthy, S., & Biaggio, A. M. (2006). Brazilian children's conceptions of peace, war, and violence. *Peace and Conflict, 12*(1), 49–63.

Dewey, J. (1916). *Democracy and education.* New York: Free Press.

Doherty, M. (2008). *Theory of mind: How children understand others' thoughts and feelings.* New York: Psychology Press.

Donovan, C. A. (2001). Children's development and control of written story and informational genres: "Insights from one elementary school." *Research in the Teaching of English, 35*(3), 394–447.

Donovan, C. A., & Smolkin, L. B. (2006). Children's understanding of genre and writing development. In C. A. MacArthur, S. Graham, & J. Fitzgerald (Eds.), *Handbook of writing research,* 131–143. New York: Guilford.

Dorph, G. Z. (2011). Professional development of teachers in Jewish education. In H. Miller, L. Grant, & A. Pomson (Eds.), *International handbook of Jewish education* (Vol. 5), 959–980. London: Springer.

Dorph, G. Z., & Feiman-Nemser, S. (1997). Beyond prepared materials: Fostering teacher learning in the service of children's learning. *Religious Education, 92*(4), 459–478.

Drakeford, M., Scourfield, J., Holland, S., & Davies, A. (2009). Welsh children's views on government and participation. *Childhood, 16*(2), 247–264.

Drever, E. (1995). *Using semi-structured interviews in small-scale research: A teacher's guide.* Edinburgh: Scottish Council for Research in Education.

Dreyfus, H. (2018, July 19). Harassment allegations mount against leading Jewish sociologist. *New York Jewish Week.* Retrieved from wwwjewishweek.timesofisrael.com.

———. (2021, March 23). Steven M. Cohen, shunned by academy, makes stealthy comeback—and provokes uproar. *Forward.* Retrieved from www.forward.com.

Duke, N. K., Bennett-Armistead, V. S., & Roberts, E. M. (2003). Bridging the gap between learning to read and reading to learn. In D. M. Barone & L. M. Morrow (Eds.), *Literacy and young children: Research-based practices,* 226–242. New York: Guilford.

Easton, D., & Dennis, J. (1965). The child's image of government. *Annals of the American Academy of Political and Social Science, 361*(1), 40–57.

———. (1969). *Children in the political system.* New York: McGraw Hill.

Eder, D., & Fingerson, L. (2001). Interviewing children and adolescents. In J. F. Gubrium & J. A. Holstein (Eds.), *Handbook of interview research: Context and method.* Thousand Oaks, CA: Sage.

Edwards, A., & Westgate, D. P. (2005). *Investigating classroom talk* (Vol. 13). Bristol, PA: Routledge.

Egan, K. (1997). *The educated mind: How cognitive tools shape our understanding.* Chicago: University of Chicago Press.

Eichler-Levine, J. (2018). American Judaism and race. In G. Lum & P. Harvey (Eds.), *Oxford handbook of religion and race in American history,* 191. Oxford: Oxford University Press.

Eisner, E. W. (2005). *Reimagining schools: The selected works of Elliot W. Eisner.* New York: Routledge.

Eisner, J. (2019, April 17). Trump and Netanyahu are breaking the bond between American Jews and Israel. *Time.* Retrieved from www.time.com.

Ellenson, D. (2008). Foreword. In O. N. Rose, J. E. Green Kaiser, & M. Klein (Eds.), *Righteous indignation: A Jewish call for justice.* Woodstock, VT: Jewish Lights.

Elliott, E. M., & Olliff, C. B. (2008). Developmentally appropriate emergent literacy activities for young children: Adapting the early literacy and learning model. *Early Childhood Education Journal, 35*(6), 551–556.

Emler, N. (2011). What does it take to be a political actor in a multicultural society? In M. Barrett, C. Flood, and J. Eade (Eds.), *Nationalism, ethnicity, citizenship: Multidisciplinary perspectives,* 135–161. Newcastle, UK: Cambridge Scholars.

Engel, S. (2011). Children's need to know: Curiosity in schools. *Harvard Educational Review, 81*(4), 625–645.

Engle, S. H., & Ochoa, A. S. (1988). *Education for democratic citizenship: Decision making in the social studies*. New York: Teachers College Press.

Epstein, I., Stevens, B., McKeever, P., & Baruchel, S. (2008). Photo elicitation interview (PEI): Using photos to elicit children's perspectives. *International Journal of Qualitative Methods, 5*(3), 1–11.

Evans, R. W., Newmann, F. M., & Saxe, D. W. (1996). Defining issues-centered education. In R. W. Evans & D. W. Saxe (Eds.), *Handbook on teaching social issues*, 2–4. Washington, DC: National Council for the Social Studies.

Fackenheim, E. (1970). *God's presence in history: Jewish affirmations and philosophical reflections*. New York: NYU Press.

Feiman-Nemser, S. (2001). From preparation to practice: Designing a continuum to strengthen and sustain teaching. *Teachers College Record, 103*(6), 1013–1055.

———. (2011). Preparing teachers for Jewish schools: Enduring issues in changing contexts. In H. Miller, L. Grant, & A. Pomson (Eds.), *International handbook of Jewish education* (Vol. 5), 937–958. London: Springer.

———. (2012). *Teachers as learners*. Cambridge, MA: Harvard Education Press.

Feiman-Nemser, S. & Schussler, D.L. (2010). Defining, developing, and assessing dispositions: A cross-case analysis. In P. C. Murrell Jr., M. E. Diez, S. Feiman-Nemser, & D. L Schussler (Eds.), *Teaching as a moral practice: Defining, developing, and assessing professional dispositions in teacher education*, 177–201. Cambridge, MA: Harvard Education Press.

Feldman, S. (1995). *Let's explore Israel: City tour (Let's explore being Jewish)*. Springfield, NJ: Behrman House.

Fertig, G. (2005). Teaching elementary students how to interpret the past. *The Social Studies, 96*(1), 2–8.

Feshbach, N. D., & Feshbach, S. (2011). Empathy and education. In J. Decety & W. Ickes (Eds.), *The social neuroscience of empathy*. Boston: MIT Press, 85–98.

Fishman, E. (2017, September 14). Why young Jews don't trust what their institutions say about Israel. *+972 Magazine*. Retrieved from www.972mag.

Foner, E. (2005). *Give me liberty: An American history*. New York: W. W. Norton.

Fortunati, L., Pertierra, R., & Vincent, J. (Eds.). (2013). *Migration, diaspora and information technology in global societies*. New York: Routledge.

Foster, S. J., Hoge, J. D., & Rosch, R. H. (1999). Thinking aloud about history: Children's and adolescents' responses to historical photographs. *Theory & Research in Social Education, 27*(2), 179–214.

Fowler, J. W. (1981). *Stages of faith: The psychology of human development and the quest for meaning*. New York: Harper & Row.

Foxman, A. H. (2007). *The deadliest lies: The Israel lobby and the myth of Jewish control*. New York: Palgrave Macmillan.

Frankel, G. (1996). *Beyond the Promised Land: Jews and Arabs on the hard road to a new Israel*. New York: Simon & Schuster.

Freire, P. (2018/1968). *Pedagogy of the oppressed*. Trans. M. B. Ramos. New York: Bloomsbury Academic.

Friedrich, N., Teichert, L., & Devadas, Z. (2017). The techno-literacy practices of young children from diverse backgrounds. *Language and Literacy, 19*(3), 21–34.

Funkenstein, A. (1989). Collective memory and historical consciousness. *History and Memory, 1,* 5–26.

Galante, R., & Foa, D. (1986). An epidemiological study of psychic trauma and treatment effectiveness for children after a natural disaster. *Journal of the American Academy of Child Psychiatry, 25*(3), 357–363.

Ganin, Z. (2005). *An uneasy relationship: American Jewish leadership and Israel, 1948– 1957.* Syracuse, NY: Syracuse University Press.

Garet, M. S., Porter, A. C., Desimone, L., Birman, B. F., & Yoon, K. S. (2001). What makes professional development effective? Results from a national sample of teachers. *American Educational Research Journal, 38*(4), 915–945.

Geertz, C. (1973). Deep play: Notes on the Balinese cockfight. In Clifford Geertz (Ed.), *The interpretation of cultures,* 412–453. New York: Basic Books.

Gehl, L. (2015). *Hare and tortoise race across Israel.* Minneapolis, MN: Kar-Ben.

Gerber, K. A., & Mazor, A. (2003). *Mapping Israel education: An overview of trends and issues in North America.* San Mateo, CA: Gilo Family Foundation.

Gervitz, G. (Ed.). (2009). *Let's discover Israel.* Springfield, NJ: Behrman House.

Gillham, B. (2005). *Research interviewing: The range of techniques: A practical guide.* Berkshire, UK: McGraw-Hill Education.

Gimenez, A., Canto, J., Fernandez, P., & Barrett, M. (2003). Stereotype development in Andalusian children. *Spanish Journal of Psychology, 6,* 28–34.

Ginsburg, H. P., Pappas, S., & Seo, K. H. (2001). Everyday mathematical knowledge: Asking young children what is developmentally appropriate. In S. L. Golbeck (Ed.), *The Rutgers invitational symposium on education series. Psychological perspectives on early childhood education: Reframing dilemmas in research and practice,* 181–219. Mahwah, NJ: Lawrence Erlbaum.

Ginsburg, K. R., & Jablow, M. M. (2005). *Building resilience in children and teens: Giving kids roots and wings.* Elk Grove Village, IL: American Academy of Pediatrics.

Giorno, C. (2016). *OECD economic survey of Israel, 2016.* Paris: Organization for Economic Cooperation and Development.

Gold, S. (2006). Jewish Israelis in Los Angeles. *Espace populations sociétiés* (2006/1), 47–60.

Goldberg, T., Schwarz, B. B., & Porat, D. (2011). "Could they do it differently?": Narrative and argumentative changes in students' writing following discussion of "hot" historical issues. *Cognition and Instruction, 29*(2), 185–217.

Goldman, K. (2020). The longing for Jewish homes, Jewish babies, and the trouble with Jewish women. *American Jewish History, 104*(2), 195–200.

Goldstein, L. S. (2015). *Using developmentally appropriate practices to teach the common core: Grades preK–3.* New York: Routledge.

González, B. R., Cantú, E. C., & Hernández-León, R. (2016). Moving to the "homeland": Children's narratives of migration from the United States to Mexico. *Mexican Studies/Estudios Mexicanos, 32*(2), 252–275.

Good, T. L., & Lavigne, A. L. (2018). *Looking in classrooms* (11th ed.). New York: Routledge.

Goodman, H., & Gold, D. (Eds.). (2015). *The Gaza War 2014: The war Israel did not want and the disaster it averted.* Jerusalem: Jerusalem Center for Public Affairs. Retrieved from http://jcpa.org.

Goodstein, L. (2014, September 22). Talk in synagogue of Israel and Gaza goes from debate to wrath to rage. *New York Times.* Retrieved from www.nytimes.com.

Gordis, D. (2019). *We stand divided: The rift between American Jews and Israel.* New York: Ecco/HarperCollins.

Gordon, H. R. (2009). *We fight to win: Inequality and the politics of youth activism.* New Brunswick, NJ: Rutgers University Press.

Gordon, H. R., & Taft, J. K. (2011). Rethinking youth political socialization: Teenage activists talk back. *Youth & Society, 43*(4), 1499–1527.

Goren, A. A. (1996). The Americanization of the halutz ideal. In A. Gal (Ed.), *Envisioning Israel: The changing ideals and images of North American Jews.* Jerusalem: Magnes.

———. (1999). *The politics and public culture of American Jews.* Bloomington: Indiana University Press.

Gottlieb, E., & Wineburg, S. (2012). Between veritas and communitas: Epistemic switching in the reading of academic and sacred history. *Journal of the Learning Sciences, 21*(1), 84–129.

Gould, P. (1973). The black boxes of Jonkoping: Spatial information and preference. In R. Downs & D. Stea (Eds.), *Image and environment: Cognitive mapping and spatial behavior,* 235–245. Chicago: Aldine.

Gould, P., & White, R. (1986). *Mental maps* (2nd ed.) Boston: Allen & Unwin.

Grant, L. (2001). The role of mentoring in enhancing the experience of a congregational Israel trip. *Journal of Jewish Education, 67*(1–2), 46–60.

———. (2007). Israel education in Reform congregational schools. *CCAR Journal, 54*(3), 3–24.

———. (2018). Educating for ambiguity. In S. M. Davids & L. A. Englander (Eds.), *The fragile dialogue: New voices of liberal Zionism,* 77–88. New York: CCAR.

Grant, L., & Kopelowitz, E. (2012). *Israel education matters: A 21st century paradigm for Jewish education.* Jerusalem: Center for Jewish Peoplehood Education.

Grant, L., Marom, D., & Werchow, Y. (2012). *Purposes of Israel education.* Consortium for Applied Studies in Jewish Education.

Grant, S. G., & VanSledright, B. A. (2014). *Elementary social studies: Constructing a powerful approach to teaching and learning.* New York: Routledge.

Greene, S., & Hogan, D. (Eds.). (2005). *Researching children's experience: Approaches and methods.* Thousand Oaks, CA: Sage.

Greenstein, F. I. (1960). The benevolent leader: Children's images of political authority. *American Political Science Review, 54*(4): 934–943.

———. (1961). More on children's images of the president. *Public Opinion Quarterly, 25,* 648–654.

———. (1965). *Children and politics.* New Haven, CT: Yale University Press.

———. (1975). The benevolent leader revisited: Children's images of political leaders in three democracies. *American Political Science Review, 69*(4): 1371–1398.

Grindheim, L. T. (2014). I am not angry in the kindergarten! Interruptive anger as democratic participation in Norwegian kindergartens. *Contemporary Issues in Early Childhood, 15*(4), 308–318.

Gringras, R. (2020). Israel in real life: The four Hatikvah questions. In J. Ariel (Ed.), *Israel education: The next edge,* 75–81. Jerusalem: Makom/Jewish Agency for Israel.

Groner, J. (2004). *Let's visit Israel.* Minneapolis, MN: Kar-Ben.

Gross, J. A. (2018, May 15). IDF says it thwarted 8 Hamas gunmen attempting to breach fence Monday. *The Times of Israel.* Retrieved from www.timesofisrael.com.

Gross, M. (2006). *Studying children's questions: Imposed and self-generated information seeking at school.* Lanham, MD: Scarecrow.

Groundwater-Smith, S., Dockett, S., & Bottrell, D. (2014). *Participatory research with children and young people.* Thousand Oaks, CA: Sage.

Guo, D., Wright, K. L., & McTigue, E. M. (2018). A content analysis of visuals in elementary school textbooks. *Elementary School Journal, 119*(2), 244–269.

Gutiérrez, K. D., & Rogoff, B. (2003). Cultural ways of learning: Individual traits or repertoires of practice. *Educational Researcher, 32*(5), 19–25.

Hackett, C., McClendon, D., Potančoková, M., & Stonawski, M. (2016, December 13). *Religion and education around the world.* Washington, DC: Pew Research Center.

Halbwachs, M. (1980/1950). *The collective memory.* Trans. F. J. Ditter Jr. & V. Y. Ditter. New York: Harper & Row.

Halevi, Y. K. (2018, April 13). Israelis, Palestinians, and the necessary injustice of partition. *Wall Street Journal.* Retrieved from www.wsj.com.

Hanau, S. (2021, March 26). 500 Jewish clergy pan comeback attempt of academic accused of sexual misconduct. *The Times of Israel.* Retrieved from www.timesofisrael.com.

Harlaar, N., Dale, P. S., & Plomin, R. (2007). From learning to read to reading to learn: Substantial and stable genetic influence. *Child Development, 78*(1), 116–131.

Harper, D. (2002). Talking about pictures: A case for photo elicitation. *Visual Studies, 17*(1), 13–26.

Hart, R. A. (2008). *Children's participation: The theory and practice of involving young citizens in community development and environmental care.* New York: UNICEF.

Hassenfeld, J. (2015). Sixty-six years of fighting: Parents and their children talk about the Arab-Israeli conflict. Paper presented at the Network for Research in Jewish Education, New York.

———. (2016). Negotiating critical analysis and collective belonging: Jewish American students write the history of Israel. *Contemporary Jewry, 36*(1), 55–84.

———. (2018). Landscapes of collective belonging: Jewish Americans narrate the history of Israel after an organized tour. *Journal of Jewish Education, 84*(2), 131–160.

Hassenfeld, Z. R. (2016). Reading sacred texts in the classroom: The alignment between students and their teacher's interpretive stances when reading the Hebrew Bible. *Journal of Jewish Education, 82*(1), 81–107.

———. (2019a). Pursuing fluency: A curricular intervention in Tanakh education. *Journal of Jewish Education, 85*(3): 293–311.

———. (2019b). The mistaken assumption: Text study has to wait. In D. T. Schuster (Ed.), *Portraits of Jewish learning: Viewing contemporary Jewish education close-in*, 1–15. Eugene, OR: Wipf & Stock.

Hassenfeld, Z. R., & Levisohn, J. A. (2019). The challenge of professional development in Jewish Studies: Why the conventional wisdom may not be enough. *Journal of Jewish Education, 85*(1), 53–75.

Hasson, N. (2016, May 3). Abu Khdeir murderer sentenced to life imprisonment plus 20 years. Haaretz. Retrieved from www.haaretz.com.

Hauver, J. (2019). *Young children's civic mindedness: Democratic living and learning in an unequal world*. New York: Routledge.

Hauver, J., Zhao, X., & Kobe, J. F. (2017). Performance as pedagogy: Children's trust and the negotiation of subjectivities in the context of deliberative dialogue. *Theory & Research in Social Education, 45*(3), 293–317.

Hedges, H. (2010). Whose goals and interests? The interface of children's play and teachers' pedagogical practices. In L. Brooker & S. Edwards (Eds.), *Engaging play*, 25–38. Berkshire, UK: Open University Press.

Hedges, H., & Cooper, M. (2016). Inquiring minds: Theorizing children's interests. *Journal of Curriculum Studies, 48*(3), 303–322.

Heisler, N. (2017, September 29). "Complicated" isn't good enough. It's time for the Conservative movement to address the occupation. *Tikkun*. Retrieved from Tikkun Daily Blog Archive, www.tikkun.org.

Heller, D. (1988). *The children's God*. Chicago: University of Chicago Press.

Herman, P. (1998). *Los Angeles Jewish population survey, 1997*. Los Angeles: Jewish Federation of Greater Los Angeles.

Hertzel, D. (2017). *Ancestors: Who we are and where we come from*. Lanham, MD: Rowman & Littlefield.

Hess, D. E. (2009). *Controversy in the classroom: The democratic power of discussion*. New York: Routledge.

Hess, D. E., & McAvoy, P. (2014). *The political classroom: Evidence and ethics in democratic education*. New York: Routledge.

Hess, R. D., & Easton, D. (1960). The child's changing image of the president. *Public Opinion Quarterly, 24*, 632–644.

Hess, R. D., & Torney, J. V. (1967). *The development of political attitudes in children*. Chicago: Aldine.

Heywood, C. (2017). *A history of childhood*. Cambridge, UK: Polity.

Hirsch Jr., E. D. (1988). *Cultural literacy: What every American needs to know*. New York: Vintage.

———. (2016). *Why knowledge matters: Rescuing our children from failed educational theories*. Cambridge, MA: Harvard Education Press.

———. (2020). *How to educate a citizen: The power of shared knowledge to unify a nation*. New York: HarperCollins.

Holtz, B. W. (2013). A map of orientations to the teaching of the Bible. In J. Levisohn & S. P. Fendrick (Eds.), *Turn it and turn it again: Studies in the teaching and learning of classical Jewish texts*, 26–51. Boston: Academic Studies Press.

Holtz, B. W., Gamoran, A., Dorph, G. Z., Goldring, E., & Robinson, B. (2000). Changing the core: Communal policies and present realities in the professional development of teachers for Jewish schools. *Journal of Jewish Communal Service, 76*, 173–185.

Horn, D. (2019, April 30). Anti-semites don't just hate Jews. They're targeting freedom. *New York Times*. Retrieved from www.nytimes.com.

Horowitz, B. (2002). Reframing the study of contemporary American Jewish identity. *Contemporary Jewry, 23*, 1–23.

———. (2012). *Defining Israel education*. Chicago: The iCenter.

Husband Jr., T. (2010). He's too young to learn about that stuff: Anti-racist pedagogy and early childhood social studies. *Social Studies Research & Practice, 5*(2), 61–75.

Hyde, B. (2008). *Children and spirituality: Searching for meaning and connectedness*. London: Jessica Kingsley.

Ichilov, O. (1991). Political socialization and schooling effects among Israeli adolescents. *Comparative Education Review, 35*, 430–447.

IDF statement on Gaza border events (2019, February 1). Retrieved from Gaza Border Events: Questions and Answers, www.idf.il.

Inbar, E., & Shamir, E. (2014). "Mowing the grass": Israel's strategy for protracted intractable conflict. *Journal of Strategic Studies, 37*(1), 65–90.

Irizarry, J. G., & Kleyn, T. (2011). Immigration and education in the "supposed land of opportunity": Youth perspectives on living and learning in the United States. *The New Educator, 7*(1), 5–26.

Isaacs, A. (2011). Israel education: Purposes and practices. In H. Miller, L. Grant, & A. Pomson (Eds.), *International handbook of Jewish education*, pp. 479–496. Dordrecht, Netherlands: Springer.

Jackson, L. A. (2009). Observing children's stress behaviors in a kindergarten classroom. *Early Childhood Research & Practice, 11*(1). Retrieved from ECRP, www.ecrp.illinois.edu.

Jahoda, G. (1962). Development of Scottish children's ideas and attitudes about other countries. *Journal of Social Psychology, 58*, 91–108.

James, J. H., Kobe, J. F., & Zhao, X. (2017). Examining the role of trust in shaping children's approaches to peer dialogue. *Teachers College Record, 119*(10), 1–34.

Jans, M. (2004). Children as citizens: Towards a contemporary notion of child participation. *Childhood, 11*(1), 27–44.

Jaspers, J., Van de Geer, J., Tajfel, H., & Johnson, N. (1972). On the development of national attitudes in children. *European Journal of Social Psychology, 2*, 347–369.

Jenkins, H., Purushotma, R., Weigel, M., Clinton, K., & Robinson, A. J. (2009). *Confronting the challenges of participatory culture: Media education for the 21st century*. A report for the MacArthur Foundation. Boston: MIT Press.

Jennings, M. K., & Niemi, R. G. (1968). The transmission of political values from parent to child. *American Political Science Review, 62*(1), 169–184.

Johnson, N., Middleton, M., & Tajfel, H. (1970). The relationship between children's preferences for and knowledge about other nations. *British Journal of Social and Clinical Psychology, 9,* 232–240.

Jordan, J. V. (2013). Relational resilience in girls. In S. Goldstein & R. Brooks (Eds.), *Handbook of resilience in children.* Boston: Springer.

Kahn, S. (2021). No child too young: A teacher research study of socioscientific issues implementation at the elementary level. In *Socioscientific issues-based instruction for scientific literacy development,* 1–30. IGI Global.

Kallio, K. P., & Häkli, J. (2013). Children and young people's politics in everyday life. *Space and Polity, 17*(1), 1–16.

Kamberelis, G. (1999). Genre development and learning: "Children writing stories, science reports, and poems." *Research in the Teaching of English, 33*(4), 403–460.

Kaplan, M. M. (2010/1934). *Judaism as a civilization: Toward a reconstruction of American-Jewish life.* Philadelphia: Jewish Publication Society in cooperation with the Jewish Reconstructionist Federation.

Katz, E. A. (2015). *Bringing Zion home: Israel in American Jewish culture, 1948–1967.* Albany, NY: SUNY Press.

Katz, M. L., & Kress, J. S. (2018). Jewish history engagement in an online simulation: Golda and Coco, Leah and Lou at the Jewish Court of All Time. *Journal of Jewish Education, 84*(2), 196–221.

Kaye, D., Nader, A., & Roshan, P. (2011). Israeli perceptions of and policies toward Iran. In *Israel and Iran: A dangerous rivalry,* 19–54. Santa Monica, CA: RAND Corporation.

Kelly, C. (2015). "Let's do some jumping together": Intergenerational participation in the use of remote technology to co-construct social relations over distance. *Journal of Early Childhood Research, 13*(1), 29–46.

Kelner, S. (2010). *Tours that bind: Diaspora, pilgrimage, and Israeli birthright tourism.* New York: NYU Press.

Kent, O., & Cook, A. (2019). A portrait of three partners. In D. T. Schuster (Ed.), *Portraits of Jewish learning: Viewing contemporary Jewish education close-in,* 1–15. Eugene, OR: Wipf & Stock.

Kessler, R. (2000). *The soul of education: Helping students find connection, compassion, and character at school.* Alexandria, VA: ASCD.

Keysar, A., & Kosmin, B. (2004). *"Eight up": The college years: The Jewish engagement of young adults raised in Conservative synagogues, 1995–2003.* New York: Jewish Theological Seminary.

Khalidi, R. I. (2014). From the editor: The Dahiya doctrine, proportionality, and war crimes. *Journal of Palestine Studies, 44*(1), 5–13.

Kim, H. K., & Leavitt, N. S. (2016). *JewAsian: Race, religion, and identity for America's newest Jews.* Lincoln: University of Nebraska Press.

Kohn, A. (1999). *The schools our children deserve: Moving beyond traditional classrooms and "tougher standards."* New York: Houghton Mifflin Harcourt.

Kolsky, T. (2010). *Jews against Zionism: The American Council for Judaism, 1942–1948.* Philadelphia: Temple University Press.

Kopelowitz, E., & Weiss, N. (2014.) *The Goodman camping initiative for modern Israeli history.* Kibbutz Hannaton, Israel: Research Success Technologies.

Koren, A., Fishman, S., Aronson, J. K., & Saxe, L. (2015). *The Israel literacy measurement project: 2015 report.* Waltham, MA: Cohen Center for Modern Jewish Studies.

Kosmin, B., & Keysar, A. (2000). *"Four up"—The high school years, 1995–1999: The Jewish development of the b'nai mitzvah class of 5755.* New York: Jewish Theological Seminary.

Krasner, J. (2003). "New Jews" in an old-new land: Images in American Jewish textbooks prior to 1948. *Journal of Jewish Education, 69*(2), 7–22.

———. (2005a). Jewish education and American Jewish education, Part I. *Journal of Jewish Education, 71*(2), 121–177.

———. (2005b). Jewish education and American Jewish education, Part II. *Journal of Jewish Education, 71*(3), 279–317.

———. (2006). Jewish education and American Jewish education, Part III. *Journal of Jewish Education, 72*(1), 29–76.

Kress, J. S., & Elias, M. J. (2008). Distancing in encompassing education settings: Lessons from Jewish education. *Journal of Applied Developmental Psychology, 29*(4), 337–344.

Kreuzer, P. (2002). *Applying theories of ethno-cultural conflict and conflict resolution to collective violence in Indonesia.* Frankfurt: Peace Research Institute of Frankfurt.

Kulick, R. (2013). Learning from each other: Collective practices in making independent youth media. In S. K. Nenga & J. K. Taft (Eds.), *Youth engagement: The civic-political lives of children and youth, 227–251.* Bingley, UK: Emerald Group.

Kurtzer, Y. (2012). *Shuva: The future of the Jewish past.* Waltham, MA: Brandeis University Press.

Kurtzer, Y., Adland, N., Baird, J., & Tucker, G. (2019). *Courageous leadership: The challenges facing Jewish leadership in a partisan age.* New York: Shalom Hartman Institute.

Kushner, H. S. (1989). *When children ask about God.* New York: Schocken.

Lambert, W. E., & Klineberg, O. (1976). *Children's views of foreign peoples: A cross-national study.* New York: Appleton-Century-Crofts.

Lankshear, C., & Knobel, M. (2003) *New literacies: Changing knowledge and classroom learning.* Buckingham, UK: Open University Press.

Lanski, A. (2021). Why Israel matters. *Sources: A Journal of Jewish Ideas, 1*(1), 93–95.

Laqueur, W. (2003/1972). *A history of Zionism: From the French Revolution to the establishment of the state of Israel.* New York: Schocken.

Lave, J., & Wenger, E. (1991). *Situated learning: Legitimate peripheral participation.* Cambridge: Cambridge University Press.

Lawrence-Lightfoot, S. (1997). *The art and science of portraiture* (1st ed.). San Francisco: Jossey-Bass.

Lee, H. (Ed.). (2009). *Ties to the homeland: Second generation transnationalism*. Cambridge, UK: Cambridge Scholars.

Lee, P. (1998a) "A lot of guess work goes on": Children's understanding of historical accounts. *Teaching History, 92*, 29.

———. (1998b). Making sense of historical accounts. *Canadian Social Studies, 32*(2), 52.

Lee, P., & Ashby, R. (2000). Progression in historical understanding among students ages 7–14. In P. Stearns, P. Seixas, & S. Wineburg (Eds.), *Knowing, teaching, and learning history: National and international perspectives*, 199–222. New York: NYU Press.

Lee, P., & Shemilt, D. (2004). "I just wish we could go back in the past and find out what really happened": Progression in understanding about historical accounts. *Teaching History, 117*, 25.

Levin, I., & Wilkening, F. (1989). Measuring time via counting: The development of children's conceptions of time as a quantifiable dimension. *Advances in Psychology, 59*, 119–144.

Levisohn, J. (2016, Spring). Redeeming Jewish literacy. *HaYidion: The RAVSAK Journal*, 12–13.

Levisohn, J., & Kelman, A. (2019). *Beyond Jewish identity: Rethinking concepts and imagining alternatives*. Boston: Academic Studies Press.

Levstik, L. S. (1989). Historical narrative and the young reader. *Theory into Practice, 28*(2), 114–119.

———. (2000). Articulating the silences: Teachers' and adolescents' conceptions of historical significance. In P. N. Stearns, P. Seixas, & S. Wineburg (Eds.), *Knowing, teaching, & learning history*, 284–305. New York: NYU Press.

———. (2008a). Building a sense of history in a first-grade classroom. In L. S. Levstik & K. C. Barton (Eds.), *Researching history education: Theory, method, and context*, 30–60. New York: Routledge.

———. (2008b). Historical response and narrative. In L. S. Levstik & K. C. Barton (Eds.), *Researching history education: Theory, method, and context*, 10–29. New York: Routledge.

Levstik, L. S., & Barton, K. C. (1996). "They still use some of their past": Historical salience in elementary children's chronological thinking. *Journal of Curriculum Studies, 28*(5), 531–576.

———. (2008) "They still use some of their past": Historical salience in elementary children's chronological thinking. In L. S. Levstik & K. C. Barton (Eds.), *Researching history education: Theory, method, and context*, 108–147. New York: Routledge.

———. (2011). *Doing history: Investigating with children in elementary and middle schools*. New York: Routledge.

Levstik, L. S., & Pappas, C. C. (1987). Exploring the development of historical understanding. *Journal of Research and Development in Education, 21*(1), 1–15.

Lichterman, P. (1996). *The search for political community: American activists reinventing commitment*. Cambridge: Cambridge University Press.

Licoppe, C., & Smoreda, Z. (2005). Are social networks technologically embedded? How networks are changing today with changes in communication technology. *Social Networks, 27*(4), 317–335.

Liebman, C. S. (1999). American Jews and Israel: Has the romance ended? *The collected speeches of Charles S. Liebman.* Retrieved from www.bjpa.org.

Limonic, L. (2019). *Kugel and frijoles: Latino Jews in the United States.* Detroit: Wayne State University Press.

Lindfors, J. W. (1999). *Children's inquiry: Using language to make sense of the world.* Language and Literacy Series. New York: Teachers College Press.

Liss, J. (2017). Preface. In S. M. Davids & L. A. Englander (Eds.), *The fragile dialogue: New voices of liberal Zionism,* xiii–xvi. New York: CCAR.

Litman, L. (2004). Voices from the field: Addressing Israel in this time of crisis. Retrieved from https://theicenter.org.

Little, J. W. (1982). Norms of collegiality and experimentation: Workplace conditions of school success. *American Educational Research Journal, 19*(3), 325–340.

Low, S. M. (1992). Symbolic ties that bind. In I. Altman & S. M. Low (Eds.), *Place attachment: Human behavior and environment.* Boston: Springer.

Lowenthal, D. (1985). *The past is a foreign country.* Cambridge: Cambridge University Press.

Macedo, S. (2005). *Democracy at risk: How political choices undermine citizen participation, and what we can do about it.* Washington, DC: Brookings Institution.

Malka, V., Ariel, Y., & Avidar, R. (2015). Fighting, worrying and sharing: Operation "Protective Edge" as the first WhatsApp war. *Media, War & Conflict, 8*(3), 329–344.

Maltz, J. (2019, July 1). J Street launches Birthright alternative, featuring "Occupation 101." *Forward.* Retrieved from www.forward.com.

Maoz, I. (2010). *Educating for peace through planned encounters between Jews and Arabs in Israel: A reappraisal of effectiveness.* In G. Salomon & E. Cairns (Eds.), *Handbook on peace education,* 303–313. New York: Psychology Press.

Marcus, I. G. (1996). *Rituals of childhood: Jewish acculturation in medieval Europe.* New Haven, CT: Yale University Press.

Martin, L. A. (2008). Elementary and secondary teacher education students' perspectives on citizenship. *Action in Teacher Education, 30*(3), 54–63.

Masalha, S. (1993). The effect of prewar conditions on the psychological reactions of Palestinian children to the Gulf War. In L. A. Leavett & N. A. Fox (Eds.), *The psychological effects of war and violence on children,* 131–142. New York: Psychology Press.

Matthews, M. H. (1992). *Making sense of place: Children's understanding of large-scale environments.* London: Harvester Wheatsheaf.

May, L. A., Stenhouse, V., & Holbrook, T. (2014). Critical moment but not critical literacy: Perspectives on teaching about President Obama. *Social Studies Research & Practice, 9*(1), 165–188.

McAvoy, P., & Hess, D. E. (2013). Classroom deliberation in an era of political polarization. *Curriculum Inquiry, 43*(1), 14–47.

McConaughy, S. H. (2013). *Clinical interviews for children and adolescents* (2nd ed.). New York: Guilford.

McGee, L. (1996). Response-centered talk: Windows on children's thinking. In L. B. Gambrell and J. F. Almasi (Eds.), *Lively discussions! Fostering engaged reading*. Newark, DE: International Reading Association.

McGintiy, K. R. (2018, June 21). American Jewry's #MeToo problem: A first-person encounter. *New York Jewish Week*. Retrieved from www.jewishweek.timesofisrael.com.

McKeown, M., & Beck, I. L. (1994). Making sense of accounts of history: Why young students don't and how they might. In G. Leinhardt, I. L. Beck, & C. Stainton (Eds.), *Teaching and Learning in History*, 1–26. New York: Routledge.

McTighe, J., & Wiggins, G. (2013). *Essential questions: Opening doors to student understanding*. Alexandria, VA: ASCD.

Meier, D. (2002/1995). *The power of their ideas: Lessons for America from a small school in Harlem*. Boston: Beacon.

Metz, K. E. (2004). Children's understanding of scientific inquiry: Their conceptualization of uncertainty in investigations of their own design. *Cognition and instruction*, 22(2), 219–290.

Miles, M. B., & Huberman, A. M. (1994). *Qualitative data analysis: An expanded sourcebook*. Thousand Oaks, CA: Sage.

Miller, P. J. (1994). Narrative practices: Their role in socialization and self-construction. In U. Neisser & R. Fivush (Eds.), *The remembering self: Construction and accuracy in the self-narrative* (No. 6), 158–179. Cambridge: Cambridge University Press.

Moore, D. D. (1996). Bonding images: Miami Jews and the campaign for Israel bonds. In A. Gal (Ed.), *Envisioning Israel: The changing ideals and images of North American Jews*, 254–267. Detroit: Wayne State University Press.

Moore, D. D., & Troen, S. I. (Eds.). (2008). *Divergent Jewish Cultures: Israel and America*. New Haven, CT: Yale University Press.

Moore, S. W., Lare, J., & Wagner, K. A. (1985). *The child's political world: A longitudinal perspective*. New York: Praeger.

Morrow, V., & Crivello, G. (2015). What is the value of qualitative longitudinal research with children and young people for international development? *International Journal of Social Research Methodology*, 18(3), 267–280.

Murphy, A., & Laugharne, J. (2013). Children's perceptions of national identity in Wales. *Education 3–13*, 41(2), 188–201.

Murthy, R. S., & Lakshminarayana, R. (2006). Mental health consequences of war: A brief review of research findings. *World Psychiatry*, 5(1), 25–30.

Narayan, R., Rodriguez, C., Araujo, J., Shaqlaih, A., & Moss, G. (2013). "Constructivism—Constructivist learning theory." In B. J. Irby, G. Brown, R. Lara-Alecio, & S. Jackson (Eds.), *The handbook of educational theories*, 169–183. Charlotte, NC: Information Age.

Nash, C. (2008). *Of Irish descent: Origin stories, genealogy, and the politics of belonging*. Syracuse, NY: Syracuse University Press.

Nasie, M., & Bar-Tal, D. (2012). Sociopsychological infrastructure of an intractable conflict through the eyes of Palestinian children and adolescents. *Peace and Conflict: Journal of Peace Psychology, 18*(1), 3–20.

Nasir, N. S. (2012). *Racialized identities: Race and achievement among African American youth.* Palo Alto, CA: Stanford University Press.

National Association for the Education of Young Children. Developmentally appropriate practice: A position statement. (2020). NAEYC. Retrieved from www.naeyc.org.

National Council for the Social Studies (2016). *A vision of powerful teaching and learning in the social studies.* Silver Spring, MD: NCSS.

Nenga, S. K. (2012). Not the community, but a community: Transforming youth into citizens through volunteer work. *Journal of Youth Studies, 15*(8), 1063–1077.

Nenga, S. K., & Taft, J. K. (2013). Introduction. In S. K. Nenga & J. K. Taft (Eds.), *Youth engagement: The civic-political lives of children and youth.* Bingley, UK: Emerald Group.

Nets-Zehngut, R. (2011). Origins of the Palestinian refugee problem: Changes in the historical memory of Israelis/Jews 1949–2004. *Journal of Peace Research, 48*(2), 235–248.

Nets-Zehngut, R., & Bar-Tal, D. (2016). Zionists but less: Competing narratives in the Israeli-Jewish popular memory of the Israeli-Arab/Palestinian conflict: Findings of a public opinion survey. *Gilui Da'at* (Hebrew), *9,* 41–65.

Nette, J., & Hayden, M. (2007). Globally mobile children: The sense of belonging. *Educational Studies, 33*(4), 435–444.

Neuman, S. B., Copple, C., & Bredekamp, S. (2000). *Learning to read and write: Developmentally appropriate practices for young children.* Washington, DC: National Association for the Education of Young Children.

Neusner, D. (Ed.). (2009). *Let's discover Israel.* Springfield, NJ: Behrman House.

Neusner, J. (1995). The conundrum of historical consciousness. *First Things, 55,* 55–57.

Newman, V. (2011). *Ella's trip to Israel.* Minneapolis, MN: Kar-Ben.

Newport, F. (2019, August 27). Polling matters: American Jews, politics, and Israel. *Gallup.* Retrieved from www.news.gallup.com.

Nguyen, K. M. (2017). *Learning to mow grass: IDF adaptations to hybrid threats.* US Army School for Advanced Military Studies, Fort Leavenworth, United States.

Niemi, R. G., & Jennings, M. K. (1991). Issues and inheritance in the formation of party identification. *American Journal of Political Science, 35,* 970–988.

Niemi, R. G., & Junn, J. (1998). *Civic education: What makes students learn?* New Haven, CT: Yale University Press.

Nieto, S. (2006). Teaching as political work: Learning from courageous and caring teachers. Longfellow Lecture at the Child Development Institute, Sarah Lawrence College, 1–11.

Noddings, N. (2002). *Educating moral people: A caring alternative to character education.* New York: Teachers College Press.

———. (2013). *Caring: A relational approach to ethics and moral education.* Berkeley: University of California Press.

Nora, P. (1989). Between memory and history: *Les lieux de mémoire. Representations*, *26*, 1–15.

Nugent, J. (1994). The development of children's relationships with their country. *Children's Environments*, *11*(4), 281–291.

OCHA (2014, September 4). Occupied Palestinian territory: Gaza emergency situation report. Retrieved from www.unispal.un.org.

O'Connor, C. D. (2013). Engaging young people? The experiences, challenges, and successes of Canadian youth advisory councils. In S. K. Nenga & J. K. Taft (Eds.), *Youth engagement: The civic-political lives of children and youth*. Bingley, UK: Emerald Group.

Olsson, L. M. (2013). Taking children's questions seriously: The need for creative thought. *Global Studies of Childhood*, *3*, 230–253.

Omer, A. (2019). *Days of awe: Reimagining Jewishness in solidarity with Palestinians*. Chicago: University of Chicago Press.

Opitz, M. F., & Ford, M. P. (2014). *Engaging minds in the classroom: The surprising power of joy*. Alexandria, VA: ASCD.

O'Toole, T., Marsh, D., & Jones, S. (2003) Political literacy cuts both ways: The politics of non-participation among young people. *Political Quarterly*, *74*(3): 349–360.

Oxley, Z. M., Holman, M. R., Greenlee, J. S., Bos, A. L., & Lay, J. C. (2020). Children's Views of the American Presidency. Public Opinion Quarterly, 84(1), 141–157.

Paley, V. G. (1992). *You can't say you can't play*. Cambridge, MA: Harvard University Press.

———. (2004). *A child's work: The importance of fantasy play*. Chicago, IL: University of Chicago Press.

Palfrey, J., & Gasser, U. (2016). *Born digital: How children grow up in a digital age*. New York: Basic Books.

Pappas, C. C. (1993). Is narrative "primary"? Some insights from kindergarteners' pretend readings of stories and information books. *Journal of Reading Behavior*, *25*(1), 97–129.

Parker, A., & Neuharth-Pritchett, S. (2006). Developmentally appropriate practice in kindergarten: Factors shaping teacher beliefs and practice. *Journal of Research in Childhood Education*, *21*(1), 65–78.

Parker, W. C. (2012). *Social studies in elementary education* (14th ed.). Boston: Pearson.

Pascal, C., & Bertram, T. (2009). Listening to young citizens: The struggle to make real a participatory paradigm in research with young children. *European Early Childhood Education Research Journal*, *17*(2), 249–262.

Passe, J. (2008). A counter-intuitive strategy: Reduce student stress by teaching current events. *Social Studies and the Young Learner*, *20*(3), 27–31.

Payne, G. (2006). Cohort studies. In V. Jupp (Ed.), *The SAGE dictionary of social research methods*, 30–32. Thousand Oaks, CA: Sage.

Payne, K. A., Adair, J. K., Colegrove, K.S.S., Lee, S., Falkner, A., McManus, M., & Sachdeva, S. (2020). Reconceptualizing civic education for young children: Recognizing embodied civic action. Education, Citizenship and Social Justice, 15(1), 35–46.

Payne, K. A., & Journell, W. (2019). "We have those kinds of conversations here . . .": Addressing contentious politics with elementary students. *Teaching and Teacher Education, 79*, 73–82.

Pearn, J. (2003). Children and war. *Journal of Pediatrics and Child Health, 39*, 166–172.

Percy-Smith, B. (2010). Councils, consultations and community: Rethinking the spaces for children and young people's participation. *Children's Geographies, 8*(2), 107–122.

Peters, J., & Newman, D. (2013). *The Routledge handbook on the Israeli-Palestinian conflict*. New York: Routledge.

Pew Research Center. (2021, May 11). *Jewish Americans in 2020*. Washington, DC: Pew Research Center.

Phillips, B. (2007). Faultlines: The seven socio-ecologies of Jewish Los Angeles. In B. Zuckerman & J. Schoenberg (Eds.), *The Jewish role in American life: An annual review* (Vol. 5). West Lafayette, IN: Purdue University Press.

Phillips, B., Lengyel, E., & Saxe, L. (2002). *American attitudes toward Israel*. Waltham, MA: Maurice and Marilyn Cohen Center for Modern Jewish Studies, Brandeis University.

Piaget, J. (1923/1926). *The language and thought of the child*. London: Kegan Paul, Trench, Trubner.

———. (1927/1930). *The child's conception of physical causality*. London: Kegan Paul, Trench, Trubner.

———. (1928). *Judgment and reasoning in the child*. London: Routledge & Kegan Paul.

———. (1954). *The construction of reality in the child*. New York: Basic Books.

———. (2007/1929). *The child's conception of the world: A 20th-century classic of child psychology* (2nd ed.). Lanham, MD: Rowman & Littlefield.

Piaget, J., & Weil, A. (1951). The development in children of the idea of the homeland and of relations to other countries. *International Social Science Journal, 3*, 561–578.

Pianko, N. (2010). *Zionism and the roads not taken: Rawidowicz, Kaplan, Kohn*. Bloomington: Indiana University Press.

Pink, A. (2019, June 13). IfNotNow made an impact with its Birthright protests. Now it's stopping them. *Forward*. Retrieved from https://forward.com.

Pirus, C., Leridon, H., & Wiles-Portier, E. (2010). Large child cohort studies across the world. *Population, 65*(4), 575–629.

Platten, L. (1995a). Talking geography: An investigation into young children's understanding of geographical terms, Part 1. *International Journal of Early Years Education, 3*(1), 74–92.

———. (1995b). Talking geography: An investigation into young children's understanding of geographical terms, Part 2. *International Journal of Early Years Education, 3*(3), 69–84.

Plowman, L., Stephen, C., & McPake, J. (2010). *Growing up with technology: Young children learning in a digital world*. New York: Routledge.

Podeh, E. (2010). Univocality within multivocality: The Israeli-Arab-Palestinian conflict as reflected in Israeli history textbooks, 2000–2010. *Journal of Educational Media, Memory, and Society, 2*(2), 44–62.

Polletta, F., Chen, P.C.B., Gardner, B. G., & Motes, A. (2011). The sociology of storytelling. *Annual Review of Sociology, 37*(1), 109–130.

Pomson, A. (2018). *Devoted, disengaged, disillusioned: The forces that shape a relationship with Israel.* Berkeley, CA: Rosov Consulting.

Pomson, A., & Deitcher, H. (2010). Day school Israel education in the age of Birthright. *Journal of Jewish Education, 76*(1), 52–73.

Pomson, A., Deitcher, H., & Held, D. (2011). *How do Jewish day school students think and feel about Israel?* Jerusalem: Melton Centre for Jewish Education.

Pomson, A., & Held, D. (2012). "Why Israel?" Re-viewing Israel education through the lenses of civic and political engagement. *Journal of Jewish Education, 78*(2), 97–113.

Pomson, A., & Schnoor, R. F. (2008). *Back to school: Jewish day school in the lives of adult Jews.* Detroit: Wayne State University Press.

———. (2018). *Jewish family: Identity and self-formation at home.* Bloomington: Indiana University Press.

Pomson, A., Wertheimer, J., & Hacohen-Wolf, H. (2014). *Hearts and minds: Israel in North American Jewish day schools.* New York: AVI CHAI Foundation.

Pontón, M.E.L., & Andrade, H. V. (2007). Children as agents of social change. *Children, Youth and Environments, 17*(2), 147–169.

Porat, D. A. (2004). It's not written here, but this is what happened: Students' cultural comprehension of textbook narratives on the Israeli–Arab conflict. *American Educational Research Journal, 41*(4), 963–996.

Punamaki, R. L. (1999). Concept formation of war and peace: A meeting point between child development and a politically violent society. In A. Raviv, L.Oppenheimer, & D. Bar-Tal (Eds.), *How Children Understand War and Peace: A Call for International Peace Education,* 127–144. San Francisco: Jossey-Bass.

Pustulka, P., Ślusarczyk, M., & Strzemecka, S. (2016). Polish children in Norway: Between national discourses of belonging and everyday experiences of life abroad. In Z. Millei & R. Imre (Eds.), *Childhood and nation,* 207–227. New York: Palgrave Macmillan.

Putnam, R. D. (2000). *Bowling alone: The collapse and revival of American community.* New York: Touchstone.

Raider, M. A., Sarna, J. D., & Zweig, R. W. (2012). *Abba Hillel Silver and American Zionism.* New York: Routledge.

Rakison, D. H., & Yermolayeva, Y. (2011). How to identify a domain-general learning mechanism when you see one. *Journal of Cognition and Development, 12*(2), 134–153.

Rantala, T., & Määttä, K. (2012). Ten theses of the joy of learning at primary schools. *Early Child Development and Care, 182*(1), 87–105.

Rauchwerger, D. L. (2018). *Dinosaur goes to Israel.* Minneapolis, MN: Kar-Ben.

Rebhun, U., & Ari, L. L. (2010). *American Israelis: Migration, transnationalism, and diasporic identity.* Boston: Brill.

Rebhun, U., & Levy, S. (2006). Unity and diversity: Jewish identification in America and Israel 1990–2000. *Sociology of Religion, 67*(4), 391–414.

Reich, R. B. (2019). *The common good*. New York: Vintage.

Reingold, M. (2017). Not the Israel of my elementary school: An exploration of Jewish-Canadian secondary students' attempts to process morally complex Israeli narratives. *The Social Studies, 108*(3), 87–98.

———. (2018). Broadening perspectives on immigrant experiences: Secondary students study the absorption difficulties faced by Mizrachi immigrants in Israel. *Journal of Jewish Education, 84*(3), 312–329.

Robertson, M., & Gerber, R. (2001). *Children's ways of knowing: Learning through experience*. Melbourne: Acer.

Roche, J. (1999). Children: Rights, participation and citizenship. *Childhood, 6*(4), 475–493.

Roffey, S. (2012). Developing positive relationships in schools. In S. Roffey (Ed.), *Positive relationships*, 145–162. New York: Springer.

Rogoff, B., Coppens, A. D., Alcalá, L., Aceves-Azuara, I., Ruvalcaba, O., López, A., & Dayton, A. (2017). Noticing learners' strengths through cultural research. *Perspectives on Psychological Science, 12*(5), 876–888.

Rogoff, B., Correa-Chávez, M., & Silva, K. G. (2015). Cultural variation in children's attention and learning. In M. A. Gernsbacher & J. R. Pomerantz (Eds.), *Psychology and the real world* (2nd ed.), 164–173. New York: Worth.

Rosenak, M. (1987). *Commandments and concerns: Jewish religious education in secular society*. Philadelphia: Jewish Publication Society.

Rosenblatt, K., Berman, L. C., & Stahl, R. Y. (2018, July 19). How Jewish academia created a #MeToo disaster. *Forward*. Retrieved from www.forward.com.

Rosenthal, S. T. (2001). *Irreconcilable differences? The waning of the American Jewish love affair with Israel*. Waltham, MA: Brandeis University Press.

Ross, D. (2015). *Doomed to succeed: The US-Israel relationship from Truman to Obama*. New York: Farrar, Straus & Giroux.

Roth, D. (2017). *Disagreements for the sake of heaven*. Jerusalem: Pardes Center for Judaism and Conflict Resolution.

Rudoren, J. (2014, July 5). Autopsy suggests Palestinian teenager was burned to death after abduction. *New York Times*. Retrieved from www.nytimes.com.

Rudoren, J., & Kershner, I. (2014, June 30). Israel's search for 3 teenagers ends in grief. *New York Times*. Retrieved from www.nytimes.com.

Rugg, H.O. (1921). Reconstructing the curriculum: An open letter to Professor Henry Johnson commenting on committee procedures as illustrated by the Report of the Joint Committee on History and Education for Citizenship. *Historical Outlook, 12*, 184–189.

Sales, A. L., Samuel, N., & Koren, A. (2008). *Mapping professional development for Jewish educators*. Waltham, MA: Fisher-Bernstein Institute for Jewish Philanthropy and Leadership.

Sarna, J. (1994). The Israel of American Jews. *Sh'ma: A Journal of Social Responsibility, 25*(478), 8–10.

———. (1996). A projection of America as it ought to be: Zion in the mind's eye of American Jews. In A. Gal (Ed.), *Envisioning Israel: The changing ideals and images of North American Jews*. Jerusalem: Magnes.

Sarre, S., & Tarling, R. (2010). The volunteering activities of children aged 8–15. *Voluntary Sector Review*, *1*(3), 293–307.

Sasson, T. (2009) *The new realism: American Jewish views about Israel*. New York: American Jewish Committee.

———. (2014) *The new American Zionism*. New York: NYU Press.

Sasson, T., Phillips, B., Kadushin, C., & Saxe, L. (2010). *Still connected: American Jewish attitudes about Israel*. Waltham, MA: Maurice and Marilyn Cohen Center for Modern Jewish Studies, Brandeis University.

Sasson, T., Phillips, B., Wright, G., Kadushin, C., & Saxe, L. (2012). Understanding young adult attachment to Israel: Period, lifecycle and generational dynamics. *Contemporary Jewry*, *32*(1): 67–84.

Sasson, T., Saxe, L., Chertok, F., Shain, M., Hecht, S., & Wright, G. (2015). *Millennial children of intermarriage: Touchpoints and trajectories of Jewish engagement*. Waltham, MA: Cohen Center for Modern Jewish Studies, Brandeis University.

Sasson, T., Shain, M., Hecht, S., Wright, G., & Saxe, L. (2014). Does Taglit-Birthright Israel foster long-distance nationalism? *Nationalism and Ethnic Politics*, *20*(4), 438–454.

Sawyer, R. K. (2014). *The Cambridge handbook of the learning sciences*. Cambridge: Cambridge University Press.

Saxe, G. (1999). Cognition, development, and cultural practices. In E. Turiel (Ed.), *Culture and development: New directions in child psychology*, 19–35. San Francisco: Jossey-Bass.

Saxe, L., & Chazan, B. (2008). *Ten days of Birthright Israel: A journey in young adult identity*. Lebanon, NH: University Press of New England.

Saxe, L., Fishman, S., Shain, M., Wright, G., & Hecht, S. (2013). *Young adults and Jewish engagement: The impact of Taglit-Birthright Israel*. Waltham, MA: Cohen Center for Modern Jewish Studies, Brandeis University.

Saxe, L., Phillips, B., Sasson, T., Hecht, S., Shain, M., Wright, G., & Kaddushin, C. (2009). *Generation Birthright Israel: The impact of an Israel experience on Jewish identity and choices*. Waltham, MA: Cohen Center for Modern Jewish Studies, Brandeis University.

Saxe, L., Shain, M., Wright, G., & Hecht, S. (2019). *Israel, politics, and Birthright Israel: Findings from the summer 2017 cohort*. Waltham, MA: Cohen Center for Modern Jewish Studies, Brandeis University.

Schacter, J. J. (1999). Facing the truths of history. *Torah U-Madda Journal*, *8*, 200–273.

Schenker, A. (1966). Zionist camping in America. *Journal of Jewish Education*, *36*(2), 103–107.

Schiff, A. (1968). Israel in American Jewish schools. *Journal of Jewish Education*, *38*(4), 6–24.

———. (1994). Towards a mission statement on Jewish Zionist education. *Journal of Jewish Education*, *61*(2), 17–19.

Schneider, J. (2014). *From the ivory tower to the schoolhouse: How scholarship becomes common knowledge in education.* Cambridge, MA: Harvard Education Press.

Schulz, W., Ainley, J., Fraillon, J., Losito, B., Agrusti, G., & Friedman, T. (2016). *Becoming citizens in a changing world.* International Civic and Citizenship Education Study. Amsterdam: IAE.

Seo, K. H., & Ginsburg, H. P. (2004). What is developmentally appropriate in early childhood mathematics education? Lessons from new research. In D. H. Clements & J. Sarama (Eds.), *Engaging young children in mathematics: Standards for early childhood mathematics education*, 91–104. Mahwah, NJ: Lawrence Erlbaum.

Shamir, E. (2015). Rethinking Operation Protective Edge. *Middle East Quarterly*, Spring, 1–12.

Siboni, G. (2014). Operations Cast Lead, Pillar of Defense, and Protective Edge: A comparative review. In A. Kurz and S. Brom (Eds.), *The lessons of Operation Protective Edge*, 27–36. Tel Aviv: Institute for National Security Studies.

Silva, J. M., & Langhout, R. D. (2011). Cultivating agents of change in children. *Theory & Research in Social Education*, 39(1), 61–91.

Sinclair, A. (2009). A new heuristic device for the analysis of Israel education: Observations from a Jewish summer camp. *Journal of Jewish Education*, 75(1), 79–106.

———. (2013). *Loving the real Israel: An educational agenda for liberal Zionism.* Teaneck, NJ: Ben Yehuda.

———. (2014, May 20). On ambivalent complexity: A response to Barry Chazan. *eJewishPhilanthropy*. Retrieved from www.ejewishphilanthropy.com.

Sinclair, A., Solmsen, B., & Goldwater, C. (2012). *The Israel educator: An inquiry into the preparation and capacities of effective Israel educators.* Consortium for Applied Studies in Jewish Education.

Sirbu, R. (2013, February 11). Why rabbis should talk about Israel. *My Jewish Learning*. Retrieved from www.myjewishlearning.com.

Smith, S. (2017). *Shul with a school: A history of the development of non-Orthodox Jewish day schools in Los Angeles* (Doctoral dissertation, New York University).

Smooha, S. (2002). The model of ethnic democracy: Israel as a Jewish and democratic state. *Nations and Nationalism*, 8(4), 475–503.

Soifer, M., & Stark, G. (2018a). *2018 Day camp census.* New York: Foundation for Jewish Camp.

———. (2018b). *Overnight Jewish camp in North America: 2018 camp census.* New York: Foundation for Jewish Camp.

Solís, J., Fernández, J. S., & Alcalá, L. (2013). Mexican immigrant children and youth's contributions to a community *Centro*. In S. K. Nenga & J. K. Taft (Eds.), *Youth engagement: The civic-political lives of children and youth*. Bingley, UK: Emerald Group.

Stearns, P. N. (2000). Student identities and world history teaching. *The History Teacher*, 33(2), 185–192.

———. (2016). *Childhood in world history* (3rd ed.). New York: Routledge.

Stein, K. (2020). Proven success in Israel education: Context, sources, and perspective. In J. Ariel (Ed.), *Israel education: The next edge*, 89–94. Jerusalem: Makom/Jewish Agency for Israel .

Stipek, D., & Johnson, N. C. (2020). Developmentally appropriate practice in early childhood education redefined: The case of math. In S. Ryan, M. E. Graue, V. L. Gadsen, & F. J. Levine (Eds.), *Advancing knowledge and building capacity for early childhood research*, 35–54. Washington, DC: American Educational Research Association.

Stodolsky, S., Dorph, G. Z., & Feiman-Nemser, S. (2006). Professional culture and professional development in Jewish schools: Teachers' perceptions and experiences. *Journal of Jewish Education, 72*(2), 91–108.

Stodolsky, S., Dorph, G. Z., Feiman-Nemser, S., & Hecht, S. (2004). *Boston MTEI: Leading the way to a new vision for teachers and schools.* Report to Boston Jewish Community and sponsoring foundations and agencies.

Stomfay-Stitz, A., & Wheeler, E. (2003). Children as peacemakers. *Childhood Education, 80*(1), 28–G(1).

Stordal, G., & Hellem, L. (2005) Children's perspectives on citizenship and nation building in Norway. Paper presented at the Childhoods 2005 conference, University of Oslo.

Svašek, M. (2005). The politics of chosen trauma: Expellee memories, emotions and identities. In K. Milton & M. Svašek (Eds.), *Mixed emotions: Anthropological studies of feeling*, 195–214. Oxford: Berg.

Taft, J. K. (2011). *Rebel girls: Youth activism and social change across the Americas.* New York: NYU Press.

Tartir, A., & Seidel, T. (Eds.). (2019). *Palestine and rule of power: Local dissent vs. international governance.* New York: Springer.

Thomas, N. L. (2010). *Educating for deliberative democracy: New directions for higher education* (No. 152). San Francisco: Jossey-Bass.

Torney-Purta, J. (2002). The school's role in developing civic engagement: A study of adolescents in twenty-eight countries. *Applied Developmental Science, 6*(4), 203–212.

Torney-Purta, J., Lehmann, R., Oswald, H., & Schulz, W. (2001). *Citizenship and education in twenty-eight countries: Civic knowledge and engagement at age fourteen.* Amsterdam: IEA.

Trencher, M. (2020, February 3). Orthodox Jews love Trump, right? Actually, it's complicated. *Forward.* Retrieved from www.forward.com.

Troen, S. I., & Fish, R. (2017). *Essential Israel: Essays for the 21st century.* Bloomington: Indiana University Press.

Troy, G. (2011, September 27). This year, any rabbis afraid to talk about Israel to their congregations should quit. *Jerusalem Post.* Retrieved from www.jpost.com.

Tsolidis, G., & Pollard, V. (2010). Home space: Youth identification in the Greek diaspora, *Diaspora, Indigenous, and Minority Education, 4*(3), 147–161.

UN Human Rights Council. (2013). Report of the United Nations High Commissioner for Human Rights on the implementation of Human Rights Council resolutions S-9/1 and S-12/1. Retrieved from www.ohchr.org.

Uprichard, E. (2008). Children as "being and becomings": Children, childhood and temporality. *Children & Society, 22*(4), 303–313.

Urofsky, M. I. (2020/1975). *American Zionism from Herzl to the Holocaust*. Lincoln: University of Nebraska Press.

VanSledright, B., & Brophy, J. (1992). Storytelling, imagination, and fanciful elaboration in children's historical reconstructions. *American Educational Research Journal, 29*(4), 837–859.

VanSledright, B., & Kelly, C. (1998). Reading American history: The influence of multiple sources on six fifth graders. *Elementary School Journal, 98*(3), 239–265.

Vasquez, V. M. (2014). *Negotiating critical literacies with young children*. New York: Routledge.

Verba, S., Schlozman, K. L., & Brady, H. E. (1995). *Voice and equality: Civic voluntarism in American politics*. Cambridge, MA: Harvard University Press.

Volkan, V. D. (2001). Transgenerational transmissions and chosen traumas: An aspect of large-group identity. *Group Analysis, 34*(1), 79–97.

———. (2002). Bosnia-Herzegovina: Chosen trauma and its transgenerational transmission. In Maya Shatzmiller (Ed.), *Islam and Bosnia: Conflict resolution and foreign policy in multi-ethnic states*, 86–97. Montreal: McGill–Queen's University Press.

Vygotsky, L. S. (1978). *Mind in society: The development of higher psychological processes*. Cambridge, MA: Harvard University Press.

Waite, S. (Ed.). (2017). *Children learning outside the classroom: From birth to eleven*. Thousand Oaks, CA: Sage.

Walker, K., Myers-Bowman, K. S., & Myers-Walls, J. A. (2003). Understanding war, visualizing peace: Children draw what they know. *Art Therapy, 20*(4), 191–200.

Walters, S. (2019). Learning to read Hebrew in a Jewish community school: Learners' experiences and perceptions. *Language Learning Journal, 47*(2), 257–267.

Wastell, S. J., & Degotardi, S. (2017). "I belong here; I been coming a big time": An exploration of belonging that includes the voice of children. *Australasian Journal of Early Childhood, 42*(4), 38–46.

Waxman, C. I. (2010). American Jewish philanthropy, direct giving, and the unity of the Jewish community. In Y. Prager (Ed.), *Toward a renewed ethic of Jewish philanthropy*. New York: Yeshiva University Press.

Waxman, D. (2016). *Trouble in the tribe: The American Jewish conflict over Israel*. Princeton, NJ: Princeton University Press.

———. (2017). Young American Jews and Israel: Beyond Birthright and BDS. *Israel Studies, 22*(3), 177–199.

Webley, P. (2005). Children's understanding of economics. In M. Barrett & E. Buchanan-Barrow (Eds.), *Children's understanding of society*, 43–68. New York: Psychology Press.

Weisberg, H. F. (2019). *The politics of American Jews*. Ann Arbor: University of Michigan Press.

Weisman, J. (2018). *(((Semitism))): Being Jewish in America in the age of Trump*. New York: St. Martin's.

Weiss, A. (Ed.). (2016). *A picture of the nation: Israel's society and economy in figures 2016.* Jerusalem: Taub Center for Social Policy Studies in Israel.

Wells, G. (1999). *Dialogic inquiry.* New York: Cambridge University Press.

Wenger, E. (1998). *Communities of practice: Learning, meaning, and identity.* Cambridge: Cambridge University Press.

Wertheimer, J. (2008). *A census of Jewish supplementary schools in the United States, 2006–2007.* New York: AVI CHAI Foundation.

———. (2009). *Schools that work: What we can learn from good Jewish supplementary schools.* New York: AVI CHAI Foundation.

———. (2018). *The new American Judaism: How Jews practice their religion today.* Princeton, NJ: Princeton University Press.

Wertsch, J.V. (2000). Is it possible to teach beliefs, as well as knowledge about history? In P. N. Stearns, P. Seixas, & S. Wineburg (Eds.), *Knowing, teaching, and learning history,* 38–50. New York: NYU Press.

———. (2002). *Voices of collective remembering.* Cambridge: Cambridge University Press.

White, H. (1975.) *Metahistory: The historical imagination in nineteenth-century Europe.* Baltimore: Johns Hopkins University Press.

Wiggins, G., & McTighe, J. (2005). *Understanding by design* (2nd ed.). Alexandria, VA: ASCD.

Wilberg, S. (2002). Preschoolers' cognitive representations of their homeland. *British Journal of Developmental Psychology, 20*(2), 157–169.

Wilson, H. (1998). *The development of national identity in 5 to 11 year old English schoolchildren* (Doctoral dissertation, University of Surrey).

Wilson, K. S. (2013). *Jews in the Los Angeles mosaic.* Berkeley: University of California Press.

Wilson-Keenan, J. A. (2015). Pathologizing the language of young children. In *From small places: Toward the realization of literacy as a human right,* 57–66. Rotterdam: Sense.

Windmueller, S. (2017, May 2). Jewish Los Angeles: Reflections and insights. *eJewish-Philanthropy.* Retrieved from www.ejewishphilanthropy.com.

Wineburg, S. (1991). Historical problem solving: A study of the cognitive processes used in the evaluation of documentary and pictorial evidence. *Journal of Educational Psychology, 83*(1), 73–87.

———. (2000). Making historical sense. In P. N. Stearns, P. Seixas, & S. Wineburg (Eds.), *Knowing, teaching, and learning history,* 306–325. New York: NYU Press.

———. (2001). *Historical thinking and other unnatural acts: Charting the future of teaching the past.* Philadelphia: Temple University Press.

———. (2018). *Why learn history (when it's already on your phone).* Chicago: University of Chicago Press.

Winer, L. N. (2019). *Teaching who they are: American-born supplementary school teachers' connections with Israel* (unpublished Doctoral dissertation, Jewish Theological Seminary).

Winnicott, D. W. (1991/1971). *Playing and reality*. New York: Routledge.

Woocher, J. S. (1986). *Sacred survival: The civil religion of American Jews*. Bloomington: Indiana University Press.

Wood, C. (2007). *Yardsticks: Children in the classroom, ages 4–14*. Turners Falls, MA: Northeast Foundation for Children.

Wootliff, R. (2016, February 4). Minors handed life sentence, 21 years for Abu Khdeir murder. *Times of Israel*. Retrieved from www.timesofisrael.com.

Wright, C., Bacigalupa, C., Black, T., & Burton, M. (2008). Windows into children's thinking: A guide to storytelling and dramatization. *Early Childhood Education Journal, 35*(4), 363–369.

Wright, J. H. (2004). *Origin stories in political thought: Discourses on gender, power, and citizenship*. Toronto: University of Toronto Press.

Wyness, M., Harrison, L., & Buchanan, I. (2004). Childhood, politics and ambiguity: Towards an agenda for children's political inclusion. *Sociology, 38*(1), 81–99.

Yerushalmi, Y. H. (1989). *Zakhor: Jewish history and Jewish memory*. Seattle: University of Washington Press.

Yin, R. K. (1994). *Case study research: Design and methods*. Thousand Oaks, CA: Sage.

Yoffie, E. (2014, September 5). Muzzled by the minority. *Reform Judaism*. Retrieved from https://reformjudaismmag.org.

Yoon, J., & Onchwari, J. A. (2006). Teaching young children science: Three key points. *Early Childhood Education Journal, 33*(6), 419–423.

Zakai, S. (2011). Values in tension: Israel education at a U.S. Jewish day school. *Journal of Jewish Education, 77*(3), 239–265.

———. (2012, November 27). Jewish education caught in the crossfire of a most uncivil war. *Times of Israel*. Retrieved from https://blogs.timesofisrael.com.

———. (2014). "My heart is in the East and I am in the West": Enduring questions of Israel education in North America. *Journal of Jewish Education, 80*(3), 287–318.

Zakai, S., & Cohen, H. T. (2016). American Jewish children's thoughts and feelings about the Jewish state: Laying the groundwork for a developmental approach to Israel education. *Contemporary Jewry, 36*(1), 31–54.

Zeng, G., & Zeng, L. (2005). Developmentally and culturally inappropriate practices in US kindergarten programs: Prevalence, severity, and its relationship with teacher and administrator qualifications. *Education, 125*(4), 706–724.

Zerubavel, Y. (2002). The "mythological sabra" and Jewish past: Trauma, memory, and contested identities. *Israel Studies, 7*(2), 115–144.

Zevenbergen, R. (2007). Digital natives come to preschool: Implications for early childhood practice. *Contemporary Issues in Early Childhood, 8*(1), 19–29.

Zevenbergen, R., & Logan, H. (2008). Computer use by preschool children: Rethinking practice as digital natives come to preschool. *Australasian Journal of Early Childhood, 33*(1), 37–44.

Zimmerman, J., & Robertson, E. (2017). *The case for contention: Teaching controversial issues in American schools*. Chicago: University of Chicago Press.

Zimmerman, L. (2016, February 17). Teaching the Israeli-Palestinian conflict: Why wrestling with Israel belongs in American Jewish education. *eJewishPhilanthropy*. Retrieved from www.ejewishphilanthropy.com.

Zimmerman, S., & Lieberman, Y. (2017). Which side are you on, my people? Ending American Jewish support for the Occupation. *Tikkun*. Retrieved from Project Muse, https://muse.jhu.edu.

Zukin, C., Keeter, S., Andolina, M., Jenkins, K., & Carpini, M.X.D. (2006). *A new engagement? Political participation, civic life, and the changing American citizen*. New York: Oxford University Press.

INDEX

Page numbers in *italics* indicate Figures and Tables

ABOUT THE AUTHOR

SIVAN ZAKAI is the Sara S. Lee Associate Professor of Jewish Education at the Hebrew Union College–Jewish Institute of Religion and Director of the Children's Learning About Israel Project of the Jack, Joseph, and Morton Mandel Center for Studies in Jewish Education at Brandeis University.

Printed in the USA
CPSIA information can be obtained
at www.ICGtesting.com
JSHW081632111223
53618JS00005B/23